THE FASCIST EFFECT

Studies of the Weatherhead East Asian Institute, Columbia University

The Weatherhead East Asian Institute is Columbia University's center for research, publication, and teaching on modern and contemporary East Asia regions. The Studies of the Weatherhead East Asian Institute were inaugurated in 1962 to bring to a wider public the results of significant new research on modern and contemporary East Asia.

THE FASCIST EFFECT

Japan and Italy, 1915–1952

Reto Hofmann

CORNELL UNIVERSITY PRESS   ITHACA AND LONDON

First published 2015 by Cornell University Press
First paperback printing 2020

Library of Congress Cataloging-in-Publication Data

Hofmann, Reto, 1975– author.
The fascist effect : Japan and Italy, 1915–1952 / Reto Hofmann.
pages cm. — (Studies of the Weatherhead East Asian Institute, Columbia University)
Includes bibliographical references and index.
ISBN 978-0-8014-5341-0 (cloth)
ISBN 978-1-5017-4848-6 (pbk.)
1. Japan—Relations—Italy. 2. Italy—Relations—Japan. 3. Fascism—Japan—History. 4. Fascism—Italy—History. 5. Political culture—Japan. 6. Political culture—Italy. 7. Japan—Civilization—Italian influences. 8. Japan—Politics and government—1912–1945. 9. Italy—Politics and government—1914–1945. I. Title.

DS849.I8H64 2015
327.5204509'04—dc23

2014032607

To my parents, Karl and Yvonne Hofmann

Contents

Acknowledgments

I am grateful to many people for support throughout the writing of this book. I owe my greatest debt to Carol Gluck, who has provided guidance and criticism at every stage of the project, giving more of her time than I could have expected. I thank Victoria de Grazia for helping me think through Italian history and for her encouragement; Greg Pflugfelder, for offering his advice on all matters whenever I needed it; Harry Harootunian, for his sharp reading of various drafts and his thought-provoking seminars; Kim Brandt, for her constructive criticism of an earlier version of the manuscript. The book benefited immensely from the comments I received from Bain Attwood, Mehmet Dosemeci, Federico Finchelstein, Takashi Fujitani, Janis Mimura, Sam Moyn, and Umemori Naoyuki.

I was fortunate to have many friends and colleagues who helped me by reading drafts or discussing ideas. I am particularly grateful to Adam Bronson, Alex Bukh, Giuliana Chamedes, Adam Clulow, Chad Diehl, Yumi Kim, Federico Marcon, Ben Martin, Ben Mercer, Dominique Reill, Sagi Schaefer, Saikawa Takashi, Sakuma Ken, Shōda Hiroyoshi, Suzuki Tamon, Brian Tsui, Max Ward, and Steve Wills. At Columbia, Mark Mazower shared his thoughts on the historiography of fascism. In Japan I benefited from participating in the seminars of Hori Makiyo and Umemori Naoyuki at Waseda University and in Nagai Kazu's seminar at Kyoto University. More recently, at Monash University, colleagues and members of my research seminar, too numerous to name individually, tuned into the final stages of the manuscript, giving invaluable feedback on several chapters. Back in the late twentieth century, at the University of Western Australia, Richard Bosworth and Rob Stuart laid the groundwork for this project as inspiring teachers and undergraduate advisers.

Warmest thanks go to Kuribayashi Machiko, who kindly granted me access to her family's private papers, welcoming me on repeat visits for over a decade. Many individuals in Italy helped in dealing with the intricate archives and libraries in Rome. A fellowship at Columbia's Weatherhead East Asian Institute gave me time to work on the manuscript—I thank Myron Cohen and Waichi Ho for making this into an intellectually stimulating experience in a friendly environment. At Cornell University Press, Roger Haydon offered expert editorial oversight.

I was fortunate to present my work at a number of scholarly meetings, including the Seminar on Modern Japan at Columbia University and the History

Seminar at Monash University. I am also grateful for having been invited to speak at the workshop "Modern Germany, Italy, and Japan: Towards a New Perspective," held at the Freiburg Institute for Advanced Studies, the Albert-Ludwigs-Universität Freiburg, and organized by Patrick Bernhard, Sven Reichardt, and Lucy Riall. I am indebted to all participants at these venues for their comments and suggestions. A version of Chapter 4 has appeared in the *Journal of Contemporary History*.

I would like to acknowledge the financial support I have received over the years. Generous grants and scholarships from Columbia University, the Weatherhead East Asian Institute, the Leonard Hastings Schoff Fund, the Whiting Foundation, and the Japanese Ministry of Education, Culture, Sports, Science, and Technology allowed me to carry out research on three continents. Monash University contributed by covering last-minute expenses.

This book would not have been possible without my wife, Siew Fung, who shared with me the ups and downs of a nomadic life, always unwavering in her loving support. Our daughters, Yza and Cya, brought much happiness. My deepest gratitude goes to my parents, Karl and Yvonne, who have helped me out in more ways than they may realize. I dedicate this book to them.

THE FASCIST EFFECT

The Fascist sympathizer Shimoi Harukichi posing with a portrait of Benito Mussolini in the early 1920s. Shimoi is clad in the uniform of the Italian shock troops (Arditi), who held the city of Fiume (Rijeka) in 1919–1920.

(From Shimoi Harukichi, Taisenchū no Itaria *[Tokyo: Shingidō, 1926].)*

Introduction

Are we in a period of "restoration-revolution" to be permanently consolidated, to be organized ideologically, to be exalted lyrically?

—Antonio Gramsci, 1935

Our revolution is a restoration.

—Mikami Taku, 1933

On different sides of the Eurasian continent—and on opposing sides of the barricades—Antonio Gramsci and Mikami Taku spoke of a common problem in similar terms. In the 1930s, when liberal capitalism had entered a period of crisis, they debated the contemporary trend to enact political reform while maintaining social relations unaltered or, to borrow the novelist Giuseppe Tomasi di Lampedusa's dictum, "to change everything so that everything would remain the same." Gramsci, the Marxist thinker imprisoned by Benito Mussolini, analyzed this condition in terms of a "revolution-restoration" (*rivoluzione-restaurazione*), a moment of crisis when neither the forces of progress nor those of reaction managed to prevail.[1] Lieutenant Colonel Mikami, interrogated in a Japanese courtroom about why he had shot Prime Minister Inukai Tsuyoshi, had organized a response to this condition by calling for a "restoration-revolution" (*ishin-kakumei*), explaining that this meant bringing about the "emperor's benevolent rule and oneness of sovereign and subject."[2] Together, these comments captured the mechanism of fascism, its role in revolutionizing the old and restoring the new in order to reconcile the tension between capital and the nation.

In interwar Japan, as elsewhere, the global nature of capitalism and its tendency to crisis clashed with the nation's attribute of exclusivity as well as its claims of harmony and timelessness. Across the world class conflict was intensifying, the gap between city and countryside had widened, and culturally, the dislocations of modern life were reflected in a sense of a fragmented everydayness and commodified social relations.[3] Fascism promised to realign the nation with capital by restoring authority, hierarchy, and community as central notions in modern politics. The result would be a new order premised, as Mussolini put it in 1922, on fascism's ability to rid the "political and spiritual life of all the parasitic encrustations of the past which cannot carry on existing indefinitely in the present because this would kill their future."[4]

Why Japanese intellectuals, writers, activists, and politicians, although conscious of the many points of intersection between their politics and those of Mussolini, were so ambivalent about the comparability of Imperial Japan and Fascist Italy is the subject of this book. Focusing on how contemporary Japanese understood fascism, it recuperates a historical debate that has been largely disregarded by historians, even though its extent reveals that fascism occupied a central position in the politics of interwar Japan. Since the 1970s historians of Japan have often dismissed the concept of fascism as Eurocentric and vague, but for Japanese of all backgrounds who came of age from the 1920s to the 1940s, fascism conjured up a set of concrete associations.[5] They discussed fascism for its nationalism, its leader, its economics of autarky and corporatism; and later, for its drive toward empire and a new world order. That they understood fascism in different ways at different times speaks for the concept's vitality more than its amorphousness, because, as this book suggests, Japanese found the many meanings of fascism relevant to their reflecting on their own political anxieties and aspirations. My aim is to rethink the history of Japan as part of a wider, interconnected, history of fascism, arguing that Japanese politics and ideology in the first half of the twentieth century were enmeshed in a dialogue with European fascism.[6]

Fascism needs to be examined through its relations. A vast scholarship exists on the relationship between fascism and other ideologies, with Marxists stressing the intimacy with liberalism, and liberal historians and social scientists emphasizing the "totalitarian" character of fascism and socialism (or communism). My intent, however, is to explore the relations between fascisms in various national contexts, focusing on Japan and Italy. This approach has at least two advantages. First, it will expose a fundamental contradiction at the heart of this ideology. On the one hand, fascism stood for particularism. It claimed to represent the deep spiritual essence of the nation, the key to unraveling a politics that represented the aspirations of a people. On the other hand, fascism's declared aim to counteract the negative effects of capitalist modernity (though not capitalism itself) implied a universal valence. The circuits of exchange between Japanese fascist thinkers and political figures and their Italian counterparts reveal the agony of coming to terms with the contradiction of fascism being at once the ideology of a country, Italy, and, especially after the 1930s, a political concept in its own right, applicable to movements, ideas, and individuals around the world, including Japan. To maintain this distinction, which Japanese made implicitly or explicitly,

I capitalize Fascism when it refers to Italy and use the lowercase *f* to indicate where it is being used as a generic ideology.

Second, recognizing that fascism was both nationally specific and structurally transnational means to reevaluate the process by which it was articulated in Japan. Interwar Japanese were keenly aware of the tensions of fascism, the way that it simultaneously emanated from Italy and emerged domestically. Intellectuals, bureaucrats, and politicians interacted with fascism on their own terms, indicating that it would be simplistic to reduce it to "influences" from Italy. At the same time, it appears unconvincing to consider what have variously been termed the "Shōwa restoration," "reformist bureaucrats," "ultranationalism," or the "New Order Movement" as singularly Japanese manifestations of fascism because, as this book shows, the protagonists of these movements and policies were so deeply involved in a conversation with European fascism. By moving away from Euro- and Japano-centric approaches, this study uncovers the making of fascist ideology as a complex interplay between ideas both local and global.

To capture the intersection between fascism in Japan and in Italy means to reevaluate the history of fascism as that of a process, not of a clearly defined model. As Gramsci remarked in those years with reference to Caesarism, a code word for fascism, the "exact significance of each form of Caesarism, in the final analysis, can be reconstructed only from concrete history, not from a sociological schema."[7] Indeed, for contemporary Japanese commentators, Italian Fascism—and fascism—represented a starting point, an inspiration rather than a blueprint. They evinced a deep ambiguity toward fascism. They may praise fascism's uncompromising faith in the nation and its goal to overcome a range of modern woes, such class conflict, moral degeneration, and the policies of autarky. But many doubted, for example, the need for a leader like Mussolini, arguing that a move away from parliamentary democracy did not necessarily mean a one-man dictatorship: in Japan a politics based on the emperor system would offer a more adequate solution. In other words, they regarded fascism as open-ended, as a new politics of the right that began with Mussolini but that would find different, and possibly more sophisticated, expressions in Japan.

Contemporary observers, especially those on the right, approached fascism with a comparative mindset. Beset with an obsession with Japanese national uniqueness, they distanced fascism from Japan, vowing to circumvent fascism, or to subsume it altogether into nativist forms of ideology articulated in such phrases as the "national polity" (*kokutai*), or the "imperial way" (*ōdō*). But, as I argue in Chapter 3, the Right's displacement of fascism into various formulations of Japanese nationalism was part of the fascist logic itself, its drive to generate a politics of cultural authenticity. The Right's discourse on Japanese difference needs to be approached critically not only to understand the concealment of fascism, but also because much of the postwar historiography on 1930s Japan replicates some of its assumptions of Japanese peculiarity. The liberal political scientist Maruyama Masao, though describing as fascist certain political movements, famously preferred the neologism "ultra-nationalism" as a marker of prewar Japan. Other scholars have proposed an array of alternative terms, such as "authoritarianism," "militarism," "Japanism," "expansionism"—or a combination thereof—all of which characterize Japan as more or less sui generis.[8] In this sense, this book aims to be an anticomparative history of fascism even though it is premised on how prewar Japanese compared the politics of Japan and Italy. The point, as contemporaries readily (if often just tacitly) recognized, is that comparisons were premised on an awareness of connections.

Finally, the focus on the fascist nexus between Japan and Italy allows for a methodology that is multiperspectival. To highlight the scope of the Japanese encounter with fascism, I survey individuals (often little-known ones), theater plays, official documents, popular literature, newspapers, and philosophical treatises. An exposition of the various fascist foci will offer a view over the landscape on which fascism thrived. Robert O. Paxton has stated that a historian of fascism will need to determine which part of the elephant he chooses to study; my attempt is to cast a wide net over the beast of fascism, capturing the textual thickness of the pachyderm's skin.[9] In this sketch, readers may wonder about the more indirect treatment accorded to German National Socialism. Though the Third Reich loomed large among Japanese civil and military bureaucrats in the second half of the 1930s and during the war, as an ideology Nazism fell within the discourse on the concept of fascism; that is, it was in many ways distinct from Italian Fascism, but it was seen as a continuation of the politics of fascism that had begun in Italy and were undergoing elaboration in Japan. For this reason, I discuss Nazism at key moments in the larger history of fascism.

This book follows a chronological order, tracing the major shifts in the history of the interaction of Japanese and Italian fascism from World War I to the years following Japan's defeat after 1945. It will become clear that during this period fascism attracted widespread attention among Japanese thinkers and politicians because it was caught up in a configuration of ideas about nation, capitalism, empire, and notions of the "West." In the 1920s, the apogee of what is often known as the period of Taishō democracy, Japanese commentators discussed fascism in terms of the social and political experience of modernity. As elsewhere, also in Japan, industrial capitalism ushered in a society where class conflict, consumerism, gender norms, and individualism clashed with established assumptions about order and hierarchy.[10] Urban workers, buoyed by socialism and the proletarian movement, took to the streets demanding better conditions. Their numbers swelled from an influx of rural laborers who moved to the cities seeking work in the expanding industrial sector but also in new service and culture industries, ranging from banks to department stores and the cafés and brothels. To conservative critics, the new identities and unevenness brought about by mass society jarred with visions of the nation as a harmonious community. Chapter 1 examines how one such figure, Shimoi Harukichi (1883–1954), found in Italian Fascism a set of social and cultural tools to realign modern mass society with the nation. An educator with a penchant for romantic literature and, later, a right-wing activist, Shimoi lived in Italy for almost two decades (1915–1933), witnessing World War I and the rise of Fascism. From this experience he conceived Fascism as a pedagogical strategy to mobilize the masses—especially youth—through patriotism and devotion to the state.

Politically, the 1920s brought about calls for constitutional democracy (*minponshugi*) and expanded suffrage. In 1918 Hara Kei became prime minister in the first cabinet headed by an elected member of the Diet rather than an appointed bureaucrat, soldier, or senior statesman. Yet even as party cabinets became the norm in the 1920s, voices critical of parliamentarism multiplied. Not just conservatives, who regarded increased popular involvement in politics as an attack on the prerogatives of the state (and the emperor), but also the younger generation of politicians who had spearheaded notions of individualism, universal suffrage, and party politics—the promoters of liberalism—found fault with these new forms of politics. Many worried that parliamentary democracy, plagued by corruption and subject to the interests of the social elites, fell short of genuinely representing the aspirations of the people.

This was the backdrop to the widespread interest in Benito Mussolini, which peaked in the late 1920s. The crisis of liberal democracy in these years has often been explained with reference to the power of the bureaucracy, hostility from the military, or the tight constraints set by a state centered on the emperor.[11] While these were surely important factors, this book suggests that the reaction to Fascism on the side of some champions of liberal and democratic ideals was often naïve, if not accommodating or, even, sympathetic. Together, Chapters 1 and 2 offer a picture of the affinities with Italian Fascism among Japanese liberals and conservatives, showing that, at a time of heightened cosmopolitanism, they assumed that Fascism, too, could be selectively interposed into Japan's liberal politics and culture of the 1920s. For example, as I argue in Chapter 2, the boom around Mussolini reflected a quest for political leadership. And, crucially, it was not so much conservatives as liberals who displayed the keenest interest in Mussolinian strategies of rule, as they sought to reinforce liberalism with fascist notions of leadership, manliness, and morality.

In the early 1930s, however, the notion that Japan needed infusions of Fascism began to fade. Chapter 3 shows that in these years various streams of right-wing thinkers and activists—such as Japanists (*nihonshugisha*), National Socialists (*kokkashakaishugisha*), agrarianists (*nōhonshugisha*)—competed to define the theory and practice of a new domestic order. Contending, as Mikami Taku did, that the bottom line for such reform was that it had to be "interpreted and carried out in a Japanese way," they disavowed Italian Fascism, as well as fascism, as a foreign ideology.[12] And yet, it is important to stress, their negation of fascism did not amount to a complete rejection.[13] It was a denunciation of the inadequacies of fascism rather than of fascism per se. Thus, in the 1930s, right-wing ideologues worked out a fascist critique of fascism that acknowledged the links with Italian Fascism.

Japan's imperial expansion into Manchuria between 1931 and 1933 played a key role in redefining the relationship between Japanese and European fascisms. The establishment of Manchukuo radicalized Japanese politics. It paved the way to the rise of "reformist bureaucrats," intensified militaristic rhetoric and policies as well as calls for autarky, and heightened patriotic fervor, giving Japanese across the ideological spectrum a sense that Japan had caught up with fascism.[14] Paradoxically, the more difficult it became to maintain clear distinctions between Fascist Italy and Imperial Japan, the more fascism appeared obsolescent. And yet, as Chapters 4 and 5 examine, it was in empire that Imperial Japan, Fascist Italy, and later, Nazi Germany found a powerful ideological common ground. Chapter 4 illustrates that the Italo-Ethiopian War (1935–1936) moved the debate around fascism from questions of nationalism and state power toward imperialism and international relations. In the minds of many Japanese observers, the Italian invasion smacked of the old, much reviled European colonialism and had nothing in common with Japan's empire in Manchuria, which they declared was a first step toward the liberation of Asians from Western rule.[15] But a consistent section of Japanese foreign-policy analysts and ideologues came to see Fascist Italy's empire as a blow dealt to the equally detested League of Nations and liberal internationalism. Thus, in the larger context of what they regarded as "white" Anglo-Saxon world dominance, they reconciled Italy's imperial ambitions in Africa with Japan's expansion in Asia.

Chapter 5 pursues the Japanese reconciliation with European fascism by exploring the discourse on the alliance between Imperial Japan, Fascist Italy, and Nazi Germany in the late 1930s and wartime. The diplomatic rapprochement among the three countries, exemplified in the Anti-Comintern (1937) and Tripartite (1940) pacts, sparked a debate on the nature of the alliance and the principles that would underpin a new world order after the victory of the Axis. Historians, philosophers of the Kyoto School of Philosophy, and political scientists probed the historical and theoretical roots of European fascism. Praising the Italian and German attack on the status quo, these theorists nevertheless subsumed fascism into the Japanese critique of the West, arguing that to "overcome modernity" it was also necessary to overcome fascism. Even so, the attempt to formulate an ideological orthodoxy that neatly separated Japanese from Italian and German fascism failed, as intellectuals and politicians felt compelled to acknowledge the links to Fascism and Nazism. In conclusion, I show that the long-standing Japanese association with fascism became an inconvenient truth for the Allies after the war, when Americans decided to rehabilitate Japan as their best friend in Asia in the fight against communism.

This book sidesteps the ontological question "Was Japan fascist or not?" preferring an enquiry into how fascism operated at different levels of analysis. It shows that interwar Japanese culture and politics was steeped in fascism, although often in a diffuse ways. A gray area emerged in which liberal thinkers, conservative politicians, and right-wing activists found themselves in agreement with fascist ideals and ends even though they did not always agree with fascist means. Academics, politicians, and bureaucrats turned down a full embrace of fascism but did not hesitate to explore fascist aesthetics, strategies of mobilization, and theories about economics and international relations as intellectual resources to develop an ideology of their own. The ambiguities of Japan's fascism are a characteristic of fascism itself, reflecting its role as a mediator between revolution and restoration as well as its hybrid nature as a product of global and national history.

1

MEDIATOR OF FASCISM: SHIMOI HARUKICHI, 1915–1928

Fascism has only three principles: the ancestral land, duty, and discipline.

—Shimoi Harukichi, 1925

In 1924, Shimoi Harukichi returned to Japan after a decade's long stay in Naples and Rome. Having witnessed the destruction wrought by World War I, he announced that under Benito Mussolini's Fascist government Italy was experiencing an unprecedented resurgence. The fourteenth-century Renaissance, he proclaimed, had been "a revival of the arts, but the renaissance that happened during the war was the great renaissance of all the nation." The result, he argued, was Fascism, a movement that "opened the people's eyes, unifying them and making them one with the state." In other words, Fascism was an Italian "spiritual movement."[1] Yet, Shimoi continued, the Fascist aesthetics of heroism, sacrifice, and war mirrored the essential traits of what he understood to be Japan's cultural essence. "Japan's way of the warrior [bushido], that ancient morality and spirit, is completely identical. I believe the Blackshirts and their truncheon are manifest in Japan's loyalty to the emperor and patriotism [*chūkun aikokushugi*]."[2] To Shimoi's mind, then, a timeless spirit of patriotism was characteristic of both Japanese and Italian history and bonded the two countries. Fascism was a manifestation of this spirit, and he made it his life's endeavor to convey this conviction to a Japanese audience.

In the 1920s Shimoi became known as the most indefatigable propagandist of Italian Fascism in Japan. However, this characterization is only partly correct.[3] Paradoxically, despite his efforts to herald the achievements of Fascist Italy, Shimoi advocated that fascist change in Japan take a different route. He admired Fascism and its Duce but did not aim to replicate a seizure of power or a leader such as Mussolini; rather, he sought to mediate the story of Italian Fascism to an audience of young Japanese in order to stir them into seeking a patriotic politics of their own. As he would proclaim in later years, "Fascism is a typically Italian phenomenon: it would be a mistake if [it] were to try to cross borders and upset the systems of other states. The life of Fascism depends on fascism itself, that is, on its own men."[4] To Shimoi's mind, the Japanese already possessed the patriotic spirit that Italians were displaying in their Fascist resurgence; they just failed to realize it. Telling the story of Italian Fascism as a narrative of ordinary heroism, patriotic sacrifice, and social order would act as a catalyst in Japan, making Japanese conscious of the values surrounding the nation and disciplining them into becoming obedient citizens.

The premise that fascist change depended on the Japanese recognizing the spiritual commonality between Japan and Italy was what distinguished Shimoi from his contemporaries. From the 1920s, Fascism did indeed attract the attention of many observers in Japan, as elsewhere in the world, but no one found in Fascism the deep links that Shimoi had detected.[5] Rather, the early Japanese debates on Fascism intersected with a discourse on political and cultural reform that swept across the ideological landscape of this period.[6] Liberal observers commented on the violence that characterized the Blackshirts. Fascist "private groups, whose actions are beyond the law," wrote the journalist Maida Minoru, threatened not only freedom of expression but, effectively representing the establishment of "dual political organs," imperiled the state of law itself.[7] Marxists, who called for social revolution, saw in Fascism a sign of bourgeois reaction. In the eyes of the communist leader Katayama Sen, then stationed in Moscow as a Comintern officer, Fascism bolstered bourgeois rule "as a reactionary force and as a powerful representative of the capitalist class [that] is hardening the ground for the capitalists in view of a renewed conflict."[8] On the other side of the spectrum, right-wingers welcomed the Fascists as a force against communism. Ninagawa Arata, an adviser to the Japanese Red Cross in Geneva and a member of the Japanese mission to the Washington Conference (1921–1922), praised the "extirpation" of Marxism at the hands of the Fascists, even arguing that they had enacted "true democracy . . . unlike Lenin, they are not despotic, nor destructive, for in reality they are constructive, democratic [*minshuteki*]."[9]

As these appraisals show, Fascism was a subject of public debate from early on. Yet in the eyes of many ideologues Fascism's practical and theoretical applicability to Japan was problematic. Fascism did not carry the clout of liberalism and socialism: in the 1920s few even considered it a fully fledged ideology with a coherent doctrine encompassing politics, economics, and culture. Indeed, initially Japanese focused their debates on the Fascists—that is, the actions of individuals, the Fascist Party, or its leader, Benito Mussolini—more than on discussing fascism as an ideology. That fascism was a term in flux is also evident from its Japanese spelling: the transliteration of the word "fascism" as *fashizumu* became standard only in the early 1930s.[10] The association of Fascism with Italy also contributed to its limits. In the Japanese cosmology of the "West," Italy did not occupy a privileged position: since Japan's first contacts with Europe, Italy remained a destination for artists, adventurers, and the handful of scholars who, by means of English literature, had developed an interest in the exotic peninsular home to Ancient Rome; Japanese politicians, economists, and intellectuals took inspiration from their German, British, and French counterparts.[11] How could Italy suddenly generate an ideology capable of competing with the intellectual traditions of its neighbors?

Shimoi made a virtue of Japan's relative lack of interest in Italy, promoting the notion that Fascism was a patriotic movement, led by robust young leaders such as Mussolini, to rescue a nation that had been betrayed by socialist revolutionaries and an ossified, liberal ruling class. This interpretation mirrored the official Fascist discourse, but at the same time it was closely connected to Shimoi's thought as it developed in the late Meiji period (1890–1911). This link is particularly evident in the theme of youth. In Shimoi's narrative of Fascism, youth is presented in the highly aestheticized terms characteristic of late nineteenth-century romanticism as the social group that, through its virility and poetic sensibility, is capable of effectuating a broader national awakening. Youth also reflected Shimoi's conviction as a conservative educator that training young people with national morals was the basis for social order. Cultural romanticism and social conservatism merged in his understanding of World War I, which he experienced in Italy. For him, the war had enabled youth to express their vitality, but in a controlled, socially safe manner: by dedicating their energy to the nation. Regarding Fascism as a continuation of the mobilization of youth during wartime, he came to understand this ideology as a kind of updated nationalism for the age of the masses.[12]

The significance of Shimoi for the history of fascism in Japan, therefore, lies not so much in his peculiarity or his many, often bizarre, enterprises to bring Japan and Italy together. Rather, by considering his role as a mediator it will become clear that his understanding of Fascism was produced between Japan and Italy through a process that reveals the marks of a right-wing activist who merged the romantic sensibility of a late nineteenth-century romantic with the anxieties of a conservative educator—all expressed in the language of Italian Fascism. In this sense, Shimoi was less idiosyncratic than he liked to style himself. Indeed, his ideas were often banal, crude refashionings of the mainstream views he encountered during his life, both in Japan and Italy. And yet the popularity of Italian Fascism that he contributed so much to generating in the 1920s is evidence that, like him, many Japanese recognized Fascism as an Italian story with wider, transnational, meanings.

A Late Meiji Educator

Shimoi may have stood out for his stance on Fascism, but before he left for Naples in 1915, he was an archetypal middle-class youth of the late Meiji period (1890s–1911). The generation of ideologues, writers, educators, and politicians who came of age in this period held a view of the world that was colored by a deep ambivalence toward modern mass society. They no longer enjoyed the degree of social mobility, of "rising in the world" (*risshin shusse*), that was open to the schooled generation that had preceded them. In response, this "anguished youth" (*hanmon seinen*), as they were sometimes called, denounced the culture of materialism associated with business.[13] They lamented the lack of a raison d'être in modern civilization, delighting instead in a romanticism drawn both from contemporary Japanese literature of the likes of Yosano Akiko, Kitamura Tōkoku, and Shimazaki Tōson, as well as from the neo-romantic German works of Hermann Hesse, Thomas Mann, and Robert Musil. Spurred by the wave of nationalism after Japan's victory over Russia (1905), they turned away from socialist critiques of society, forming instead a discourse on social redress based on civil morality and loyalty to the state and emperor.[14]

From an early age, Shimoi demonstrated an eagerness to rise in society, as is evident from his move from Asagura-chō, a village in rural Fukuoka prefecture on the southern island of Kyūshū, to Tokyo. Born in 1883 as Inoue Harukichi, Shimoi was the son of an impoverished former samurai whom the agricultural crisis of the 1890s had forced to seek employment in the coal mines near his hometown. It has been speculated that, through his father's connections, Shimoi became familiar with right-wing organizations such as the ones headed by Tōyama Mitsuru, many of which originated around Fukuoka.[15] Although in later years Shimoi would indeed be close to Tōyama, in his younger years his primary concerns were with gaining an education. Shimoi's father, Kikuzō, was able to provide Harukichi with a privileged education. He attended both compulsory primary school and the optional middle school, from which he graduated in 1902. By all accounts Harukichi was a bright student and, following a practice common for the times, Shimoi Kasuke, a wealthy trader in timber from Tokyo, adopted him and arranged for him to marry his daughter Fūji in 1907. It is unclear why Kasuke, despite having a son of his own, Eiichi (who, influenced by Harukichi, would become an Italian literary scholar), intended to make Harukichi his successor. In any case, it was an unfortunate decision. Although Harukichi strove to make it to the capital, he had no intention of becoming a businessman.

In fact, Shimoi disdained the prospect of pursuing a materialist career. Two reasons account for this attitude, both related to his training at the First Normal School in Tokyo, which he entered in 1907. As Donald Roden has shown, two very different streams of thought coexisted at this institution. There was the conservative side. The normal schools had been established in the 1880s by the architect of the Meiji education system, Mori Arinori, as stepping-stones to the Imperial universities and as the training ground for teachers and bureaucrats who were to educate and administer future generations of Japanese in the spirit of Meiji ideology. The instruction in these schools was strict, with an emphasis on inculcating moral values that would create an orderly society and self-abnegating national leaders.[16] On the other side, at the normal schools students were also immersed in the romantic culture of late Meiji, exploring their feelings as individuals through literature and literary clubs. Indeed, even before entering these schools, many students were steeped in popular adventure novels that promoted ideals of heroism, courage, and chivalry.[17] This romanticism antagonized the perceived material civilization of the West—and its Japanese supporters—turning instead to a valorization of the timeless qualities of the Japanese nation. In this environment Shimoi reworked the relationship between the conservative "morality of doing" and the voluntaristic individualism that derived from romanticism, conferring on the educator the role of remaking national subjects through the mobilization of the spirit of Japan.[18]

The occasion for putting these assumptions into practice came with the *Ōtsuka kōwakai*, a movement Shimoi founded at the Tokyo Normal School to further the publication and dissemination of children's stories. The publication of children's stories had undergone a rapid expansion in late Meiji, when efforts were made to modernize them. The resulting genre incorporated the kind of nationalism that emerged as a result of Japan's ascendancy in East Asia, but under one key promoter, Iwaya Sazanami (1870–1933), it also revamped traditional folktales, merging them with contemporary themes of military valor, individual heroism, and devotion to country and emperor. Amid the sense of social crisis of the early 1910s, folktales expressed an ideal of community in which individuals lived in harmony with each other and the nation.[19] For this reason Shimoi's group saw the genre as a way to reeducate Japan's youth in civil morality.

With this goal in mind, Shimoi wrote what would become his first, and very successful, publication, *Ohanashi no shikata* (How to Make Tales), a manual on how to tell moralistic stories based on folktales. Revamping the production of folktales, then, was not Shimoi's only goal in *Ohanashi no shikata*. Perhaps more crucial to its author was the task of educating educators. "Oral folktales [*tsūzoku dōwa*] are one great form of education. Yes, an education. But even though they are about education, educators are surprisingly indifferent to them. I want them to become passionate."[20] Hence oratorical methods of delivery were the focus of the book. In other words, modernizing folktales for the age of the masses meant stressing how something was narrated, not what was narrated. The pitch of one's voice, the choice of words, expression, the use of gestures, and the structure of the tale—these were all points that Shimoi elaborated in order to provide educators with the means to capture the attention of Japan's youth. Rhetoric (*yūben*) was an important part of Meiji educational culture and was taught in classes and clubs as a means to create independent and elite political subjects. Shimoi wanted to reform this project. In his view and that of other ideologues of late Meiji, in the age of mass society it could no longer be assumed that the individual would identify with the nation; indeed, left in the hands of individuals, rhetoric could prove to be a threat to the nation. So, in order to revitalize the connection between the individual and the nation, Shimoi believed that rhetoric should reside in the hands of the teacher, a figure that stood safely halfway between civil society and the state. "I pray that through this new field in education—folktales rhetoric [*tsūzoku kōwa*]—educators will take the opportunity and press on to become a vanguard [*kyūsenpō*]."[21]

As it turned out, Shimoi relinquished his goal to be at the forefront of Japan's educational innovation, preferring instead an appointment as a lecturer in Japanese at the prestigious Royal Oriental Institute in Naples, where he moved in 1915. Personal advancement abroad trumped concerns over Japan's social morality. In later years he would claim that it was his love for Dante, whom he had discovered as a student, that led him to Italian shores. More likely, however, the romantic, decadent, and antique image of Italy, as portrayed in the English and German literature that Shimoi had read at the normal school, had aroused his curiosity. A determination to rise in society, romanticism, and a sense of adventure convinced him that his own interests were just as important as those of Japan.

Poetics: Naples, World War I, and Gabriele D'Annunzio

"It is much easier here than in Japan to achieve success as a literary person [*bungakusha*]," Shimoi wrote to his younger brother Eiichi in 1920.[22] He could say this with some confidence, as in the half-decade he spent in Naples Shimoi had risen from an obscure Japanese educator to a "poet" whose reputation extended from Italy to his country of origin. During this time, he demonstrated a remarkable capacity to connect to Italian, and especially Neapolitan, elites. Though he came to the attention of such prominent individuals as Prime Minister Antonio Salandra and the chief of general staff, General Armando Diaz, it is clear that Shimoi even more ardently cherished the hope of entering into the local intelligentsia, particularly literary and artistic circles. Within these, it was poets whom he befriended with greatest dedication. His background as a "literary youth" only partly accounts for this inclination. More critical to his acceptance was the unexpected and keen interest in Japanese poetry on the part of local poets. Whether of the modernist kind, such as the Neapolitan group that formed around the journal *La Diana*, or the romantic bent, such as Gabriele D'Annunzio, Italian poets wanted to know more about Japan and pursued Shimoi as a source of knowledge about the country. Although he was neither a scholar nor a poet, Shimoi was only too happy to receive such epithets, convinced that Italians had recognized his intellectual talent.

Sidelining his background as an educator for a career as an amateur poet and literato had a profound effect on Shimoi's perception of the present. As emerges from his publications, he developed a highly aestheticized appreciation of the changes brought to Italian culture and society during this period. He came to this understanding, first of all, through his experience of World War I. Poets, it appeared to him, had played a crucial role in producing the patriotic sentiment that united Italians to fight for their country. At his arrival in 1915, Italy was on the brink of entering the conflict, and several literati, most famously the futurist Filippo Tommaso Marinetti, the Florentine modernists Giovanni Papini and Giuseppe Prezzolini, as well as the romantic Gabriele D'Annunzio, were extolling the virtue of the war as a way to rejuvenate Italians and Italian culture.[23] But Shimoi also believed that he had contributed personally to the surge of national sentiment through his collaboration with *La Diana*; by introducing the journal to Japanese poetry and culture, he claimed a place in the revitalization of Italian poetry and patriotism. This mediation led him to the conclusion that Italians and Japanese shared an inborn patriotic spirit that emerged from the compatibility of their literary traditions. In short, he claimed to have uncovered a privileged aesthetic and spiritual link between Japan and Italy.

La Diana was a prime example of the vibrant avant-garde movements of early twentieth-century Naples. In the late nineteenth century Naples had undergone a decline in comparison to the rapidly industrializing Milan, bureaucratizing Rome, and tourist-trapping Florence and Venice.[24] Yet it remained a large city with a proud history of grandeur. *La Diana* was founded in 1915 by the Buenos Aires–born Gherardo Marone (1891–1962), a young law school graduate who had turned to letters. In line with other, more established, contemporary modernist journals such as *La Voce*, Marone's publication addressed the burning question of the day: how to reinvigorate Italian culture, and Italians along with it. The name of the journal, which translates as "reveille," was probably chosen with that idea in mind, and, for Marone, the war signaled that wake-up call. Championing the "moral value of every great war," he argued that such a conflict "no longer generates class conflict . . . but a superb idea which, purifying and sublating the spirit, reaches the ideal of pacification."[25] *La Diana* was a loose group that included a mixed crowd of poets, artists, and literati, who broadly subscribed to this ideal. Among the contributors were high-profile national intellectuals such as the philosopher Benedetto Croce and the poets Umberto Saba, Giuseppe Ungaretti, and Corrado Govoni, as well as little-known figures such as Lionello Fiumi—and the thirty-two-year-old Japanese Shimoi Harukichi.

Shimoi, who had never written poetry before, managed to command the attention, even the admiration, of these poets because he arrived in Naples at a time of transition in the Western discourse on Japan. Fin de siècle Europe had exoticized Japan in the cultural wave known as Japonisme. The late nineteenth-century impressionist painter Van Gogh, for example, drew inspiration from Edo period (1600–1868) Japanese arts and woodblock prints. In Italy, the composer Giacomo Puccini's opera *Madame Butterfly* also reveals interest in traditional Japanese culture, just like the early aesthetic sensibilities of D'Annunzio.[26] Japan's military victory over Russia in 1905, however, prompted some European intellectuals to enquire about the country's modern literature. To most Italians, of course, contemporary Japanese works remained out of reach for lack of translations; only a handful had traveled to the country. In this context Marone saw in Shimoi a direct point of access to Japanese culture unmediated by Paris or London, the two cities from which Japonisme had spread across Europe. Shimoi was quick to understand Marone's overtures and without much ado climbed into this new intellectual niche.

What excited the Neapolitans was the haiku, a seventeen-syllable poem. The haiku spoke to *La Diana*'s attempt to carve out a middle ground in Italian modernism because it balanced conciseness with emotion, exemplifying a free verse that did not capitulate to what many considered futurism's soullessness.[27] Shimoi, together with Marone, set out to translate the work of a number of contemporary modernist poets, focusing on Yosano Akiko and Yosano Tekkan's *Myōjō*, the journal of the New Poet Society (*Shinshisha*), published in Tokyo between 1900 and 1908. Translations of the two Yosanos and other Japanese authors appeared regularly in *La Diana* after 1916. The initial reception was positive and prompted Marone and Shimoi to publish a separate collection, *Japanese Poems* (*Poesie giapponesi*), in March 1917. The booklet caused a small sensation, both within the circles of *La Diana* and in the broader literary field. Giuseppe Ungaretti, soon to become one of Italy's most distinguished, and nationalist, twentieth-century poets, was sent a copy of the publication while he was in the trenches. He wrote to Marone thanking him for the volume. "Now I shall enjoy them; and with you accede to the world of enchantments."[28] The poems were reviewed in a dozen newspapers in Italy, and Giovanni Papini appraised the poems in the prestigious Parisian symbolist journal, *Mercure de France*.[29] The literary critic Goffredo Bellonci had misgivings about the poems, claiming that the poets translated by Shimoi and

Shimoi Harukichi, Naples, ca. 1916.

(From Gaetano Macchiaroli, ed., Gherardo Marone *[Naples: La Città Nuova, 1996].)*

Marone did not actually exist and were, in fact, written by Marone himself. It was necessary to call in the Japanese embassy to vouch for the existence of these Japanese poets.[30]

La Diana stirred Shimoi's belief that Italy and Japan stood jointly at a turning point in their modern histories. It seemed to him that *La Diana* and *Myōjō* headed an altogether parallel project to revitalize national culture through aesthetic forms capable of safeguarding the old in the new. *Myōjō*, they argued, exemplified the desire to overcome past literary forms. Just as *Myōjō* had devised new forms for the age-old *tanka*, so *La Diana* sought to revive older Italian styles without compromising Italy's national essence, as stated by Shimoi and Marone in their introduction to *Japanese Poems*: "A sudden revolutionary movement in the fields of art, which began in the first few years of the twentieth century, created in Japan a new poetic era, the contemporary and most interesting one . . . which stands up to the most dignified European avant-gardist movement."[31] Ungaretti confirmed this sentiment in a letter to Marone.

> My dear Gherardo, for a century, in the series of schools that have been succeeding each other in our Western countries, poetry has been renovating itself, refreshing itself, purifying itself in contact with all kinds of poetry; I do not know the Japanese who have preceded yours, and I do not know what and how much we owe to them; but it seems to me that you wanted to prove that a Westerner of a certain refinement could, nowadays, doubtlessly write like Yosano Akiko and vice versa.[32]

As far as Shimoi was concerned, his two years of collaboration with the Neapolitan modernists had been a success. He had achieved a social status he could not have dreamed of in Japan. Moreover, to his mind, he had played a central role in shaping the poetics of *La Diana* and, in turn, in revitalizing Italy's national culture. In so doing he also came to see himself as the pivot in an as yet fledgling spiritual connection between Japan and Italy. Yet when the war caused *La Diana* to cease publication in 1917 Shimoi did not despair. Naples felt far from the trenches where, it seemed to him, Italians were fighting for their country's survival. The front in Italy's northeast appeared more exciting than the salons of Naples. Why else did Italian poets from D'Annunzio to Marinetti and Ungaretti flock to the front line? The contained, introspective lyricism of *La Diana* could not express Shimoi's war fever.

La Diana had confirmed for Shimoi that poets played a key role in the rejuvenation of the national spirit, but it had not convinced him, as an educator, that they could also transform ordinary Italians. It was the experiencing of war, Shimoi felt, that spread the patriotic fervor proclaimed by these poets among the wider population. In late 1918 he toured the Italian front. It seemed to him that patriotism emerged spontaneously in the everyday lives of soldiers and civilians alike. For this reason World War I became central to Shimoi's thought, leading him to praise war for the aesthetics of camaraderie, sacrifice, and death that it generated among soldiers.[33]

Shimoi expressed these feelings in *The Italian War* (*La guerra italiana*, 1919), his memoir of the front. It was, in many ways, an unremarkable publication. It replicated the tropes of the nationalist literature that glorified masculine courage, camaraderie, and devotion to one's people, articulated perhaps most crudely in Ernst Jünger's accounts, which appeared throughout Europe in the years after the conflict.[34] Yet, despite its banalities, it reveals how the war marked a period of shifting alliances for Shimoi.

The Italian War suggests the desire, and the confidence, on the part of Shimoi to distance himself from his Neapolitan milieu. In the book he sought to garner a readership that was both national and not strictly intellectual. For this reason he sprinkled the book with his correspondence with the highest political and journalistic personalities, whose letters of reference he needed in order to visit the Italian front (he did not actually fight, despite being sometimes anxious to give this impression). Francesco Saverio Nitti, the finance minister, stated that Shimoi was a "distinguished Japanese writer and sincere friend of Italy." The minister therefore asked Giovanni Visconti Venosta, the secretary of the head of the joint chiefs of staff, to "introduce [Shimoi] to General Diaz and to find a way to have him visit our front with due care." Guelfo Civinini, a nationalist journalist of some repute who wrote for the conservative Milanese daily *Corriere della Sera*, introduced Shimoi to the Supreme Command's Section for Photography and Cinematography.[35]

The Italian War was a work of transition also in Shimoi's poetic taste. While bearing the hallmark of romantic lyricism, it also displays elements of futurist origin. Shimoi effusively wrote about his perception that order, self-sacrifice, and camaraderie helped soldiers to set aside regional identities and class conflict and embrace each other as Italians. In writing the book, he claimed that he was offering the "simple but sincere words of affection and admiration of a Japanese" to those "old fathers who offered their sons in the name of the sacred fatherland [*patria*] . . . to the simple soldiers [who] after the sorrowful life of four years in the trenches . . . return now to their ploughs and hammers, content and happy."[36] In the war, he argued, Italians found the nation in their everyday lives. He praised the bravery in ordinary people, "those many heroes, young and old, [who] every day are actors in moving scenes without being remembered by anybody."[37] A scene of an old man, women, and children sitting near their dilapidated house around a makeshift hearth expressed Shimoi's ideal of nationalism: "Love of the hearth is the sacred origin of love of the fatherland."[38]

But now futurism slipped into his writing, revealing how Shimoi found in war not only an occasion to contemplate people's patriotism but also an exciting transformative experience. As if to vindicate Marinetti's boast that war was the world's only hygiene, Shimoi found the war "majestic": "The word 'war' conjures up an idea of agitation, confusion, disorder, disquiet . . . but here dominates a perfect calm. You won't find the disorder that there is in Rome or Naples. What an ideal order! Discipline is being maintained; the streets are all clean; women, boys, old men all work in silence and full of faith. What a beautiful scene!"[39]

Shimoi also evoked that other object of futurist fetish, the automobile. For him speed denoted modern efficiency while encouraging the transformation of everyday customs. When "flying in a car," he remarked, a military salute was more practical than greeting by taking off one's hat.[40] Nor was futurist masculinity absent from his sentiments. Crossing a river he observed, "what a masculine excitement [*eccitazione maschia*]! Traversing a stream flowing at two-and-a-half meters per second, in an iron boat, under tremendous enemy fire!"[41]

The most significant turning point in *The Italian War* was Shimoi's relationship—personal, poetic, but also fictitious—with Gabriele D'Annunzio. Shimoi found him irresistible, a poet who wedded romanticism to an uncompromising and eroticized nationalism while also being a man of action. A high-profile figure in national politics, D'Annunzio volunteered to fight in the war at age fifty-five, flying bombing raids on enemy cities. To Shimoi, he represented a warrior-poet engaged with the real problems of the nation. Shimoi's infatuation grew deeper after the two actually met, though in unclear circumstances, on the front. In a letter with which Shimoi prefaced *The Italian War*, D'Annunzio wrote in his usual effusive tone: "We spoke of Italy, the painful one, we spoke of our sacrifice, our blood, of the desperate days and our undefeated hope. Do you remember? I suddenly saw two vivid teardrops flowing from your stranger's eyes. And then I recognized you as a brother; and my heart opened."[42]

It remains unclear how sincere D'Annunzio declarations were. Shimoi, however, was determined to exploit the poet's overtures in an effort to reconceive his life after World War I. First, he followed D'Annunzio in the expedition to Fiume. The case of this city, claimed by both Italy and the newly formed Kingdom of Yugoslavia, became a cause célèbre for Italian nationalists. To them, Fiume exemplified all that was wrong in postwar politics. They argued that the government had failed to gain adequate territorial compensation for Italy's war effort and the over six hundred thousand Italians who had died in the conflict. The acquisition of Austrian-held Trentino, Trieste, and Istria was not enough, leading D'Annunzio to announce that Italy's was a "mutilated victory." He was irate over what he saw as the government's lack of determination to resolve the contention over Fiume in Italy's favor. In September 1919 he took matters into his own hands and invaded the city with his army of war veterans, the *legionari*, declaring it an independent Italian state under his command. Only in December 1920, after a bombardment by the Italian navy, did he surrender the city.

For Shimoi, the Fiume episode signaled that an age had arrived in which artists, and especially poets, spearheaded moral reform by forging national unity through performing exemplary acts of patriotism. D'Annunzio's leadership left a profound mark on him. Contemporaries and historians alike have commented on the innovative style pioneered by D'Annunzio during the yearlong occupation. He crafted a militaristic-authoritarian rule and combined it with a symbolic apparatus that included the Roman salute, dramatic speeches delivered from his balcony, and a cult of his persona. Shimoi, like many veterans who participated in the occupation or observed it closely, as Mussolini did, was deeply impressed. Disregarding the *legionari*'s debauchery—they violated such taboos as sexual freedom, homosexuality, drug use, and nudism—in later years Shimoi emphasized the heroic narrative of Fiume, claiming a part in it.[43]

There was another, more material side to Shimoi's experience at Fiume. He realized that his presence in the city was opening the door to fame for him in his home country. Japanese newspapers reported on the independent republic formed by the boisterous Italian poet, commenting in great detail on the presence of a Japanese there and his seemingly crucial role. Japanese literary circles had been familiar with D'Annunzio since the early nineteenth century. His novel *Triumph of Death* (1894) was translated into Japanese by the critic Ikuta Chōkō in 1913 and met with great acclaim. Now, too, his image as a daring aviator and showman prevailed among a broader and more popular audience.[44] Shimoi, drawn into the international dimension of D'Annunzio's invasion, instinctively understood the potential of this association and exaggerated his position as his close collaborator, capturing the attention of the Japanese readership.

Shimoi's second aim was therefore to popularize D'Annunzio—and by implication himself—in Japan. To do so, he attempted to convince D'Annunzio to fly from Italy to Tokyo. It was not an entirely absurd idea. He could count on D'Annunzio's interest in Japan and his inclination for daring flights (in the war, he had flown over Vienna, dropping propaganda leaflets). Authorities in both countries supported the idea. The Italian government, to whom D'Annunzio was an embarrassment and a nuisance, reasoned that its interests would be served if the poet left the country and tried to facilitate the flight.[45] Even the journalist and leader of the nascent Fascist movement, Benito Mussolini, enquired about the possibility of obtaining a seat on a plane.[46] Japanese authorities also responded to the idea with enthusiasm. The military, in particular, were eager to study the advanced Italian airplane technology. On September 12, 1919, the cabinet secretary allocated the generous sum of 77,600 yen for receiving the poet and for the logistics associated with the event.[47] The army minister, Tanaka Giichi, expressed his support, stating that the Italians could use Japanese military facilities in Korea and on the main islands and that the army would provide refueling and technical support.[48] In addition, the minister believed that, thanks to D'Annunzio's proven credentials as a man "of patriotic thought," the event would not only "improve relations between the two countries" but would also be "important for the awakening of the Japanese people."[49]

D'Annunzio himself, however, was only half-committed. While appearing genuinely interested in the enterprise, he subordinated the flight to his political plans in Italy. On three occasions between late 1918 and early 1920 he and Shimoi discussed the possibility of his flying to Tokyo, but each time he called off his participation. In March 1919 he wrote to Shimoi expressing his excitement about the idea of flying to Tokyo on his "stork of fire" but turning down Shimoi's "magnificent invitation" due to the death of a copilot.[50] A second plan was in preparation but was set aside when, in September 1919, D'Annunzio led his *legionari* into Fiume. He finally called off the idea in January 1920. "I had hoped to see the peach blossoms in bloom in the land of Tokyo, and to be able to compose verse in competition with one of your delicate poets in an idleness which would have been sweet after such a long, iron discipline." Finding more pressing business in Fiume, however, he urged Shimoi to "carry to your brothers in the country of the rising sun Fiume's salute and Fiume's violets which, today, are the most fragrant in the world."[51] Three days later, perhaps as a consolation, D'Annunzio hosted a dinner in honor of "the guest from the Orient." Flattering Shimoi, he praised how "in his little chest he had a big Italian heart, and today, under the star of Fiume, a most fiery Fiume heart." He took the occasion to express his admiration for Japan's "rebirth": "What historical fact is comparable in its greatness to the Asiatic resurrection, to the sudden rejuvenation which is renovating sacred Asia, that region of broad and sublime unity?"[52]

Thanks to the official and public excitement over the possible flight to Tokyo, Shimoi achieved the status of a minor celebrity in Japan.[53] The Japanese press followed the event closely. Maruyama Tsurukichi, secretary in the Government-General of Korea and "friend" of Shimoi, explained that Shimoi was a worthy graduate of the Normal School, a "writer" (*sakka*) and "Dante scholar," who had received an award from the Italian consulate in Tokyo to teach at the Oriental Institute in Naples, where he had exerted himself to introduce Japanese culture.[54] Articles also reported on Shimoi's activities during World War I and at Fiume, where he and the "great poet" D'Annunzio became "like brothers."[55] Curious journalists interviewed Fuji, the wife of "the poet of Naples," as well as his son Fujio and daughter Fujiko, both too young to remember their long-departed father, enquiring about Shimoi and their feelings about the seemingly imminent reunion.[56]

Photographs of Shimoi appeared for the first time in Japanese media. Fond of posing in kimono for an Italian audience, Shimoi found his Fiume uniform more suitable for his compatriots.[57]

One Japanese whose passions were stirred by news of the flight was the romantic poet Doi (Tsuchii) Bansui. In the January 1920 edition of the magazine *Chūō kōron* he published a long poem (*chōshi*) entitled "On the flying horse" (*Tenba no michi ni*) dedicated to Italy and the Italian poet. Doi, in Shimoi's view "a brother of D'Annunzio in opulence of style, taste for exuberance, and the hallucinating airiness of his constructions, launched his words of fire for the Italian poet."[58]

> Neither weapons nor treaties,
> —shadowy methods of tricksters
> will merge the remote continents;
> only the hand of poetry.
> And it shall be you, king of the eternal spaces,
> Poetry of Italy incarnate,
> To preach in the skies
> To the most distant peoples, life.[59]

Statements such as Doi's prompted Shimoi to change his outlook on Italy, Japan, and his own position between the two. He had arrived in Naples as a middling educator with the intention to further his career abroad. That he left his family behind in Japan was no doubt because he did not foresee remaining in Italy for long. But the collaboration with *La Diana*, the experience of war, and his relationship with D'Annunzio had a profound effect on him. It seemed to him that Italy had become a land of opportunity, with high-profile politicians writing on his behalf. Perhaps more significant was his conviction that Italy and Japan shared a poetic sensitivity, as he had witnessed during his work with Marone, and as the lyricism of the likes of D'Annunzio and Doi confirmed. Shimoi concluded that World War I had effected a world-historical change, wherein poets were thrown back at the vanguard of history by playing a key role in forging national unity, and that he himself had helped to bring this about.

Politics: Rome, Fascism, and Benito Mussolini

So intrigued were Japanese about Shimoi that in May 1921 the daily newspaper *Asahi* dispatched a journalist from Paris to investigate this much discussed figure at first hand. The correspondent described Shimoi's cultural ambassadorship as an "epic work," calling him "Italy's Lafcadio Hearn," after the English-American writer who popularized Japan in the West in the early twentieth century. "I have no doubts," he wrote, "that Shimoi . . . has a true grasp of Italy's spirit [*seishin*] thanks to his Japanese heart [*ki*]."[60] Showered with praise, Shimoi decided to continue his work as mediator after World War I, but changed his target. After a brief attempt to popularize Japanese literature and art in Naples, he stood his campaign on its head and focused instead on introducing Italian culture to Japan. This shift in the direction of his efforts coincided with a move from poetics to politics. To be sure, Shimoi's aesthetics had always had a political undertone as a conservative social critique. But now politics became a conscious factor in his search for a rationale for an Italo-Japanese spiritual alliance, one that led him toward Benito Mussolini and Fascism.

Shimoi's wartime experience and postwar soul-searching made him deeply interested in Mussolini's rapid rise to political prominence. "First-hour" Fascists, as the early activists are known, had been staunch interventionists who believed in the necessity for Italians to fight in World War I and who, in peacetime, continued the struggle against internal enemies, namely socialists, communists, and left-wing trade unions. During the so-called two Red years (1919–1920) Fascist squads, often led by ex-army shock troops (and often with the aid or compliance of the authorities) unleashed brutal campaigns against the political Left, intimidating, torturing, and killing their opponents. Mussolini, himself an ex-soldier and interventionist, succeeded in wielding loose control over the early Fascist movement, transforming it into a political party, the Fascist National Party (PNF) in October 1921. Having gained, by May 1922, a membership of over three hundred thousand, Mussolini now had a base that enabled him to compete in national politics. With few serious opponents among his own party and the Liberals or Socialists, he was appointed prime minister by King Victor Emmanuel III in October 1922 (Fascist propaganda preferred to mark the event through the "March on Rome," when bands of provincial Fascists moved into the capital). After governing as prime minister until 1924, Mussolini expanded his personal powers, outlawing the opposition and becoming, by 1926, dictator of Italy.[61]

It took Shimoi some time to adjust to the "new man" in Rome and to set a new agenda for himself. Immediately after the war, he returned to Naples to pursue his work of introducing Japanese culture to Italy. Now, however, he conceived it as a venture in which he was the main protagonist. Supported by his fame and for a while by the Japanese Embassy, he became a regular tour guide for Japanese visitors to Italy, high and low alike. For instance, he accompanied the romantic writer Tokutomi Rōka who, during his journey around the world, visited Naples in July 1919. Tokutomi later related how Shimoi informed him of his and D'Annunzio's plans to fly to Tokyo and how, startled, he had set to work immediately on a celebratory poem to send to the Italian poet.[62] In July 1921, the

Japanese Embassy appointed Shimoi a "temporary employee" (*rinji shokutaku*), probably as translator, during the visit of Crown Prince Higashinomiya, the future Shōwa emperor. The august traveler "praised" the "activities" of his subject, who displayed two large Italian and Japanese flags on boats anchored off the island of Capri where the monarch was to pass as he set sail to leave Naples.[63]

Also a reflection of Shimoi's prewar activities was the journal *Sakura* (Cherry Blossoms), published between June 1920 and March 1921. Like *La Diana*, *Sakura*'s aim was also to "diligently convey to Italy and Europe the greatness of Japanese poetry." Shimoi took charge, calling himself *direttore* (director), and relying on old *La Diana* hands for support. The young Neapolitan poet Elpidio Jenco wrote about Yosano Akiko, and the young composer Vincenzo Davico expressed his appreciation of a *tanka* poem of hers. Most active was Shimoi himself, now translating excerpts from the novels of Mori Ōgai (1862–1922) and Kunikida Doppo (1871–1908), as well as poems of Higuchi Ichiyō (1872–1896). But he also enlisted new collaborators, most conspicuously Dan Inō, the son of the wealthy industrialist Dan Takuma and later a professor of art history at Tokyo Imperial University, who visited Naples on a study tour to Italy.[64]

The most striking novelty in *Sakura* was the turn toward classical literature and folklore. Shimoi himself introduced the oldest collection of Japanese poetry, the eighth-century *Manyōshū*.[65] Dan wrote on the Edo period (1600–1868), including woodblock prints (*ukiyoe*) and painting. Other articles dealt with comic drama (*kyōgen*), Buddhist temples, and traditional beliefs. Premodern Japanese houses were described as "full of grace, poetry and dreams."[66] This was a marked a departure from *La Diana*'s modernism. If in *La Diana* Shimoi's aim had been to prove that Japan's modernity was coeval with that of Italy, in *Sakura* he wanted to show that a characteristic of Japan since time immemorial was the way in which poetry was present in the everyday life of its citizens in the form of an aesthetics of home and community. In Japan, he contended, "poetry became a supreme spiritual element, a daily practice of life."[67]

There was more to this argument than nostalgia. Rather, Shimoi believed that the Japanese spirit inherently tended toward harmony, and that this realization was crucial to overcome the social and cultural conflicts of the 1920s. In Japan, he asserted, even a duel between implacable enemies would end with a reconciliation of the two, "brothers in Poetry."[68] Validating the timeless past of Japanese literature for an uncomfortable present was therefore Shimoi's goal in *Sakura*. As he wrote in the introductory issue, he wanted to "uncover, especially, the purity of the Nipponic soul, which is a marvelous and moving human phenomenon, today that the world and human beings are a precise and uniform system of logarithmic tables. To reveal poetry: to reveal man."[69] This discovery, he contended, had a particular meaning for Italians, because they shared the Japanese inclination toward poetry, as they had demonstrated during the war. "The literary sensibility of the most different races becomes parallel," Shimoi and Jenco had claimed in a publication of these years.[70]

Shimoi soon became aware that introducing Japan to Italy was more difficult than he had imagined. Money was in short supply and irregular, partly due to his own romantic disdain for the material aspects of life. In late 1920 he quit his post at the Oriental Institute in Naples to dedicate his energies to his cultural project, meaning that he was left without a steady income.[71] For some time he received pay from the Japanese Embassy and the Japanese Ministry of Education, but these subsidies were also highly irregular.[72] What limited means Shimoi had he spent on books, boasting in 1921 that he was the owner of over three thousand works on Dante.[73] More damaging to his ambitions was the fact that Shimoi had overestimated the Italian interest in Japan. By 1920 the brief modernist fascination with Japan that had characterized *La Diana* was over. Torn between nationalism, Fascism, and socialism, Italians had little time for *Japonisme*, *Myōjō*, or its postwar counterparts.

Shimoi came to realize that he had reached a turning point. As Mussolini solidified his rule, he became aware of the growing Japanese interest in Fascism and Mussolini and proceeded to shift his efforts to promoting Italian culture and politics to Japan. As early as September 1922, a month before the March on Rome, Shimoi had introduced a commission of three Japanese parliamentary deputies to the future Duce, the visitors assuring Mussolini that the "liberal public opinion of the Japanese was following with vivid cordiality and interest the Italian Fascist movement."[74] Shimoi took these sorts of remarks as a sign of opportunity. From 1924 to 1927 he traveled between Italy and Japan four times, each time with great media fanfare, to give a "detailed account of Italian current affairs" and culture.[75]

It was during this period—and moving between Italy and Japan—that Shimoi began to prioritize politics over literature. The Calpis affair, one of his many enterprises during this period, best exemplifies this shift by illustrating Shimoi's change of alliance from D'Annunzio to Mussolini. A lactose-based drink, Calpis was founded by Mishima Kaiun, an adventurous businessman who is said to have developed the recipe from a drink offered him in Inner Mongolia in the early 1900s. Mishima was an aggressive proponent of marketing techniques, and in June 1924 he attempted to recruit D'Annunzio for a commercial stunt. He charged Shimoi with the task of proposing the idea to D'Annunzio. Mishima wrote that D'Annunzio was uniquely capable to "unify the soul of the [Japanese] people and clarify the goals of our country toward whose reconstruction the people will have to strive." Japan, he argued, lacked a great man of comparable status. For this reason he asked D'Annunzio to "donate to the youth of Japan a poem of any length and any form"

Shimoi at his home during a return visit to Japan, ca. 1924. Sitting on his left is his wife, Fuji; standing on his right is Tōyama Mitsuru, an exponent of the Japanese radical Right.

(Photo courtesy of Kuribayashi Machiko, Tokyo.)

and, possibly, to "accept Japan's invitation to visit us as a guest of the nation." He concluded that "Shimoi will personally explain our desires to you."[76] But by this time D'Annunzio, aging and comfortable in his lakeside residence in Gardone, had lost his interest in the long voyage and in Japan. When he was asked by Shimoi for his decision, he replied, tersely and mockingly, that he would not go, but that nonetheless his "heart [was] on top of Mount Fuji and you [would] see it ablaze from afar."[77] Shimoi returned to Tokyo without the much-coveted salute.

But Shimoi was not a man to give up easily. Following an audience with Mussolini in March 1926, he succeeded in getting from the Duce what the Comandante had denied him. Mussolini composed a message addressed to Japan's youth. He praised Japan's "high level of civilization" and warned young Japanese to turn away from socialism ("modern demagogic materialism") and to be true to the "millenarian spirit of [their] race." Just as Fascism was based on the "conscious acceptance of discipline, hierarchy, and patriotism," so Japan's spirit was present in bushido.[78]

With Calpis taking care of sponsorship, Mussolini's message reached a vast audience of officials and ordinary Japanese. The message was first delivered with great pomp in Tokyo's Hibiya Park where, according to the Italian ambassador,

Shimoi Harukichi presenting Mussolini with a samurai armor, 1926.

(Photo courtesy of Kuribayashi Machiko, Tokyo.)

a crowd of some ten thousand had gathered, including prestigious political representatives, bureaucrats, and young people whose regular "thundering applause" was matched by a final Fascist salute.[79] Shimoi wrote to Mussolini, telling him that the message had drawn widespread attention and gained new admirers. He reported, no doubt with exaggeration, that airplanes dropped "one million" leaflets of the message while three hundred thousand copies of a version of it, including a photograph of Mussolini, were distributed on the ground, and that Calpis had paid for the message to appear in "all daily newspapers of the Empire."

(Although probably an overstatement, Mussolini's message did appear even in a newsletter of a youth organization in rural Akita prefecture.)[80] The organizing committee was composed of three respectable Meiji personalities: entrepreneur Shibusawa Eiichi, politician and bureaucrat Gotō Shinpei, and educator Sawayanagi Masatarō. They wrote to Mussolini, hailing the event as a way to "bring back to the righteous path those youth who had been led astray" and expressing their gratitude for the "immense fervor and formidable [spiritual] revival that [Mussolini's] message provoked in Japan's youth."[81]

From Shimoi's point of view, the Calpis affair had been a success. Obscure when he left Tokyo in 1915, by the mid-1920s he was recognized and readily associated with Italy, Fascism, and Mussolini.[82] His passion for Italian culture, extending from Dante to D'Annunzio, had ended in an embrace of the Fascist politics of Mussolini and was pursued in the brash, indefatigable manner characteristic of someone who grew up as an ambitious late-Meiji youth. D'Annunzio and Mussolini had a profound effect on him. Shimoi had learned from them how to utilize modern techniques of mass communication, which he put to good use, as demonstrated in his organization of the Hibiya event. His capacity to straddle aesthetics and spectacle, high culture and mass politics set him aside from other nationalists.[83] He saw no contradiction between his work as a *professore* of Italian culture and his political life as an activist for Fascism. On the contrary, Shimoi was convinced that only by linking culture and politics in new ways could Japan's own resurgence be brought to full fruition.

Paedagocis: Youth and the Myth of World War I

"Japan's situation is getting worse day by day, with all kinds of problems resembling exactly those of Italy ten years ago. To know the road taken by Italy is the best guidance to think about the road that Japan ought to take."[84] Shimoi expressed these feelings in 1926, in *Taisenchū no Itaria* (Italy during the Great War, 1926), the work that best exemplified his program of cultural and social reform for Japan in the 1920s. He read the conflicts he found in Japan through the lens of his experiences in Italy and believed that the response that Italians had devised could stimulate a Japanese resurgence. Nevertheless, it was not his intention to replicate Italian Fascism. Rather, he had a more specific goal in mind—namely, to mobilize Japanese youth on behalf of the nation. Mobilization was the thread that ran through his interpretation of Italy's "second Renaissance." What *La Diana*, D'Annunzio, and Fascism had in common for Shimoi was the call on young men and women to set aside their differences by stirring them to unite for their country. He felt that no one was better qualified to teach these lessons than him. In this way *Taisenchū no Itaria* reveals how Shimoi's mindset as a conservative Meiji educator, which was based on the principles of obedience and discipline, had merged with the aesthetics of Fascism that he had embraced in Italy after World War I, which called for rebellion, violence, and death.

Italian Fascism saw itself as a youthful movement that would rejuvenate national politics and bring about social order.[85] Shimoi could relate well to this discourse. Since the early 1900s conservative critics had alerted Japanese readers to a morally decadent and socially destitute youth—what one of them, the nationalist journalist Tokutomi Sohō, later called "colorless youth" [*mushoku seinen*].[86] In 1920s Japan, as elsewhere, the social landscape of youth had grown ever more complex. After the economic expansion during World War I, rural youngsters migrated in large numbers to Japan's major industrial cities. In places such as Tokyo and Osaka these youth became part of the masses that made up the country's working class, unemployed and, sometimes, petty criminals.[87] Educated urban youth often embraced socialism, feminism, or consumerism, causing disquiet among commentators like Sohō, who argued that youth had to be taught the ideal of linking individual interest to that of the state. As Sohō put it, "Without ideals [*risō*], there is no ambition; without ambition there is no self-denial [*kokki*], no endeavor [*doryoku*] and one easily ends in self-abandonment [*jibōjiki*]."[88] Mussolini and Fascism, it seemed to Shimoi, had overcome these modern evils by organizing Italian youth around the time-honored values of the nation.

Taisenchū contained Shimoi's strategy to mobilize Japanese youth. The book was a mythic account of World War I characterized by a narrative of heroism and sacrifice that linked the patriotic fervor of the prewar years to the spirit that was born on the battlefields and continued in peacetime under Fascism.[89] A project that bears the hallmark of Shimoi's expertise in children's tales, the book outlines the main events and protagonists of Italy's war as a moral story directed at a young readership. While it revives the themes in Shimoi's earlier work, *The Italian War* (1919), *Taisenchū* presents the war as an aesthetic adventure that is character building and formative. "Poetry is dead," remarked a French soldier in 1917.[90] Shimoi could not have disagreed more, for, in his view, it was alive and well in the politics of Fascism.

George Mosse has argued that Italy was at the forefront in the wider transformation of the relationship between poetry and politics around the time of World War I.[91] *Taishenchū* illustrates this point not only in Shimoi's move from D'Annunzio to Mussolini but also in his contention that ordinary Italians—especially young men, but also women and children—had rediscovered poetry in their everyday lives by fighting in World War I. He glorified Nazario Sauro and Cesare Battisti, irredentists who were executed by the Austrians for their pro-Italian activities; Enrico Toti, the maimed "one-legged" hero who had made a name for himself by riding his bicycle to Lapland before dying as a volunteer in the trenches; Luigi Rizzo, the naval officer who sank the Austro-Hungarian battleship *Szent István*; Francesco Baracca, a virtuoso air-force pilot killed in action; and E. A. Mario, the Neapolitan writer, poet, and folk musician who after the war composed the patriotic song "The Legend of the Piave." Shimoi was fond of portraying his affection for these soldiers as well as the peasants and women he met near the frontlines, for whom, he argued, war was at the same time art and materiality.[92] On one side, there was the harshness of daily life—hunger, cold, and death—and on the other, the production of poetic life. All Italians were poets, he explained. On one occasion he caught a group of soldiers in the trenches reading the nineteenth-century poet Giovanni Pascoli as bombs flew over their heads. Elsewhere, he recounted the story of one soldier who, in spite of his minimal education, had become "an incandescent poet" at the front, always stirring up the emotions of the men around him.[93]

In a European context, *Taisenchū* may have seemed a banal example of a right-wing memoir of World War I. But in a country that had not known the trenches or total mobilization, and where firsthand accounts of the conflict were few, the book stood out. Shimoi's melodramatic and gripping style, aided by over fifty photographs, struck a chord with young Japanese. During the 1920s the market for popular literature boomed, and it is telling that between 1925 and 1927 Shimoi published eight books with some of the most representative presses of this period.[94] *Fassho undō* (The Fascist Movement) was published by Minyūsha (1925), the house founded by the conservative critic and journalist Tokutomi Sohō, who by then had come to display a keen interest in Fascism and Shimoi. *Mussorini no shishiku* (Mussolini's Lion Roar) appeared as a special edition of Kōdansha's *King* (1929), the main magazine of mass culture in the second half of the 1920s. (In March 1930 the publishers were still advertising the book, then in its twenty-third edition.)[95] Shimoi claimed that his *Gyorai no se ni matagarite* (Riding on the Back of a Torpedo, 1926), a book on Italian special squads, was "chosen as a reading for the empress and the prince regent, a distinction that is given only rarely and only to books of national interest."[96]

Although all these publications replicated Shimoi's personal myth of World War I, some went further in presenting in great detail the way in which, according to its author, Fascism had changed Italians and what Japanese could learn from it. Under Mussolini's rule, young Italians spontaneously respected the "ancestral land," unlike Japanese youth, who did so only because they were told to in school.[97] Italians had become efficient. They no longer engaged in long, formulaic greetings like the Japanese but jumped to their feet and raised their arms in a Roman salute, exclaiming "To us!"(*A noi*)—a sign, Shimoi felt, of their willingness to work hard, and a salute that ought to be adopted by Japanese, as "*Wareware ni*" sounded equally good.[98] Italians had become champions of "manliness" (*otokorashiishugi*); Japanese were stuck with an effeminate obsession with "safety first" (*anzen daiichi*).[99] Italian women were good wives, wise mothers, and understood that the home (*katei*) was the "way" (*michi*) of the woman. Their Japanese counterparts lacked these morals. They acted like "Americans, copying their women's movement, and, advocating women's suffrage, they go outside the house at will strolling around, they make speeches in their shrill voices, hang around in that flippant manner—and they call themselves 'culture women' . . . I hate these women."[100] It is difficult to gauge the effect of Shimoi's books on his readers, but, at least as far as one editor was concerned, Shimoi's work demonstrated the close resemblance between the sentiments of Italians and Japanese, and had "penetrated particularly the hearts of our youth and urged the awakening and arousal of their spirit."[101]

In addition to his publications, Shimoi used another strategy to mobilize Japanese along the lines of Fascism. Resorting to the oratorical skills he had learned from D'Annunzio and Mussolini, he became a grassroots activist. Traveling through the entire archipelago, he boasted that he had given "more than four hundred speeches" to workers, peasants, ex-military, and students, and made a point of mentioning that each one lasted on average three and a half hours.[102] In many of these speeches he attacked the labor movements and their requests for shorter working hours. In Italy, he pontificated, there were no debates about the eight-hour day. Mussolini had done away with this simplistic socialist conception of the limitation of the worker's time. The Duce himself dedicated as little time as possible to leisure or meals, working some twenty hours a day. "If one works thinking of one's dignity, work is not at all a hardship—it becomes a pleasure. It is possible to work eight hours, nay ten hours, even twelve hours."[103] Shimoi earned himself a reputation as a strikebreaker. On one occasion, the chairman of the Japanese Communist Party, Sano Manabu, referred to an incident at Ashio's copper mines when management had called on Shimoi to dissuade workers from forming a union. Sano added that "when [Shimoi] started his speech, a threatening crowd of workers chased him off the premises."[104]

Shimoi's forays into other organizations whose membership was composed mainly of young men offer further evidence of the extent of his work and goals in the mid-1920s. He forged connections with the military. According to the Italian ambassador, in these years Shimoi received the support of the army and navy ministries, although it is not clear in what form.[105] He also founded a "patriotic movement," the *Kōkoku seinentō* (Imperial Country Youth Party). To train its young members, he followed musters he had learned in Italy. His goal, as he wrote to Mussolini, was to counter "the penetration of Russian communism in the industrial and agricultural centers, as it leads to painful agrarian conflicts,

Shimoi Harukichi at the height of his fame, ca. 1927. Among the bystanders are the right-wing patron Tōyama Mitsuru and the conservative journalist Tokutomi Sohō, standing next to Italian embassy officials. The event was sponsored by Yebisu Beer.

(Photo courtesy of Kuribayashi Machiko, Tokyo.)

strikes, class conflict . . . under arrogant red organizations."[106] While his movement was short-lived, the significance of this experiment lies in what Shimoi had in mind. He explained that it was based on the Fascist type but, crucially, was "adapted to the national characteristics of Japan, that is, it is based on the sentiment of the ancestral land unified through the monarchy." In other words, in Japan political and social reform was centered on the emperor, who "was and must be forever the center of national solidarity."[107]

Black Shirts, White Tigers: The *Byakkōtai* Affair

On December 6, 1928, the provincial town of Aizu Wakamatsu, three hundred kilometers northeast of Tokyo, celebrated the arrival of a Roman column sent to it as a gift of friendship by Benito Mussolini. The event commemorated the "white tigers" (*byakkōtai*), a group of young Aizu warriors. They had fought on the losing side during the Bōshin War of 1868, the conflict between the newly established

Shimoi at the head of a youth movement, unnamed but possibly the Kōkoku Seinentō, the short-lived group he had founded in the mid-1920s. Such groups became more common in the late 1920s and 1930s, but it is likely that Shimoi drew inspiration from Fascist youth organizations such as the Balilla or the Fasci Giovanili di Combattimento. Shimoi, dressed in white, is third from the left in the front row, ca. 1926.

(Photo courtesy of Kuribayashi Machiko, Tokyo.)

government under Emperor Meiji and the shogunate, with which the Aizu Domain was allied. After imperial troops defeated their clan's armies, the young patriots committed suicide rather than fall prisoners to the enemy. What sparked the Duce's interest in the episode was a casual reference by Shimoi. Mussolini, it seems, expressed admiration for the *byakkōtai* and made a vague promise that he would back up his sentiments with a concrete gesture.[108] Rumors spread, probably circulated by Shimoi, provoking great excitement among Aizu notables, who inflated the story of the Italian leader's interest into a matter of national importance. The *byakkōtai* affair turned into a diplomatic problem between Japan and Italy, but it also became an opportunity for Japanese to revisit patriotically a divisive and, until then, unresolved, incident in their recent history.

Although publicized by Shimoi, the driving force of the *byakkōtai* affair was a coterie of influential bureaucrats from Aizu. Desirous of the honor and recognition that a gift from Mussolini would bring, they pressured government officials into persuading the Fascist regime to live up to its leader's word. In February 1928 Baron Yamakawa Kenjirō, a local and former head of Tokyo Imperial University, urged Prime Minister Tanaka Giichi to intervene so that the celebrations would be held. Preparations had already started in Aizu, Yamakawa informed him, but there were as yet no signs of the monument; and "Shimoi is nowhere to be found."[109] Swayed by this appeal, Tanaka sent his deputy to persuade the Italians to complete the work. If shipping a monument was not possible, the diplomat asked, would Mussolini at least consider sending a "solemn message."[110] Eventually, the Italians gave their approval. After some quibbles over the text of the engraving, the 8.35 meters high, 25-ton column, dug out from the Roman Forum, finally left Naples in October 1928.[111]

In the hands of Japanese government officials the *byakkōtai* commemoration became a major national event. A high-profile committee provided the pomp and circumstance for the inauguration of Mussolini's gift to Aizu and Japan. Tanaka Giichi was himself a member, as were Shidehara Kijurō, the foreign minister, and Matsudaira Tsuneo, the ambassador to Britain and an Aizu native. Baron Ōkura Kishichirō, head of the Ōkura conglomerate, represented industry; the military contributed by sending the emperor's aide-de-camp; and to give the committee a touch of aristocratic gravitas Prince Konoe Fumimaro was the committee's president, while Prince Takamatsu, the emperor's third brother, lent the celebration his august patronage. It was the "first time an imperial prince [had] assumed such a role," the Italian ambassador, Pompeo Aloisi, informed his superiors in Rome, assuring them that this had to be considered "a special act of deference from the emperor" to Mussolini.[112]

The unveiling of the antique column, adorned by the regime with its two most distinctive symbols, an eagle and two fasces, had three major consequences. First, cultural effusions over the *byakkōtai* promoted a diplomatic rapprochement between Japan and Italy. In his speech, Konoe articulated his conviction that "this monument, besides enlivening a constant inspiration of the civil virtues of the nation, will also be a spiritual symbol and an act that strengthens ever more the friendship between Japan and Italy."[113] It was a nicety that was not altogether out of place. On July 12, 1929, Shidehara Kijurō met Aloisi, remarking that "on various international questions . . . the Italian and Japanese governments, which have so much similarity in their foreign policies, keep friendly relations."[114] Prince Takamatsu echoed the minister's diplomatic sentiments. After a tour of duty to London in November 1929, he made it a point to visit Rome for an audience with Mussolini to express his gratitude for the gift of the Roman column.[115] And, the following year, Ōkura Kishichirō sponsored an important exhibition of Japanese modern art in Rome.

The Roman column sent to Aizu-Wakamatsu by Mussolini in 1928. At its lower end are the fasces, symbols of Fascism, which were removed during the Allied Occupation (1945–1952).

(Photo courtesy of ASMAE.)

The event had another effect. Thanks to its high profile and broad coverage in the press and newsreels, Fascism and Mussolini extended their reputation in Japan beyond the major metropolitan centers. One Japanese official commented that the news of Mussolini's column was "spread by newspapers, and not just in the area of Aizu, but in the whole country, and, in particular, it has raised interest and expectations among young people."[116] Indeed, people flocked to the occasion in large numbers. When his train was nearing Aizu, Aloisi was stunned to see that, despite it being six o'clock in the morning, there were "not only all civilian and military authorities of the province, but the entire population who, for about six kilometers was shouting 'alalà' [a Fascist salute] as I passed to go to the hotel." The town was adorned with Italian flags—the first time a foreign flag had been flown there, he asserted. Iimoriyama, the hill designated as the site for the monument, would become one of Japan's "most regularly visited places of pilgrimage."[117]

Finally, the *byakkōtai* affair offered a chance to bring Aizu's uncomfortable past into national history. In the sixty years since the end of the Bōshin war the "white tigers," having fought against the emperor's army, had remained "enemies of the court" (*chōteki*) in official discourse. To be sure, since 1868 Aizu locals had gradually managed to enter the higher ranks of officialdom. Yamakawa and Matsudaira were two examples.[118] But the *byakkōtai* was not granted a place in the complex of national myths. The 1928 event made this possible. With the presence of representatives of all major organs of the state, the commemoration of the *byakkōtai* through the Roman column amounted to an implicit acknowledgment of the "white tigers" as national heroes. Konoe Fumimaro was unwittingly touching on the hidden meaning of the event when he commented that "this rejoicing and satisfaction should not be confined to the members of the *byakkōtai* but be enjoyed and felt by the nation as a whole because the spirit of the chivalry of our Japan was upheld abroad by the premier of Italy."[119] In short, Fascist recognition of the *byakkōtai* strengthened Japanese national unity.

The *byakkōtai* affair marked the apex of Shimoi's career as Fascism's impresario in Japan. His role in the event was limited to bringing the "white tigers" to the attention of Mussolini and was not publicly acknowledged, but he no doubt took it as a validation of his convictions about the spiritual bonds between Japan and Italy. For him, the story of the *byakkōtai* proved that the two countries could mutually reinforce each other. The *byakkōtai* had moved the Duce, convincing him to express his admiration for the young warriors in the form of a Roman—and Fascist—column. This symbol provoked great interest in Japan, to the point that it allowed Japanese to overcome a past history of division and conflict. Ultimately, it appeared to Shimoi, the event led to the kind of national mobilization that he had been advocating. By emphasizing youth, both as the subject of commemoration and the object of mobilization, he believed that the *byakkōtai* affair vindicated the pedagogical project he had devised in late Meiji.

And yet the *byakkōtai* affair also terminated Shimoi's vision of social and cultural reform based on Italo-Japanese intimacy. His latest—and boldest—attempt to mediate between the two countries interfered with the diplomacy of two states, which led to animosity toward him at all levels. The Japanese ambassador in Rome informed his foreign ministry that Shimoi's "deceptions" had "touched on the honor of Mussolini." His superior agreed, inflamed at Shimoi's "profiteering" and the "great trouble" he had caused.[120] In Italy, Antonio Beltramelli, a biographer of Mussolini and once a faithful friend, reported that it had become clear to him that Shimoi was a fraud, that he had been investigated by the Neapolitan police, and that he had been "a cocaine dealer."[121]

Events surrounding the *byakkōtai* celebrations ushered in a new phase in Japan's relation with Fascism. The relatively spontaneous eruption of the affair signified not only that, by 1928, Japanese had acquired a great deal of familiarity with Italian Fascism but also that they no longer needed Shimoi's mediation. From the early 1920s Shimoi had perhaps done more than anyone else to popularize Italian Fascism, commodifying its exponents—D'Annunzio and Mussolini—and rephrasing its ideology into a language of patriotism that could be readily understood by a mass Japanese audience. In this sense, Shimoi's fascism was produced neither in Italy, nor in Japan, but in both contexts. If the escalating interest in Fascism was partly Shimoi's success, as he had helped to create it, it also caused him a setback, for he could not control it. As he searched for new roles, a wider public turned to scrutinize Fascism, starting with its leader, Benito Mussolini.

2

THE MUSSOLINI BOOM, 1928–1931

Andrea: Unhappy is the land that breeds no hero.
Galileo: No, Andrea: Unhappy is the land that needs a hero.

—Berthold Brecht, *Life of Galileo*, 1938

"Among today's world leaders, whom do you like best?" a newspaper asked Japanese in a national survey in 1927. The readers' response left no doubt: Benito Mussolini, the Italian dictator and Duce of Fascism.[1] Their answer was confirmed by a veritable boom around Mussolini in the late 1920s. Featured in theater plays, biographies, commercial advertisements, and films, he emerged as a popular celebrity as well as a political leader much discussed by the Japanese public. To be sure, in this period Mussolini was making headlines around the world. In such liberal countries as France, the United States, and Great Britain journalists and intellectuals found much to admire in this man, whom they often compared with Napoleon, Caesar, or Cromwell. As a Columbia Productions poster later put it, Mussolini "might be the answer to America's needs."[2] But in Japan, perhaps more than elsewhere, the timing of Mussolini's popularity is noteworthy. The year 1928, when the interest in him peaked, coincided with Japan's first election held under universal male suffrage. How can we explain the thirst for knowledge about the life and deeds of a dictator at a time when Japan had reached one of the liberal pinnacles of Taishō democracy? For many contemporaries this was no paradox.

In the second half of the 1920s, politicians, journalists, and critics began to argue that liberalism had reached an impasse. Progressive reformers who had once supported such liberal ideals as party cabinets, freedom of expression, and meritocracy as a way to curb the power of unelected institutions—the bureaucracy, the elder statesmen (*genrō*), or the military—came to the conclusion that a decade of liberal politics had done little to change the status quo.[3] They saw the Peace Preservation Law (1925) and the institutionalization of the two major political parties, the Seiyūkai and the Minseitō, as symptoms that the government remained in the hands of established elites who repressed the will of the people rather than representing it. Conversely, conservatives criticized the liberal reforms, contending that these principles had led to a moral selfishness that caused the people, whom they principally understood as "imperial subjects," to disregard the higher ideals of the state. Though at loggerheads over the value of liberalism, both groups agreed that the underlying problem was the individual's role in modern mass society. For reformists, liberalism had failed to develop a "new consciousness" that would have stirred the individual into seeking a more popular government; for conservatives, liberalism had enabled individuals to challenge the institutions of the state and their legitimate place in a hierarchical arrangement of power.[4]

The preoccupation with Mussolini outside the circles of the radical Right grew as a result of the Duce's capacity to straddle both liberal and conservative ideals of the individual. Some Japanese with a liberal bent were drawn to Mussolini because he had displaced the entrenched elites thanks to his skill to mobilize the people, an endeavor, they pointed out, that Japanese politicians were either reluctant to undertake or incapable of replicating. Mussolini's populism, his background as a journalist, and his gifts in oratory, led them to believe that he was the opposite of those whom Tokutomi Sohō, the nationalist commentator, vilified as "specialized politicians," functionaries who served state and emperor but lacked any connection to the people.[5] Conservatives, anxious about *raison d'état*, commended Mussolini's determination to repress the Left and curtail individual freedoms in order to reinforce the existing social order and the prerogatives of the state. The Duce appeared to be a talented statesman who swayed Italians into obedience by inculcating in them a love of nation and state. Mussolini, then, appealed not so much as a despot, but as a man who had developed cultural and political strategies that could be appropriated—on the side of conservatives, to curtail liberalism and, on the side of liberals, to revamp a liberal democracy that was in crisis.

In this way, the debate about Mussolini spoke to the quest for an individual capable of healing the rifts in modern mass society by forging consent between rulers and ruled.[6] In other words, it was a discourse about political and cultural leadership. Indeed, writers and politicians of late Taishō and early Shōwa displayed an acute interest in the lives of leaders past and present, discussing them in terms of "great men" (*ijin*), the character of a "genius" (*tensai*), or the attributes of a "hero" (*eiyū*). To some extent, they longed for a talented, hard-nosed politician who would rise above the perceived mediocrity of Japan's ruling class. In 1928, for example, Tsurumi Yūsuke, an acclaimed Anglophile author, politician, and orator, published *On the Hoped-for Hero* (Eiyū taibō-ron), in which he lyrically lamented that only a great man could put an end to his country's stagnation: "Genius, arise! Hero, arise!"[7] But often leadership was thought of as an aspect that had to be cultivated in ordinary Japanese. Educators, in particular, worried about the leveling effect of modern mass society and sought in the lives of leaders evidence that all Japanese could achieve great things, even if these accomplishments belonged to the general sphere of their everyday lives. In an age of consumerism and materialist ideologies, they argued, Japanese could excel in moral leadership, such as upholding the value of the family or the sanctity of the state.

Mussolini had a broad appeal because he seemed to possess both extraordinary and ordinary features of modern leadership. Max Weber famously argued that these qualities were merged in a "charismatic leader," but this type of individual was hardly what Japanese political and moral commentators were looking for.[8] Rather, they believed that Mussolini's ordinariness—his lower-middle-class background and his manliness—should inspire Japan's elites to be closer to the people; and that, conversely, his extraordinary talents as a strong statesman were capable of arousing in the people the sentiment that heroism was within everyone's reach.

Much about Mussolini was, of course, a myth, carefully crafted in Rome by the regime, reinforced by the Duce himself, and seconded by admirers at home and abroad.[9] Thus the significance of the Mussolini boom lies in the fact that Japanese writers, ideologues, educators, and politicians participated in the production of the global myth of Mussolini even as they debated the Duce in the context of the political and cultural anxieties of Japan. But this does not mean they accepted the verities of Mussolini uncritically. Quite the contrary was the case. Even as they evinced a range of interests in the figure of Mussolini, they appropriated the facets of his character selectively, often balancing his virtues with a wide scope of criticism that was absent in Shimoi Harukichi. Still, sharing with Mussolini a desire to rebuild national communities, liberals and conservatives operated in a gray area, a space that could accommodate Fascist leadership strategies in order to strengthen the bond between individuals and the state at a time when liberalism was in crisis.

An Italian Hero

Several liberal and conservative commentators were deeply ambivalent about Mussolini. A leader, they contended, had to be a revelation of the national past, not a revolution coming from the global present, and Mussolini served the reality and needs of Italy. Tsurumi Yūsuke made this point when he stated that a hero was organically connected to his people, who would spontaneously follow him because he was a "comprehensive leader" (*sōgō shidōsha*), one who embodied all the qualities of the nation. Optimistically, he added that, because "the heroic spurt of blood that brought about the Meiji Restoration [in the 1860s] is still throbbing in the veins of the Japanese nation [*minzoku*]," they would naturally produce an indigenous leader without the need to rely on foreign models.[10] Progressive spokesmen like Tsurumi were among Mussolini's fiercest critics, and yet, it is important to emphasize, their skepticism reflected not so much an uncompromising defense of democratic politics as considerations of national characteristics.

The idea that Mussolini was good for the Italians but bad for everyone else betrayed two conflicting tendencies of liberal thought about the Duce. Steeped in the tastes of Anglo-American liberalism, the Japanese liberal intelligentsia also shared its racist stereotypes of Latin peoples, among which Italy was assessed as a particularly backward country. Italians were often perceived as lazy, dirty, and unrefined. Indeed, Tsurumi surmised, for Italians life was a very "practical" (*genjitsuteki*) thing. Contrary to the Germans' "abstract conception of the world," Italians thought of "eating, drinking, singing, and loving." Their nature was such that

> they cannot think with their own heads. Therefore when an extraordinary man thinks in their stead, they accept him unreservedly. They do not live in an abstract world, but in a pragmatic one. So they logically acknowledge that a lion is stronger than a cat. . . . If a Caesar emerges they are conscious that Caesar is greater than ordinary people. If a Michelangelo emerges, they recognize that Michelangelo's art is finer than that of the common run of men. If a Mussolini emerges, they will recognize immediately that he is greater than an Antonio or a Giovanni.

For this reason, Italians gave birth to such a figure because they have "no opinion, no education, and no strong individual consciousness . . . they are not fit for democracy."[11]

Backwardness, however, also meant that the primordial instincts of Italians were more or less intact. And "élan vital [*seimei no yakudō*]" was a virtue much praised by Tsurumi. He admitted that Italians possessed the "bursting vital energy characteristic of primitive people," a quality that made them "remarkably young" compared to their senescing European neighbors (who, Tsurumi observed, had at the very least "reached middle age"). He admired Italians' bravery and their readiness to spring into action. "They are not like the Swiss, who save every penny, breeding cows in their pastures and trying to make some money with milk. With their adventurous hearts, Italians leap into danger."[12]

Linking the instincts of the nation with those of the individual was a Darwinian association that was widespread among Taishō liberals, many of whom argued that Mussolini expressed the Italian collective instinct.[13] Nitobe Inazō, a Christian author, diplomat, and politician as well as mentor to Tsurumi, went so far as to remark that Mussolini represented a turning point in Italian history. After he visited Italy during the early years of Fascism, it seemed to him that he had witnessed "verily the beginning of the Italian revolution, the second stage of the French revolution." He left Italy with only one regret, "not having had the chance to meet this hero [*gōketsu*]," Mussolini.[14] For Nitobe, the Duce represented the dead past of Italy at the same time as he embodied the vital impulses necessary for this nation to thrive.

The association of Mussolini with Italy could lead to another critical perspective. Mussolini was an extremist, the argument ran, because he assigned too much weight to either state authority or popular instinct, causing excesses that might have been necessary in Italy but were undesirable in Japan. Liberals feared that Mussolini commanded too much state power. "Mussolini might be great [*erai*], but in that they accept his repression, Italian citizens prove that they are unable to take care of their own lives and that they can hardly be considered honorable citizens." This was the assessment of Nakano Seigō, a journalist and aspiring politician better known for his outspoken sympathies for Fascist Italy and Nazi Germany in the mid-1930s but who, at this time, advocated representative democracy.[15] Nakano's comments were really directed at the increasingly authoritarian politics of General Tanaka Giichi, prime minister from 1927 to 1929. Although Nakano was no backer of the Japanese Left, he criticized the viciously anticommunist Tanaka Giichi and his home minister, Suzuki Kisaburō, who in 1928 had ordered a crackdown on the Japanese Communist Party. "Suzuki," Nakano held, "reeks of Mussolinian violence [*bōryokushugi*]." The phenomenon of Mussolini, Nakano claimed, had to be understood in the context of the inferior moral development of Italians. By trying to imitate him, Tanaka and Suzuki "let themselves be misled by the trend of a small-sized, simple and convenient Mussolini, just like the fad for small-sized taxis [*entaku-kei*]." Japanese, Nakano was quite sure, did not deserve a Mussolinian treatment. "Our citizens, as one could see in the election some time ago, have a lot of common sense. They are not a baseless [*kudaranai*] people. They will not let themselves be ruled either by the tip of the brush of Marxism or by Mussolini."[16]

If liberal politicians connected Mussolini to an expansion of state repression, conservatives worried that he was a figure who undermined the state's authority. Although they welcomed the Duce's crushing of the Left, they found it intolerable that a crowd of petty-bourgeois parvenus like Mussolini and his followers could displace existing political elites and take over the high offices of the state. Ultimately, they were terrified that an ordinary man could impinge on the prerogatives of the sovereign. "Will Mussolini become a monarch?" asked a seasoned commentator of international affairs, Inahara Katsuji. The journalist believed that

Mussolini had created the Fascist Grand Council, a new constitutional organ, as a way to establish a Machiavellian dictatorship. Just like Lenin, Mussolini "sees ends, not means."[17] In such a situation, Inahara continued, "Mussolini would supervise Mussolini, that is, a farce."[18] The problem, however, was not so much that he escaped popular control, but that his institutionalization would cause the "meaning of the existence of the monarch himself [to] become extremely shallow."[19]

The relationship between a figure like Mussolini and a monarch was particularly sensitive in Japan because it became embroiled in an existing controversy over the place of the emperor in the Japanese state. The so-called organ theory debate originated in differing scholarly interpretations of the Meiji constitution but by the late 1920s had spilled over into more heated public disputes. One side, led by the scholar Minobe Tatsukichi, argued that the emperor was merely an organ of the state; Minobe's opponents, especially Hozumi Yatsuka and Uesugi Shinkichi, professed that the emperor transcended the state and that, therefore, he was not accountable to the people. In February 1928, no doubt as a response to the popularity of Mussolini, Uesugi published an article on the Duce in the current affairs journal *Chūō kōron*. "On Mussolini, Enemy of Reason and Justice" rebuked Mussolini and those Japanese who, according to its author, sympathized with him. For Uesugi, Mussolini was a "monster dictator" whose politics contradicted the Japanese "kingly way" (*ōdō*), which was based on the "love and justice" that emanated from the emperor. He did not worry about Mussolini's repression of people's democratic rights, but that he was the outcome of the masses possessing too many rights and aspirations in the first place. Parliamentary democracy gave an unnecessary voice to the people, as was the case in Europe, whose "five-hundred million idiots [*baka*]" were trapped in "a great chaos of thought." Japanese needed neither democracy nor Mussolini, but the emperor's benevolent rule, which embodied the "idea of virtue, develop[ed] civilization, construct[ed] the state in eternity, and . . . perfect[ed] the people's quality as human beings [*jinkaku*]."[20] Ultimately, the problem with Mussolini was that, although his attempt to harmonize the relationship between the people and the state was laudable, he failed to strike the right balance, causing variously populist excesses that desecrated state authority or, conversely, government repression at the expense of the people.

A Modern Hero

The critical view of Mussolini coexisted with a more positive interpretation granting that the Duce possessed certain qualities that Japanese politicians of the 1920s lacked. In particular, in these years liberal "reformists," backed by large swaths of public opinion, attacked the political class on two accounts.[21] First, they argued that Japanese leaders, in their embrace of Wilsonian internationalism, had given proof of their unwillingness to stand up for the national interest. They had sacrificed Japan's rightful colonial interests in Asia, and in particular in China, in order to develop a foreign policy that was too conciliatory with the West. Second, politicians were accused of being corrupt and removed from ordinary people. As a critic later summed it up, Japanese politicians had a poor hand at being popular, because "they do not know the techniques."[22] What intrigued these critics was Mussolini's capacity to win popular support despite being a dictator. The search for Mussolini's universal lessons meant not only that he had to be partly removed from his national context; it also meant that, in order to appropriate some of his strategies, Japanese depoliticized him, separating him from the ideology of Fascism.

Echoing the views of their German contemporary, the conservative legal scholar Carl Schmitt, Japanese critics of parliamentary democracy lamented the absence of a figure capable of making decisions. As early as 1923, the vice minister of the army General Ugaki Kazushige praised that "extraordinary man [*kaiketsu*], Mussolini" for having formed a resolute political leadership.[23] Critics, liberal and conservative alike, felt that the shortcomings of Japanese leaders were particularly acute when it came to foreign policy.[24] They chastised party cabinets, whether from the Seiyūkai or Minseitō, for being indecisive and bent on compromise for the sake of the politics of internationalism promoted by the League of Nations and the Western powers. The Washington Conference of 1922, in which Japan agreed to limit the size of its naval armaments, was one case that caused great domestic uproar. Even more sensitive with the population was the government's open-door policy in China, and especially in North China and Manchuria, areas that many in the military, but also in the government, had earmarked as Japanese spheres of interest.[25]

With these concerns in mind, Japanese advocates of a "strong foreign policy" (*kyōko gaikō*) praised the "iron man" (*tetsuwan*) Mussolini and his stance on foreign affairs. In a two-part article on Italian politics, the *Asahi* newspaper journalist Maida Minoru (1878–?), a veteran Europe correspondent, commented on Mussolini's firm grip on his country's foreign policy. He emphasized the Duce's military intervention during the 1923 Corfu incident, when Mussolini had ordered a naval and aerial bombardment of the Greek island after the killing of an Italian general and then refused to collaborate with the League. Maida hailed it a success for the Duce, noting that determination in foreign policy helped him to remain popular at home and gain respect abroad.[26]

Another journalist interested in Mussolini's approach to foreign policy was the *Osaka Mainichi* correspondent, Nakahira Akira, who found in the Duce a leader who dared to challenge established norms and stand up to the Great Powers. Admitting that Mussolini's territorial ambitions in North Africa, Ethiopia, and the Balkans destabilized Europe, he nevertheless legitimized Mussolini's ambitions. Italy, Nakahira argued, was oppressed by the international status quo sanctioned by the League of Nations. Its major powers, France and Britain, obstructed Italian colonial expansion as a solution to the country's lack of resources and its excess population. According to Nakahira, because Japan faced the same problems, "one must learn from the Fascist attitude of facing the world and majestically stress the clear consciousness of one's needs. . . . Just like Italy, our country should call out its demands on the Asian continent."[27]

Mussolini's attitude in foreign affairs was not the only aspect of his leadership to evoke discussion. Journalists wrote with admiration about Mussolini because of his political style and the techniques he developed to rule Italians. In the 1920s the Fascist regime developed a sophisticated aesthetic apparatus around the person of Mussolini with the intent to promote what is often called a "cult of personality." Through photographs, films, and biographies the regime attempted to create a mythic image of the dictator as a "new man" with exceptional qualities, emphasizing his energy and ability to dominate, and thus to unify, the people.[28]

Several pundits yielded to this image of the Duce. In the context of the perceived mediocrity of Japan's political class, they contrasted Mussolini to Japanese politicians who, in their view, indulged in long-winded discussions that failed to inspire ordinary Japanese. In 1924, the political scientist Yoshida Yakuni, a scholar of Machiavelli, witnessed a speech of Mussolini's and was struck by his rhetoric. "To imagine what Mussolini's speech was like, one should think that it was just like his looks . . . his voice, reverberating like a bell, could be heard from afar . . . powerful and abounding with energy, not in the slightest does his voice provoke a feeling of ennui in the listener."[29] Nagai Ryūtarō, an exponent of the liberal reformists and, in the 1930s, the holder of several cabinet posts, hailed Mussolini's oratory as an example of a patriotic leader's devotion to nation and state.[30] So impressed was Nagai by the Duce's oratory that in 1927 he translated Mussolini's maiden speech. Nagai argued that Japanese misunderstood Mussolini, a "giant" (*kyojin*) of the contemporary world, when they called him an "arrogant" leader. In his view, the Duce's "arrogance [was] not due to haughtiness but, on the contrary, to his ardor burning for emperor and country." Having offered to the sovereign "his passionate efforts and his intention to achieve their perfection," Mussolini encapsulated the highest principles of government.[31] His dedication, Nagai continued, should be a lesson for the Japanese. "In the present day, Japan awaits the emergence of an arrogant great politician, just like Mussolini, fearing the heavens yet not fearing man, who can carry out a great, resolute revival of the state."[32]

Mussolini developed another strategy of rule that fascinated Japanese: personal audiences with the leader. Receiving visitors, Italians and foreigners alike, occupied a large part of Mussolini's working day and was an integral part of his regime. He used audiences for paternalistic exchanges of favors, but also as a symbolic device that represented the union of the people and their leader, as if to emphasize that one man alone could represent ordinary Italians more effectively than parliament. The staging of the audiences was closely regulated by his secretariat, the Segreteria Particolare del Duce, which meticulously briefed Mussolini about his visitors. If they had published a book, for example, guests frequently commented that they spotted a copy of it on Mussolini's desk. It was a ceremony that was not left to chance and usually produced the desired effect on Mussolini's visitors.[33]

Japanese were quick to recognize that one distinctive characteristic of Mussolini was the fact that he could be visited. A minor but regular presence at Palazzo Venezia, the Renaissance palace in central Rome that was home to Mussolini's offices, a diverse crowd of Japanese artists, diplomats, politicians, journalists, and political activists visited Mussolini throughout the two decades of his rule.[34] For many, being able to look Mussolini in the eye was awe-inspiring and confirmed the image of the Duce as a virile statesman. Okada Tadahiko, a former prefectural governor, head of the police department (*keihōkyoku chō*), and member of parliament for the Seiyūkai, was impressed by the leader's physique, his "piercing eyes," "large mouth," and "sturdy chin." When Okada wished Mussolini good health, he was immediately taken aback by the Duce's retort: "My health doesn't matter. The point is thinking about the future of Italy." An awestruck Okada replied that "these words truly illustrate a politician's resolve. I will keep them as a tale of my travels for the day when I return to Japan."[35]

Some historians have connected the cult of the Duce to what they regard as the sacralization of politics under Fascism.[36] It is striking, however, that the reports left by Japanese indicate that Mussolini impressed them for his ordinariness rather than his godlike stature (after all, in Japan, religion and politics mixed in a far more unequivocal manner in the figure of the emperor). A number of visitors commented on how an amiable Mussolini made them feel at ease. Takaishi Shingorō, a correspondent for the *Osaka Mainichi*, was granted an audience in 1928 accompanied by two other staff members from the newspaper and an American journalist with connections to Mussolini. At first anxious over the political topics that he would have to broach, Takaishi was relieved that his host displayed a keen interest in the promotional brochure about the city of Osaka that he had brought along. "Prime Minister Mussolini's interest in the magazine exceeded our expectations," he recalled. "He flipped through every single page from the beginning to the end and pointed to photos, asking for explanations . . . and we would answer that Osaka is an industrial and commercial city." With his "passionate questions," Takaishi went on, he made everyone feel comfortable—he even "happily" conceded to allow us to take a photograph and to give us an autograph. "The concerns we had before the audience and my plans about how to proceed in the conversation disappeared like snow in the spring in front of Prime Minister Mussolini's humanity, his figure, and true feelings."[37]

The picture of Mussolini is therefore a complex one. While some Japanese reviled him, it was also common to find comments glorifying him for his achievements. Yet perhaps most significant was the tendency, as exemplified by Takaishi, to humanize the Duce. By stressing his everyday characteristics, Japanese often disregarded that Mussolini was a dictator; after all, their primary concern was not Mussolini's politics but the personality of the leader. Nagai Ryūtarō was most emphatic on this point. In an article published in 1927, titled "From Wilson to Mussolini," Nagai argued that Mussolini ushered in a new stage in the history of politics because he had understood that a nation (*minzoku*) had a personality with a particular "desire for life" (*seikatsu yōkyū*) that required a particular form of "political organization."[38] Mussolini personified the global trend toward a "personality of a nation," which, overriding Woodrow Wilson's principle of national self-determination, would give birth to a new world order based on "coexistence and prosperity [*kyōzon kyōei*]." In line with these ideas, which he shared with Tsurumi Yūsuke, Nagai could not imagine a replica of Mussolini for Japan. Because he reflected the essence of Italy, Nagai concluded, "we cannot be satisfied with a model like Mussolini, but must make an effort to build a culture based on the peculiar personality of the Japanese people."[39] It was a statement that contradicted his earlier longing for a strong, "arrogant" politician; but it also reflected the wider ambivalence about the need for a figure like Mussolini.

A Moral Hero

In several quarters Mussolini was of interest less for his virtuosity as a political leader than as a model of ordinary moral leadership. Outside the realm of politics, the discourse on him reflected the aspiration of cultural critics, educators, and writers to reconstitute an individual subjectivity that was untouched by the commodification of modern life. As Miriam Silverberg has argued, in Japan the cultural revolution in the everyday life of the 1920s resulted in a tension between the individual as a consumer subject and as an imperial subject, with critics attacking materialistic individualism for undoing national cohesion.[40] To them, Mussolini appeared to be a man who had found a way to a socially safe individualism, one that subordinated materialism to spirit and was premised on the mobilization of the self for the nation. It is therefore ironic that the Mussolini boom of the late 1920s was enabled by mass culture and consumerism, the very phenomenon that many of his admirers were committed to eliminating. His presence in radio, magazines, cinema, commercials, and popular theater suggests that, from the onset, mass culture could be reconciled with conservative politics.[41] Indeed, Japanese consumer culture was overwhelmingly sympathetic to the Duce. Its producers pored over the life of Mussolini, presenting it as an example of individual success that was sanctioned by civic morality. In other words, they insisted that Mussolini had found a successful formula to combine individual success with the advancement of the nation. In so doing, they replicated the official Fascist narrative even as they made a conscious effort to direct their message to Japanese youth.

The two genres in which Mussolini became most visible in Japan were kabuki plays and biographies. Plays, perhaps, are a better indicator of the degree of stardom he had achieved in the late 1920s and, in turn, the role of mass culture in contributing to his myth. In the boom year of 1928, five theater pieces on the Duce were produced. The most striking adaptation of Mussolini for a mass audience was that of Kishida Tatsuya (1892–1944), a playwright for the all-female and greatly popular Takarazuka Revue.[42] The second was the play "The World's Great Man: Mussolini," written by Tsubouchi Shikō, the nephew of the famous novelist and literary critic Tsubouchi Shōyō.[43] Another was "Mussolini," a high-profile piece written by Osanai Kaoru (1881–1928), the playwright and Japan's leading director at this time, and featuring Ichikawa Sadanji II, the foremost actor of the interwar period.[44] The left-wing writer Maedakō Hiroichirō (1888–1957) produced a drama (*gikyoku*) also entitled "Mussolini." One other play by Numada Zōroku, a minor producer, was performed in Kyoto but is considered lost.

How can the production of these plays about Mussolini be explained? What did some of the most prominent actors and directors find appealing in the figure of the Duce? A number of answers are plausible. However much the plays contributed to the broad interest in Mussolini, his fame had preceded his appearance in kabuki theater. The activities of Shimoi, especially the Calpis affair and the uproar around the *byakkōtai* affair, as well as the general interest in the politics of Mussolini, probably made producers aware that there was a market for plays about him. At the same time, as James R. Brandon has shown, the production of plays based on contemporary political themes and personalities was not new. The Russo-Japanese War (1904–1905) saw the birth of "new wave" (*shinpa*) theater, which characteristically responded to contemporary events in order to both inform and entertain Japan's fledgling mass audiences.[45] Later, the 1920s witnessed a boom of popular theater (*taishū engeki*) that led to "new drama" (*shingeki*), a genre that attempted to respond to social change through realism and

Ichikawa Sadanji as Mussolini in Osanai Kaoru's play *Mussorini*.

(From Engei gahō, *no. 6 [1928].)*

The actor Furukawa Toshitaka as Mussolini in Tsubouchi Shikō's 1928 play *Mussorini*. To his left is Mori Eijirō and to his right Alfonso Gasco, Italian consul general in Kobe.

(From Takarazuka kokuminza kyakubon kaisetsu, *no. 4 [1928]: 7.)*

psychological analysis. Mussolini, who made headlines and offered a distinctive persona, was ideally suited for both genres: he spoke the language of the people, was prone to pathos, and had a life that was already mythologized—ready-made for a mass audience. Also, the aesthetics of his regime facilitated the transposition of Mussolini into theater. The quintessential fascist political space, the *piazza* (city square), could conveniently be replicated on stage, along with Fascist rituals and paraphernalia such as marches, songs, and symbols. Kishida Tatsuya's play, for example, reenacted the Fascist choreography that was associated with the dictator, especially the Blackshirts. Moreover, as a musical, it also reproduced Fascist songs, including the hymn of the Fascist Party (and unofficial Italian anthem) "Giovinezza" (Youth).[46] The Duce, in short, possessed many of the qualities that 1920s playwrights sought.

Writers and actors were not immune to the wider fascination with Mussolini. With the exception of Maedakō Hiroichirō, all playwrights expressed some degree of admiration for the Duce. Maedakō, a member of the literary current known as "proletarian literature" (*puroretaria bungaku*), presented an argument that reflected the Comintern theses on fascism, according to which Mussolini embodied bourgeois reaction against the proletariat. For this reason, but also at the behest of Italian authorities, his play was banned from being performed publicly (it did, however, appear, heavily censored, in the journal *Kaizō* in 1928).[47] In con-

The actor Furukawa Toshitaka emulating Mussolini's stare.

(From Nihon gikyoku zenshū, *43, 481.)*

trast, Kishida Tatsuya praised Mussolini, especially for making Italy into a safe place to visit. The "kind" Blackshirts were to be credited for the "disappearance of Italy's infamous fraudsters and mandatory tips." In the opening scene of his play, the main actor calls Mussolini "god of loyalty and patriotism [*chūkun aikoku*]."[48] Osanai Kaoru, though known for his left-leaning position, echoed

Mussolini's hatred of socialists, denouncing them in his play as "empty theorists, cowards, incompetents, and fence-sitters." Ichikawa Sadanji, too, was well-disposed toward the Duce. Having been granted an audience with him in 1927, he described the encounter in the warmest of terms, lauding the Italian "great man," whose "piercing glint in the eyes narrate half of the history of his life."[49]

Although none of these playwrights can be considered a Fascist, their fondness for Mussolini and their desire to represent him through his emotions led them to replicate large parts of the Fascist self-narrative. This approach is particularly visible in Tsubouchi Shikō's declaration that he aspired to tell Mussolini's story not "by stressing ideologies" but through the Duce's own "feelings."[50] Relativizing—if not effectively legitimizing—Mussolini's thought and actions, Tsubouchi's "Mussolini" was a portrayal of a hero who, by virtue of his sense of loyalty to the nation, rescued his country from political and moral collapse. His narrative stressed how the patriotism of Mussolini and the Fascists had restored social order in Italy. Even Fascist violence, Tsubouchi, argued, had to be understood in this context. Whereas the socialist Maedakō criticized the bourgeois readiness to resort to violence to repress proletarian organizations, Tsubouchi turned this argument on its head. In his story, it was the socialists, not the Fascists, who bore the brunt of the responsibility for the disorder that caused widespread violence. In other words, the Left's attempt to bring about social revolution prompted the nationalist reaction of Mussolini. One telling example of this inversion of violence is a scene set in a tavern. Three drunk socialists begin molesting a waitress and threatening her brother, a young soldier who has just returned from the war.

> SOCIALIST: I hate you for having been a soldier.
> BROTHER: Why?
> . . .
> BROTHER: I am a man who has loyally done his duty as a citizen for the state and King Emmanuel. . . .
> SOCIALIST: What benefits did we draw from your fighting? You lot are the running dogs of capitalist wartime profiteers [*narikin*].

This exchange is emblematic of Tsubouchi's picture of a society in disarray that Mussolini rescued by reasserting law and order. Tsubouchi declared the Fascists an inevitable, and welcome, outcome. In his play the Italian Left is described as a pawn of the Soviets and, as such, a threat to the stability of the state; the liberal establishment, led by weak statesmen—in particular Luigi Facta, the prime minister who preceded Mussolini—is shown to be ineffective in managing the situation, paving the way for social chaos. As one war veteran puts it: "I was in the army. I heard some rumors [about this situation], but I didn't imagine things to be like this. It's absolute disorder [*muchitsujo*]."[51] The Fascists, then, come to the rescue. In the words of a Blackshirt, "we, with barely fifty comrades, have shown how to do what the government has been unable to do."[52]

Tsubouchi cut a figure of a Mussolini in whom physical prowess and psychic vitality fed off one another. When Mussolini is hospitalized for injuries he had suffered in a battle during World War I, one roommate expresses his disbelief that he could have survived the misfortune.

> Absolutely, that man's physique [*shintai*] is different from ours. Immortal, that's what he is. Bullets don't seem to bother him. He has thirty-one of them in his body, but with that condition I've no idea what's going to happen. That man is superior to Garibaldi.[53]

Wheeling Mussolini into his hospital room, the nurse informs the onlookers that the prominent patient has high fever.

> ALL: 42 degrees?
> NURSE 3: Even the doctor was surprised. And even with 42 degrees he is writing and reading without interruption—that can't be the work of man [*ningenwaza*].
> SOLDIER 2: [*To Mussolini*] Hey, you, what are you writing?
> NURSE 3: He's writing a report to the nation [*kuni*]. . . .
> SOLDIER 4: Hey, Mussolini, what are you reading so desperately?
> MUSSOLINI: Russian.

Mussolini, irritated by all this talk, proceeds to lecture the incredulous crowd on the spiritual origins of his strength.

> MUSSOLINI: What are 40 degrees? Let's look at a man's [*danshi*] will [*iki*], at the will of a man! I will not die, I will not die, I absolutely will not die. I, on the battlefield, when I faced the enemy, was never afraid. . . . The battle is, first of all, with oneself. The person to carry it through is me. The person to rescue the state of Italy is me. Me!

Hearing these words, a soldier wonders whether Mussolini is "more of a dreamer than D'Annunzio," but is immediately challenged by two companions. Mussolini, they explain, is a "passionate patriot," "a man of vigor" (*seiryokuka*). The skeptical soldier ought to understand that, unlike the socialists and other weak-headed parliamentarians, Mussolini is not a man who delights in lengthy discussions. His vision is about "showing complete discipline for the nation" (*honbun kiritsu*), having "duties [*gimu*] not rights [*kenri*]," and engaging in "action [*jikkō*] not debates [*giron*]."[54]

For Tsubouchi, Mussolini deserved a place in the genealogy of great Italian men. Constructing a national narrative of heroism, Tsubouchi drew a straight line from

Giuseppe Garibaldi, the nineteenth-century hero of Italian national unification, to Gabriele D'Annunzio, and ultimately, to Mussolini. Indeed, it is D'Annunzio, the venerable poet, who salutes the youthful Mussolini as his heir.

> D'Annunzio: Oh! Our brave man [*yūshi*] Mussolini! Everyone, here he is, here is the hero [*eiyū*] who will rule the Italy of the future. . . .
> D'Annunzio: So, since you are already in command, I am now thinking of returning home [*kokyō*]. What are your plans after this?
> Mussolini: I am aiming at Rome, a march on our capital Rome. . . . my highest aim is to perform a great surgery to bring Italy back to life.
> D'Annunzio: A march on Rome, ah, that's interesting, just hearing this cheers my heart. You already have made up your mind [*iki*], what else can I say?
> Mussolini: Thank you.
> D'Annunzio: I pray for your success, young patriot!
> Mussolini: I pray for your health, ardent great poet!
> D'Annunzio: Adieu, adieu.[55]

Emphasizing what they perceived as Mussolini's extraordinary qualities—an iron will, patriotism, loyalty—playwrights proposed these traits as desirable for a moral redress of ordinary Japanese, especially youth.

That in Japan the imagined life of Mussolini reflected less the cult of a political leader than the cultivation of youth through moral leadership also emerges in several biographies of the Duce that were published in these years. As Luisa Passerini has suggested in her study of Italian biographies of Mussolini, in the 1920s there was a wider aspiration to extrapolate the individual from a discourse on the social: contemporaries felt that "individuals had become anonymous, but biographies recovered them, giving them a stamp of official recognition."[56] What was more distinctively Japanese, though, was how the biographical proliferation of works on Mussolini bridged the late Meiji discourse on the despondency of youth with the 1920s question of declining social mobility. Responding to the concern that also animated Shimoi Harukichi, biographies of Mussolini lent themselves to the recasting of young Japanese as leading protagonists in a heroic national narrative—whether as aspiring leaders or as individuals committed to simple acts of everyday heroism.

Given that biographies were a popular genre in the 1920s, it is not surprising that Mussolini was only one of many "great men" (*ijin*) who had his life recounted by Japanese writers. In this sense, he was placed with a multitude of legendary men (and, occasionally, women): William Gladstone, Fukuzawa Yūkichi, and Jeanne D'Arc are just a few names of these individuals, Japanese but often also foreign, who were of interest to biographers. Years later, Nakagawa Shigeru, a prolific biographer, included a study of Mussolini in a vast collection of some eighty volumes on "great men" stretching across continents and centuries.[57] Biographers had a predilection for patriotic figures of the past, usually statesmen, but they also wrote about contemporary men who epitomized individual success. In 1928, for example, a little-known biographer from Osaka named Okumura Takeshi published *Wonder Man Mussolini* and, in the same year, *Henry Ford: King of the Automobile*.[58] But for biographers Mussolini's life had a distinctive quality. It simultaneously evidenced national fervor and strenuous efforts to rise in society. Here was an individual whose life bridged a narrative of patriotism associated with men of the past and a narrative of success characteristic of the present, and this helps to account for the proliferation of his biographies.

To write their works, Japanese biographers relied on a wide range of accounts of Mussolini published in English, German, and French. This international corpus encompassed a spectrum that ranged from hagiographic official biographies to publications that were outspokenly critical of Fascism and its leader. The classic Italian biography of the Duce by his lover, the journalist Margherita Sarfatti, considered a "progenitor" of other Mussolini biographies, was partly translated into Japanese in 1926, and local biographers drew freely from this adulatory tribute.[59] But a number of works on the Duce were decidedly unfavorable, and Japanese biographers read those as well. Sawada Ken, who in 1928 wrote the closest thing to a standard Japanese biography of Mussolini, counted among his sources the works of several pro-Fascist writers, such as Giuseppe Prezzolini, Luigi Villari, and Pietro Gorgolini.[60] But he also cited Luigi Sturzo, a priest and politician in exile in London and New York; the liberal historian, journalist, and novelist Guglielmo Ferrero, placed under house arrest by the Fascist regime and later an émigré to Geneva; and Ivanoe Bonomi, lawyer and liberal prime minister.[61]

Yet, despite the available range of diverse points of view on Mussolini, Japanese wrote positive biographies of the Duce. Although authors often had reservations about his domestic repression, antiunion violence, and censorship, they could not resist flattering commentary when it came to his persona. "Mussolini, man of doubt! Great sphinx of reaction! Go as far as you can!" wrote one editor.[62] Japanese biographers were unconvinced by critical political commentary—or perhaps they chose to disregard this aspect. Instead, selectively separating the public from the private Mussolini, they drew a portrait of the Italian leader whom, for all his shortcomings, they saw as a great man, often in his very ordinariness. Emphasizing the earlier years of his life, these works focused on how the young Benito built up a strong personality despite—indeed, thanks to—a life of hardship. They stressed his poverty, his countryside upbringing, his emigration to Switzerland, and finally, his conversion from socialism to nationalism. Thus, as no Japanese wrote an anti-Fascist counter-biography, this powerful means of defining the image of Mussolini was left to conservative commentators, who adapted for Japanese consumption the hagiographic clichés originating from the official image of Mussolini in Italy.

The view that Mussolini possessed the moral qualities desirable to foster in Japanese youth was an explicit theme in the biography of Sawada Ken (1894–1969). He had begun his career after World War I as a commentator on international affairs but in the 1920s shifted his attention to biography, just as he turned markedly to the right. In writing the lives of great individuals, Sawada drew portraits of leaders who, to his mind, advanced the interests of their nations regardless of whether they were democrats or dictators. In line with this conviction, Sawada narrated the lives of the American heroes of mass production Henry Ford and Thomas Edison; the Japanese bureaucrat, entrepreneur, and politician Gotō Shimpei; and the fascist leaders Benito Mussolini and Adolf Hitler, the latter two books going through three editions.[63]

In his biography of Mussolini, *The Story of Mussolini* (*Mussorini-den*, 1928) Sawada championed the Duce as a model of moral leadership that could inspire Japanese youth to overcome the mediocrity of the present. "In present-day Japan, are we not in a time that necessitates a man with a strong personality like Mussolini? The trickery of conservative bigots. The malady in debates of the communists. The evasions of decrepit liberals. Are we not looking forward to the construction of a new Japan by the power of our strong youth?"[64] Mussolini, Sawada argued, was not without his faults, but he ought to be admired for shouldering the responsibility of making a clean sweep of the mess created by the political establishment. "There are many points for which we should criticize Mussolini's politics. I acknowledge this. But if we blame Mussolini's politics, we should turn the blame largely on the generation of politicians that has preceded him. They should be our concern and the targets of our attacks."[65] For Sawada, instilling youth with Mussolinian morality would mean creating a generational change. "The force to rescue Japan, the force to build up a new Japan is no longer in the hands of the gentlemen in frock-coats or the sickly, visionary, armchair experts mimicking Western letters. . . . That force is in our patriotic youth."[66] Mobilizing youth through the example of Mussolini, however, would not give way to Fascism but enact a political reform that was autochthonous. "Ah, where is Japan going? Quo vadis, Japone! . . . May Japan's heroic children produce a truly Japanese, neoliberal, constitutional [*rikkenteki*] hero."[67]

Sawada's call for a "neoliberal political movement" (*shinjiyūshugi seiji undō*) is noteworthy. In his view, liberalism did not need to be replaced with a dictatorship but could be rejuvenated through the kind of national mobilization of the individual that Mussolini had pioneered. As far as the quest for leadership was concerned, there was compatibility between Fascism and liberalism, even though the former needed an overbearing Duce while the latter required a new generation of national leaders who would act within the parameters of Japan's social and political status quo.

Similar concerns motivated the novelist and journalist Usuda Zan'un (1877–1956) to write a biography of Mussolini, also in 1928. In earlier years, Usuda had written a series titled *Popular World History* published by Waseda University, of which he was a graduate. This experience convinced him that the best way to spread knowledge about the world was by writing about individuals who embodied their nations, and he believed that Mussolini did that more than any other living figure. As is suggested by the title of his book, *I Am Mussolini* (*Wagahai wa Mussorini de aru*), Usuda wrote a fictional autobiography. Much had been written about the Duce, he admitted, but it was largely "political commentary [*hyōron*]." So far no biography had examined the man's life in detail. So, in writing *I Am Mussolini*, he aimed to write the story of the life of "a central figure in [our] times" through his "character and conduct," by "diving into Mussolini's womb as if he were Buddha [*tainai kuguri*]." The result was a narrative that repeated the recurring themes surrounding Mussolini—his family background, his performance at school, his experience as a migrant in Switzerland. The use of the first person "I" added psychological pathos.[68]

Usuda's biography was peculiar in one respect. As no doubt most readers were aware, the title echoed that of a work by the famous novelist Natsume Sōseki, *I Am a Cat* (*Wagahai wa neko de aru*, 1906). This novel was a satire, narrated from the perspective of a cat, of late nineteenth-century Japanese society, which was torn between Western and Japanese thought. By evoking this book, Usuda was arguing that similar questions of national identity were as yet unresolved. But by making Mussolini his main character, he also indicated that here was someone who had overcome the dilemma through his loyalty to the Italian people and the state. Like Sawada's biography, Usuda's *I Am Mussolini* was written with a conscious allegorical intent.[69]

In biographies for youth, then, Mussolini served as a means to reimagine the relationship between the individual and the nation. But there was another category of biographies: those intended for children. In interwar Japan, as Mark Jones has shown, the notion of childhood became a central site of class competition. Educators, journalists, and child experts produced three visions of the modern child. One, associated with the aspiring middle classes, championed the "superior student" (*yūtōsei*), a notion that emphasized a child's capacity to overcome difficulties and strive for meritocratic success. Another was the ideal of the established elites, who advanced a romantic image of a "childlike child" (*kodomorashii kodomo*), one that shunned materialistic advancement in favor of cultivating a child's emotions and experiences in the world. The third was the "little citizen" (*shōkokumin*), a child raised by a "wise mother" who "valued the child as a national possession trained to possess moral fortitude and physical vigor."[70] What emerges from biographies of Mussolini for children is that they were able to deploy the young Benito for all three categories. The Duce, in other words, represented both the ideal of a talented boy who strove to make it in the modern world and that of a child who was reared with "traditional" family values and who therefore was an exemplary citizen.

As was the case for those who wrote biographies of Mussolini for youth, biographers for children had also practiced their trade for some time before turning to the Duce. Some authors were established writers of children's literature, such as Abe Sueo (1880–1962), Matsudaira Michio (1901–1964), and Ashima Kei (1895–?); they had published biographies of Isaac Newton and Charles Darwin, but also of modern Japanese figures such as the Meiji educator and politician Tsuji Shinji (1842–1915). Others were of a minor stature, often associated with provincial and local educational associations. Ueda Sakuichi, who wrote a biography of Mussolini in 1926, was a member of the Osaka People's Education Research Association (Kōmin kyōiku kenkyūkai).[71] And like other biographers, these authors, too, elevated Mussolini to the status of a great man. To one editor Mussolini proved that "it is a mistake to argue that the age of reverence for heroes [*eiyū sūhai*] has already come to a close."[72]

What distinguished these biographers was the fact that they associated Mussolini's heroism with moral values that transcended class boundaries. In the effort to promote social harmony, they sought certain traits of Mussolini that would appeal to all Japanese, regardless of whether they were urban workers, bureaucratic elites, or peasants. One characteristic of Mussolini that all of them emphasized was his commitment to the family (thus ignoring his reputation as a womanizer). Traditional Japanese family values and obligations, it seemed to middle-class intellectuals, were being eroded by modern lifestyles. They contended that new forms of leisure like jazz and cinema, participation in political activities, and the lure of the department store led to the birth of a generation at the mercy of either American or Soviet materialism, steeped in the pursuit of individual or class interests. Mussolini provided a counterimage of familial devotion in which generational and gender hierarchies were respected, teaching that the family was the individual's real unit of social identification.

In biographies of Mussolini written for children, family bonding often revolved around parental figures, evoking an ideal of authority based on the notion of filial piety (*oya kōkō*). As in official Italian biographies, Mussolini's mother, Rosa, often emerges as the symbol of what many middle-class Japanese would identify as a "good wife, wise mother" (*ryōsai kenbo*).[73] In these biographies Mussolini frequently expresses his affection toward his mother. "Since my childhood I devoted my greatest love to my mother."[74] In a departure from Italian models, however, Rosa is described as a wife who, in spite of the domestic difficulties caused by her violent, alcoholic husband, loyally takes care of him and the young children, "managing the household and trying not to neglect her obligations toward other people." Even Mussolini's father, despite his vices and temperament, remained a figure from whom the young Benito had something to learn. One biographer made an explicit connection between the father's occupation—he was a blacksmith—and the son's iron will.[75] Conversely, Mussolini could be made to embody the father figure. Abe, for example, begins with an episode of a young boy who, weeping, misbehaves because his mother will not introduce him to Mussolini. The Duce, suddenly appearing on horseback, takes the child for a ride. The boy, initially unaware of the identity of the good uncle (*ojisan*), is exhilarated with joy when he is told that the man who was riding with him was no less than the Duce himself, shouting "Italy, banzai!"[76]

Mussolini's masculinity was another recurring theme in biographies written for children. It was well known that in reality Mussolini's virility easily gave way to violence; but also in this respect biographers found ways to mitigate the Duce's excesses. Dwelling on other aspects of his character, they reinforced the image of a moral Mussolini who balanced personal impulse with camaraderie. Matsudaira Michio, for example, narrates that Mussolini was a "bully" (*gaki taishō*) prone to picking fights with schoolmates, even as he presents him as a "warmhearted [*ninjō no atsui*] youngster with plenty of chivalry." Matsudaira explains that one day the young Benito and a friend decide to help themselves to the apples of a nearby peasant. Catching him in the act of climbing the tree, the peasant accidentally fires a shot into the friend's leg. Benito, instead of running for it, attends to his friend, using his handkerchief to bandage the wounded leg. "How does it feel? Is it still painful? Hmm, don't cry, you are a brave fellow [*yūshi*]. Only your honor has been injured. Is there a man [*yatsu*] who, being injured in his honor, cries? Come on, let's go. You can't walk? All right, I'll carry you on my shoulders." Mussolini's capacity for this male to male bonding is such as to bring even the angry peasant to express his admiration. "That brat, I think one day he'll become something [*erai mono*]. He's so different from the usual brats."[77]

Biographers interwove Mussolini's life with one further social issue that was coming to prominence in the 1920s: the relationship between city and countryside. State-minded and bureaucratically inclined individuals like educators were particularly sensitive to the growing economic disparity between the major urban centers and rural villages because they romanticized the peasant community as a space resistant to modern class conflict.[78] They worried that modern life was luring vast numbers of young Japanese to the cities, where they replaced their ideals of social harmony with a spirit of competition. In the context of this discourse

Violent yet virile, Mussolini bullies a classmate. Biographies for children commonly featured imaginary representations of the Duce's life.

(From Matsudaira Michio, Mussorini *[Tokyo: Kin no seisha, 1928].)*

on the "village" (*nōson*), biographers found in Mussolini a counterpoint to the perceived crisis. Presenting him as a rural migrant—and overstating the poverty of his family—they emphasized the hardships he had faced as he sought to improve his life, intimating that he responded to the challenges of mass society in an exemplary way.

From his travails, biographers constantly pointed out, Mussolini accumulated wisdom, not wealth; a sense of national harmony, not ideas of class conflict. Abe, for example, called Predappio, Mussolini's hometown, an "impoverished village" (*kanson*) whose inhabitants were "hard workers" and who had a distinct "love for their hometown" and "pride in their region."[79] A sense of community, therefore, was innate in Mussolini. This attachment to the people, Abe explained, was the reason why Mussolini renounced socialist theories of class conflict in favor of a vision of harmony among Italians. The lesson for Abe's young readers was that poverty should not become a reason for resentment. Far from it, poverty actually generated spiritual wealth. Would Japan's future leaders come from the countryside? The countryside, for all its current misery, was fundamental to the nation, as it contributed to its greatness by offering to the state moral resources in the form of patriotic young men.

Linking community, sacrifice, and violence, biographies of Mussolini only barely concealed a discourse on blood and soil. The harmonious social vision put forth in these texts rested, ultimately, on the assumption that young men had to be ready to die for their nation. Respect "the state," "devote yourself to the soil [*tochi*], the people [*kokumin*], history, and spirit [*seishin*] . . . throw away your passions, and strive to fulfill the passions of Japan," Ashima exhorted his young readers.[80] It was no coincidence that illustrations in many books portrayed a warrior Mussolini on horseback, not wearing the uniform of the Blackshirts but that of the army. Military service, and the willingness to die for Japan, was the ultimate expression of an individual's elevation of the nation above all other forms of identity. "Through obedience, discipline, and training, the self will become grand for the first time, leading us to a great freedom. Mussolini teaches us this."[81]

Thus, whether as a political leader or as an ideal of leadership, Mussolini had a meaning beyond Italy. No one made this point clearer than Furukawa Toshitaka, who had impersonated Mussolini in Tsubouchi's play. "Unfortunate was Italy's need for Mussolini, but fortunate was Italy's finding of Mussolini. Is Japan not also falling into a misfortune by requiring someone of the earnestness and ability of Mussolini?"[82] This question was the driving force of the Mussolini boom, asked by liberals and conservatives alike.

Their answers were ambiguous. In fact, it is remarkable that the popularity of Mussolini coexisted with a wide range of reservations about his style, rule, and politics. For Mussolini was portrayed as tragic and comic; heroic and bombastic; transcendental and commercial; popular and vulgar; timeless and quotidian; politician and celebrity; Italian and global. In Japan there was little interest in merging cultural and political leadership in one person, let alone adopting a readymade foreign leader. And yet, the misgivings about the Duce's style, rule, and repression went hand in hand with his fame as a youthful and vigorous leader. As both liberals and conservatives sought a solution to the shortcomings of parliamentarism—and the underlying degeneration of politics—they found in Mussolini a set of personal qualities and institutional strategies usable to forge consent among rulers and ruled. Their eagerness to learn from Fascist notions of leadership demonstrates that Mussolini also had a meaning beyond fascism. The spirit, courage, and will that were characteristic of Mussolini, argued the biographer Ashima Kei, were necessary in any country at any time—also in Japan. "But if people with such spirit and courage were to arise in Japan, they would not become heroes like Mussolini. Instead they would become outstanding great men (*kyojin*) in all fields of society."[83] As the interwar crisis came to a head in the 1930s, fuelled by the Great Depression and expressed by imperial expansion in Asia and turmoil at home, the call for heroes and heroism entered a new phase.

3

THE CLASH OF FASCISMS, 1931–1937

Fascism [*fassho*] is hardening day by day; the political parties are in panic; truly the sky is threatening.

—"Chokugen," *Yomiuri shinbun*, May 13, 1932

The Names of Fascism

Only two days after this anonymous line appeared in the daily *Yomiuri shinbun*, officers in the Imperial Japanese Navy, in collaboration with the right-wing League of Blood (Ketsumeidan), killed Prime Minister Inukai Tsuyoshi as part of a wider plot to overthrow parliamentary rule and impose a "Shōwa Restoration." What the media quickly nicknamed the May 15, 1932, Incident was funneled into a broader—and more ominous—debate. Fascism, it was feared, was raising its head in Japan. Indeed, anyone who had observed Mussolini's rise in Italy and Hitler's successes in Germany would have recognized Japan's own fascist symptoms. From 1930 to 1936 military radicals, often consorting with civilian right-wing associations and ideologues as well as the criminal underworld, embarked on an unprecedented campaign of violence. Hoping to foment a coup d'état, they killed and intimidated leading politicians and industrialists in a series of high-profile "incidents," prompting one Western observer's deft remark about Japan's "government by assassination."[1] The state unleashed the Special Higher Police (*tokkō*) on "subversive" groups, especially communists, but also on all those suspected of "thought crimes." In Manchuria, annexed by the Kwantung Army in 1931 and made into the "jewel in Japan's crown," a coalition of bureaucrats and soldiers experimented with autarky, developing centralized, technocratic industrial planning.[2] Even though none of these events triggered a dictatorship, their combination left contemporaries in no doubt that in the first half of the 1930s Japan had entered a process of "fascistization" (*fassho-ka*).

Fascism no longer carried the same meanings as in the 1920s. In a shift from an earlier discourse that identified fascism with Italy, Japanese intellectuals, politicians, and bureaucrats now associated it with a world trend. Recognizable fascist movements were springing up seemingly everywhere, its members donning a rainbow of shirts—white in Syria, green in Egypt, blue in China, orange in South Africa, gold in Mexico. Politically, Hitler took office in Germany in 1933; in China, Chiang Kai-shek launched the New Life Movement (1934) to counter socialism, liberalism, and democracy; two years later, Spain's Francisco Franco staged a military coup with the support of the right-wing Falange movement.[3]

Moreover, it became clear that fascism could no longer be reduced to a form of rejuvenated nationalism, as Shimoi had described it. Fascism's expansion around the world in the 1930s coincided with an increase in capitalist class conflict, which fascism promised to resolve by appealing to the force of the organic national community. To reconstruct the nation as a harmonious unit, fascist regimes and theoreticians devised an array of strategies, including the corporate state, anticommunist and anti-union policies, militaristic mobilization of the civilian population, and cultural rebirth. Thus Japanese commentators sought a broader understanding of fascism, one that accommodated its manifestation as an ideological force in several milieus.

By the early 1930s, then, fascism had entered the political lexicon of the twentieth century as a concept in its own right. Yet the centrality of fascism in the Japanese political and cultural debates in this decade has gone largely unnoticed.[4] Fascism stirred a protracted controversy that raged among intellectuals, activists, and politicians from across the political spectrum. As a global ideology, it unsettled assumptions about the Japanese state and national identity at their core. If, as some liberal and Marxist critics argued, fascist symptoms were to be taken seriously, the uniqueness of the Japanese state, based as it was on the filial relationship between the emperor and his subjects, had to be questioned: Could the emperor system operate as a fascist dictatorship? Comparing the fundamental principles of Japanese politics with foreign developments may not have been contentious in earlier decades; but at a time of heightened nationalism these assertions could not be left unchallenged, especially by those on the right who called for a return to the true spirit of Japan and rejected foreign influences of all kinds, including fascism.

The clash of fascisms was therefore a struggle for the control over the many meanings the term had assumed. Whereas antifascist forces expanded the definition of fascism to include the ideological and political changes in Japan, the functionaries of Japanese fascism—the motley crowd of ideologues, bureaucrats, politicians, and military—fought for a narrowing of its meaning by making fascism congruent with Fascist Italy—or, at least, by setting very clear limits to the extent to which fascism could be relevant in Japan. By 1937, in many respects, it was the discourse of the Right that had asserted itself. An increasingly military-dominated government enforced the ideological orthodoxy of the "national polity" (*kokutai*). In asserting the notion of Japanese uniqueness through the "unbroken imperial line" that was implied in the *kokutai*, officials recast this old term to serve the contemporary purpose of a counterpoint to the argument that Japan was becoming fascist.[5] In this sense, the official line overlapped to a large extent with the arguments of the Right, which, undeniably, had contributed to the formation of imperial discourse. With critical voices silenced or co-opted, the debates on fascism waned.

Nazism as Fascism

Adolf Hitler's appointment as German chancellor in January 1933 changed the course of European—and world—history. Under his rule, Germany turned into a dictatorship, fomented World War II, and annihilated millions of Jews, as well as other individuals deemed by the regime as racially or politically undesirable. Yet, what in hindsight stands out as a turning point did not necessarily appear so to contemporaries. To be sure, Japanese took note of Hitler's singularly intransigent and bellicose leadership; his regime's bold claims to reconstruct Germany's economy on the blueprint of an economy that was neither liberal nor socialist; and the anti-Semitism that pervaded his ideology, National Socialism. But many remained unconvinced that the Nazis represented something new, largely because they recognized a host of commonalities with Italian Fascism. Just like the early Blackshirts, so Hitler's Brownshirts, the SA, assassinated and terrorized political adversaries; both Fascists and Nazis developed mass parties by gaining the support of the middle classes as well as sections of the liberal elites; and Mussolini and Hitler were appointed to lead a government by their respective heads of state. Until the mid-1930s, then, Nazism stirred fewer emotions than might have been expected in hindsight. As far as the Japanese were concerned, the politics and ideology of Nazism complemented Italian Fascism and confirmed the concept of fascism as the trend of the times.

The Third Reich, however, had a very eager audience among young elite intellectuals and bureaucrats. These groups' interest in Nazism was not coincidental, because they had mediated German–Japanese interactions since the late nineteenth century. Then, legal scholars modeled the Meiji constitution on the German one while the founders of the Imperial Army borrowed the organizational structure of the Prussian military. Japanese students attended German universities to learn about technology, the economic theories of the German Historical School, medicine, and philosophy.[6] This trend continued—indeed, expanded—after World War I. More Japanese learned German during the interwar period than in Meiji, and Germany was the prime destination for government-sponsored students.[7] Starting in the early 1920s, bureaucrats and military planners studied Germany's wartime mobilization of its human and economic resources to learn lessons for a future total war. Thus, examining how the Nazis reformed Germany was part of a longer history of intellectual relations between the two countries.

The young Japanese technocrats, also known as "reformist bureaucrats," were drawn to Hitler's Germany because of Nazi ideas and policies of scientific management.[8] The Great Depression wreaked havoc on societies around the world and, to the technocrats' mind, it had also discredited the principles of free market that underpinned liberal capitalism. They sought a solution to this crisis by giving the state a leading role in the economy. State planning, it appeared, had been a policy in the three countries that had weathered the Great Depression most successfully: namely, the Soviet Union with its five-year plans; Fascist Italy's corporatism; and, after 1933, Nazi Germany's efforts to build a "national economy" (*Volkswirtschaft*). Soviet planning, though experimented with in Manchuria, was problematic because it smacked of communism. Italy's corporatism was appealing because of its attempt to break the deadlock between the interests of capital and labor. The legal scholar Alfredo Rocco theorized that the state would create social harmony by integrating nationalism with legal and industrial reforms. Hijikata Seibi (1890–1929), an economist at Tokyo Imperial University and a pioneer in the research of Fascist economics, endorsed Fascism's "machinery of control" (*tōsei kikō*).[9] Many Japanese, however, were disturbed by the Italian model because it seemed to invoke a large degree of state involvement, which some commentators described as quasi-communist. By contrast, Nazi policies seemed to respect private initiative and safeguard the interests of capital to a greater degree. As Janis Mimura has shown, there were widespread plaudits for the national economics of academics like the Werner Sombart and Friedrich von Gottl-Ottlilienfeld, whose theories predated the Nazi rise to power but found an articulation into policy in the Nazi state.[10] Technocrats such as Kishi Nobusuke, a rising star in the bureaucracy and future postwar prime minister, admired the German rationalization movement, its industrial relations and "management technologies."[11]

Yet many technocrats were unconcerned about the distinction between Nazism and Fascism, especially when economic policies were mixed with the larger question of state reform. A case in point is that of the political scientist Rōyama Masamichi, a colleague of Hijikata at the Imperial University and an exponent in the Shōwa Research Association (Shōwa Kenkyūkai). Founded in 1933, the research group came to include high-level intellectuals, such as the philosopher

Miki Kiyoshi, the political scientist Sassa Hiroo, and the economist Ryū Shintarō, and provided policy advice to the higher echelons of the government: after 1937, the association counseled Prime Minister Prince Konoe Fumimaro on a wide range of issues from Japan's policy toward China to the domestic New Order Movement.[12] Rōyama had observed Italian Fascism since the 1920s and, by the 1930s, had hailed it as a positive ideology because it created new principles for a "national economy" while dispensing of the parliamentary system. To him, Nazism merely built on what Italian Fascism had already started, reaffirming the need to link nationalism to policy reforms. Consequently, he often used "fascism" as shorthand for both Italian Fascism and German Nazism.[13]

When discussing the practicality of Fascism and Nazism as models to be appropriated, technocrats may well have distinguished between Italy and Germany; but, ideologically, the two generally fell under the umbrella term of "fascism." This trend is confirmed elsewhere. Before *Nachi* became the standard Japanese word for Nazi, newspapers often translated National Socialist Party as *kokusui-tō*. *Kokusui*, meaning "national essence," was the same word that had been used to translate "Fascism" in the early 1920s.[14] A decade later, the sociologist Shinmei Masamichi formalized the genealogical affinity between Nazism and Fascism in a series of articles he wrote in Germany, where he was studying. He concluded that fascism was a world phenomenon and that "we should regard the NSDAP as the most typical frontline of fascism."[15]

Thus, when Nazism came of age, fascism was already in place. When it came to classifications, Nazism rarely stood on its own, as emerges also from the indexes of studies on fascism that were published during these years. In 1933 the left-wing Tokyo Research Institute for Social Science published the *Guide to the Study of Fascism* (*Fashizumu sankō bunken*), a sixty-page reference work that included studies of Italian Fascism, Nazism, and a range of similar movements and ideologies in Europe and Japan. Even the Japanese state followed this pattern. Several ministries, including the Home Ministry, the Ministry of Education, and the Ministry of Justice, kept watch on right-wing publications and associations. Often, as in the case of the Police Bureau of the Home Ministry, officials classified the spectrum of the Right under the general rubric of fascism, which they then divided into subcategories wherein they sought minute differences between Fascism, Nazism, and, indeed, such domestic movements as Japanism (*nihonshugi*) and national socialism (*kokkashakaishugi*).[16] As a result, although Italy lacked the clout of Germany, it was the Italian ideology that defined its German counterpart—and, in due time, the Japanese version.[17]

Theorizing Japanese Fascism

On October 27, 1930, Benito Mussolini proclaimed that fascism, as an "idea, doctrine, and realization, is universal."[18] Japanese liberal and left-wing intellectuals could not have agreed more with the Duce. Mussolini's popularity around the world, Hitler's headway in Germany, and, at home, the anti-parliamentary tide as well as the rumblings about autarky, made contemporary observers aware that Fascist Italy merely foreshadowed a larger, global, trend. As early as 1927 the progressive current affairs journal *Kaizō* published an article entitled "critique of fascism," a roundtable discussion in which intellectuals weighed the possibility that fascism might also take root in Japan. In the words of the anarchist writer Ishikawa Sanshirō, one of the participants, "Musso's [*Musso kun*] Fascist movement may be a dictatorship, but it is the expression of a new era."[19] By the early 1930s, intellectuals realized that the conventional political lexicon failed to capture the ideological shifts to the right and proceeded to analyze their present through the concept of fascism.

Japanese liberal and Marxist critics produced theories of fascism in an attempt to answer this question: How could one explain that even though fascism arose at the same time around the world, in Japan it was assuming a configuration of its own? It was a problem that presupposed a comparative analysis with Italy and Germany as the prime points of reference. As even the research branch of the Japan Industrial Club was willing to admit, "Italy offers the raw materials for the study of world fascism."[20] The result was a number of sophisticated analyses of fascism in Japan and in general. Intellectuals affirmed the commonalities between fascism in Japan and the two European countries without, however, elevating Italian or German fascism as a quintessential model. For example, on the crucial issue of the seizure of power they were unconvinced that it was necessary for a movement or a party, such as the Fascist Party or the NSDAP, to take over. Rather, they suspected that fascism could infiltrate political and social institutions gradually, without causing a neat rupture. Moreover, they recognized that, ideologically, Japanese fascism concealed itself as mainstream nationalism and, in this guise, won over the support of actors beyond the radical Right, including liberals and socialists. In so doing, during the first half of the 1930s, an antifascist discourse emerged that reflected the wider concern about Japan's slide into fascism and that depended on a conscious comparison—and connection—with Fascist Italy and Nazi Germany.

In their assessment of fascism, liberal intellectuals were primarily concerned with offering a diagnosis of the crisis of liberal democracy. The threat to political parties and "constitutional politics" (*rikken seiji*) posed by a broad and heterogeneous fascist "movement" (*undō*) had become apparent to most people, including the figurehead of 1920s liberalism, the political scientist Yoshino Sakuzō. In 1932, shortly after the Manchurian Incident and only months before his death, Yoshino published "Fascism in Japan" in the semiofficial English-language journal *Contemporary Japan*. The article reveals his pessimism about the future of democracy in Japan. "[Fascism] has come to Japan, and although its various exponents in this country have carefully explained that it is something very different from Fascism anywhere else, the principles upon which it relies, the methods it adopts, the nature of its support and the ends it pursues are the same as those of similar movements in other parts of the world." Fascism, he concluded, was obviously a "commodity" for export.[21] Yet the article is of interest also because it exemplifies the attempts made in the early 1930s to widen the scope of the concept of fascism. Abstracting from the Italian variety, Yoshino proposed a remarkably generic definition of fascism as the "rule of the disciplined and resolute few as against that of the undisciplined and irresolute many."[22]

In his analysis of fascism in Japan, Yoshino argued that a broad, if as yet dispersed, fascist movement had enveloped Japanese politics, and that, given the right circumstances, it could indeed seize power.[23] Although he singled out the military as the most radical carriers of fascism, he also applied the term to a wider array of social actors, suggesting that fascism could garner support from mainstream politics. Fascism included "anti-democratic," "national," and statist ideas and was animated by "various groups" that, "in spite of their occasional repudiation of the title, can reasonably be called Fascists."[24] Yoshino pointed to three groups. The first were the "proletarians of the right" who spearheaded the theoretical and practical development of a socialism with Japanese characteristics: national socialism (*kokkashakaishugi*). The concept was coined in the mid-1920s by the thinker Takabatake Motoyuki, but it was his successors, especially Akamatsu Katsumarō and Tsukui Tatsuo, former Marxists like Takabatake, who attempted to convert his ideas into practice by forming a political party through a (botched) alliance of right-wing social democrats, ex-communists, and peasant parties. Yoshino noted the resemblance in name to Hitler's National Socialism, adding that its "undemocratic program" was typical of the "left-wing" predilection for "direct action." The second were the military, which, he remarked, had in recent years launched an offensive against party politics under the pretense that the incapacity of politicians to provide adequate backing to the army's and navy's needs threatened Japan's national survival. In the minds of many officers, the logic was that the "only way to prevent politics from controlling the Army, and thus imperiling the national safety, was for the Army to influence, if not control, politics," a vision for which they received the support of crucial political personalities such as Adachi Kenzō, who had occupied the positions of Communications and Interior ministers, and who, in 1932, formed the National Alliance with fellow fascist sympathizer Nakano Seigō.[25] Third were the "right-wing" (*uyoku*) organizations, such as the Amur River Society (Kokuryūkai) and the Greater Japan Production Party (Dai Nihon Seisantō), which stressed the spiritual values of Japan as a remedy to Western individualism and materialism.[26]

Yoshino made another, comparative, observation. He argued not only that Japan had its share of fascist groupings but also that the country's larger political condition was altogether similar to that of Italy ten years earlier. In both countries there reverberated a rhetoric of "patriotism": "As Mussolini invokes the glories of Rome, so his Japanese counterparts invoke the glories of Yamato; as he praises the sterner ways of the Roman past, so they laud the sterner ways of Old Japan; as he denounces the imported systems of Northern Europe, so they denounce the imported systems of the West."[27] Yoshino believed that four factors were necessary for the success of fascism: proletarian backing, military backing, a crisis in national affairs, and sufficient "national emotion." Strikingly, however, only three of these factors existed in Italy, whereas "in Japan today we have all four." Yoshino did not elaborate on this distinction, but it is safe to assume that the fourth element was the military, which had not played a major role in Italian Fascism's rise to power. In other words, Japan was more prone for fascism in 1932 than Italy had been in 1922. "Hence our fascist movement," Yoshino bemoaned, "or rather movements—for up to the present they are not entirely correlated—constitute an extremely powerful force, and one which, in the opinion of many, may ultimately succeed in bringing about a fundamental change of régime."[28]

Although this was another example of Yoshino's attempt to extrapolate fascism from its Italian context, it was an assessment with no ambition to construct a theory of fascism. He occupied an intermediate position between the older, 1920s view of fascism as reactionary politics and the sociological interpretations that were put forth by a younger generation in the 1930s. It was the critic and public intellectual Hasegawa Nyozekan who made the most radical liberal assessment of fascism in Japan. Hasegawa's reflections on the subject appeared in 1932, collected in *A Critique of Japanese Fascism* (*Nihon Fashizumu hihan*).[29] He argued that, to seize power, fascism did not need to overthrow the existing institutions, as Yoshino had maintained, but could grow "legally" within a political system: fascist essence could coexist with democratic forms.

Because fascism mutated in time and space, for Hasegawa a theory of fascism had to account for its change, both domestic and international. Although he was no Marxist, he detected the roots of fascism's dynamism in socioeconomic factors, grounding his theory on the assumption that capitalism caused the kind of class conflict of which fascism was an expression. The central problem, he argued, was that, because both Italy and Japan were "late developers," their capitalism was "halfway" (*chūtohanpa*) and, as a consequence, also their bourgeoisie was immature. Sensing its own fragility, the bourgeoisie strove to keep the left-wing parties out of parliament, leaving the socialists with no other solution than a violent overthrow of bourgeois democracy. Calls for social revolution, however, alienated the petty bourgeoisie from the proletariat, precipitating the two classes into a bitter class conflict. In the desperate attempt to avoid its proletarianization, the petty bourgeoisie, in fighting for a political space of its own, found that fascism best expressed its ambitions and grievances. Fascism, Hasegawa argued, arose out of a "standstill" in class conflict as the "instinctive, primitive, and infantile" manifestation of the "unenlightened" petty bourgeoisie.[30] Yet, even as he singled out the petty bourgeoisie as the carrier of fascist ideology, Hasegawa believed that this class would act differently in different countries and, as a consequence, generate different fascist formations.

Hence, Hasegawa redefined the notion of fascism by displacing Italy as its archetype. While he conceded that Mussolini's rise at the head of a large, petty-bourgeois, fascist movement constituted "primitive" fascism (*genshiteki*), he suggested that another road was possible whereby an interclass amalgamation between the petty bourgeoisie and the bourgeoisie could lead to fascism through the already existing parliamentarian institutions—what he called "cool fascism." What distinguished Italy was that a large, organized, Left served as a concrete enemy for the petty bourgeoisie, which, in opposition, organized itself around fascism. In Japan, however, the socialist movement had "stalled in a position of extreme powerlessness," leaving the petty bourgeoisie without a clearly defined social enemy.[31] Thus the petty bourgeoisie and its ideology were absorbed into the "two great [bourgeois] parties," the Minseitō and the Seiyūkai, which, despite their weakness, dominated politics to such an extent that "third forces" were unable to challenge them.[32] Yet this co-opting of the petty bourgeois came at a price: the embrace of fascism by the bourgeoisie. "Eventually," Hasegawa argued, "bourgeois democracy has overcome the confrontation with the petty bourgeoisie, but it was a conditional overcoming."[33] For if the petty bourgeoisie ended up playing to the interests of the bourgeoisie, bourgeois politics in turn would absorb the ideology of the petty bourgeoisie—that is, fascism.

Hasegawa expanded this point into the foundation for a general theory of fascism, suggesting that "legal fascism" (*gōhōteki fashizumu*) was at work not only in Japan but also across the world. In short, he stood Yoshino's comparison on its head, regarding Fascist Italy, not Imperial Japan, as a peculiar manifestation of fascism. Outside of Italy, he argued, "if we look at the modern world, we cannot see one example of a capitalist state whose power [*seiken*] is based upon the violence and ideology of the middle class."[34] In most other countries fascism became a "prop for the big bourgeoisie."[35] For Hasegawa, this phenomenon was visible in England, where Oswald Mosley's fascist party was operating inside parliament;

in Germany, where Hitler's future depended on his willingness to assume a bourgeois strategy and make his movement into a proper political party; and even in Italy, where Hasegawa observed a "transformed fascism" (*henshitsu fashizumu*) whose petty bourgeois origin had evolved into representing the interests of the bourgeoisie.[36]

Hasegawa departed from Yoshino in that he outlined a theory in which fascism was not merely a political struggle between democratic and antidemocratic forces but the result of social conflict. And yet both agreed on one fundamental point. They located the nature of fascism outside the philosophical tradition of liberalism and its social representative, the bourgeoisie. Yoshino may have blamed the political leadership for its corruption and its lack of democratic sentiment and Hasegawa singled out the bourgeoisie for its porosity to fascist ideology, but neither implicated this class as having played a decisive role in the rise of fascism. They regarded the petty bourgeoisie, the military, the proletarian movement—all those classes and groups that they surmised to be untouched by liberalism—as the true carriers and implementers of fascism. Yoshino excluded the ruling classes a priori; Hasegawa excused the bourgeoisie's role by arguing that it was weak and incomplete. Both of them foreshadowed postwar liberal interpretations of fascism, exemplified in Maruyama Masao's work on fascism, which emphasized the backward character of fascism and absolved the most "progressive" class, the bourgeoisie, from responsibility.[37]

The task of elaborating the link between the bourgeoisie, capitalism, and fascism was left to Marxists. By the 1930s, intellectuals associated with the Japanese Communist Party had largely accepted the official Comintern thesis on fascism. Espoused in Japan by two never identified Soviet scholars, Tanin and Yohan, this view reduced fascism to the violent dictatorship of the bourgeoisie, even if it included the monarchy and the social democrats as its willing supporters (notoriously, the latter were termed "social fascists"). This dogmatic thesis was challenged by the philosopher and cultural critic Tosaka Jun in a series of writings in the early 1930s, but especially in "The Japanese Ideology" (*Nihon ideorogiiron*). Tosaka expanded the existing understanding of fascism in two ways. First, he challenged the Comintern thesis by showing that fascism ruled, not just through dictatorial repression, but also by generating consent. Echoing his Italian contemporary, Antonio Gramsci, Tosaka argued that the power of fascism resided in its capacity to produce "hegemony" by making the nation central to people's common sense (*jōshiki*). Second, he complicated Hasegawa Nyozekan's thesis about "cool fascism."[38] For Tosaka, fascism went beyond the economic and political domains. Fascism did not only take over political institutions in a barely perceptible manner; its capacity to work at the level of people's common sense also meant that it crept into a nation's culture. In this sense, the sophistication of Tosaka's analysis lies in his explanation of the insidiousness of fascism.[39]

Because Tosaka assumed that fascism was globally consistent but locally diverse, Fascist Italy and Nazi Germany were important points of reference. He argued that it was crucial to recognize the conjuncture—"the general international situation"—of fascism in the early 1930s. Hitler consolidated his power, Mussolini interfered in Austria, Roosevelt built America's own "national industrial rationalization" (*sangyō kokka tōsei*), and the Japanese military set up Manchukuo for the same purpose. Japan's "nationalist movements" (*kokusui undō*) mirrored the Italian Fascists and the German Nazis. Yet if Japanese fascism—what he variously called "Japanese ideology" (*Nihon ideorogiiron*) or Japanism (*nihonshugi*)—was an inflection of a worldwide phenomenon, it also represented the messy combination of several domestic fascisms. Although they had different characteristics and called themselves by various names, such as Pan-Asianists, advocates of the "kingly way" (*ōdō*), or national socialists, for Tosaka they were all constituent parts of *nihonshugi*. These right-wing movements, then, were complemented by other "technicians" of fascism: the military (especially the officer corps), the bureaucrats, and intellectuals like the philosopher and historian Watsuji Tetsurō. All these streams gave Japanese fascism an ambiguous quality. On one side, their "random" (*manzen*) character and lack of ideological coherence made it difficult to form a united political force. On the other, their obsession with that empty and "harrowing principle, 'Japan,'" had an enormous advantage: because it could be arbitrarily filled with abstract and spiritual meaning through the symbols and myths of the nation, *nihonshugi* wielded a formidable populist appeal, and not just among the masses. "Indeed, in the last two or three years," Tosaka wrote, "the Japanese ideology has been produced in great quantities and has begun to pervade the press, as well as the fields of literature and science."[40]

For Tosaka, the spread of fascism would not have been possible without the complicity of liberalism. Challenging the assumption that liberalism presented a self-contained theoretical body that distinguished it from fascism, Tosaka argued that the two ideologies overlapped in a discourse on the nation. Liberalism had two fundamental problems. First, in Japan it had never been more than "passive." With the exception of thinkers like Yoshino Sakuzō, Hasegawa Nyozekan, and Kawai Eijirō, political liberalism had few outspoken adherents, even though journalism had made some of its principles into the "common sense" of the petty bourgeoisie. But in this form it was a "moody liberalism" (*kibunteki jiyūshugi*) that, when entering into crisis, swung toward fascism. Second, when liberalism failed to solve materially the social contradictions of capitalism, it reached for an "idealist" (*kannenteki*) solution based on national ethics, spirituality, and national history:

in the effort to maintain the social status quo, the ruling classes exhorted the people to unity and harmony by appealing to their sense of Japaneseness. Liberalism, therefore, was "unarranged [*zatta*] thought" with almost no theoretical resistance to *nihonshugi*. "That liberals and liberalism do not walk over to *nihonshugi* is not because of their logical reasoning [*ronriteki konkyo*] but because of their mood; that they do not walk over to materialism is because of their logic."[41]

When capitalism entered a crisis, Tosaka continued, liberalism and fascism converged, because both sought spiritual (or culturalist) solutions to material (or social) problems. The result was a hybrid, *nihonshugi*. Contrary to Hasegawa's point that the established political parties had fallen under the onslaught of the Right and militarists, Tosaka argued that the bourgeois forces had transformed themselves from within, all the while maintaining intact Japan's parliamentary forms. It was a "constitutional fascism" (*rikkenteki fashizumu*) that "perplexes people with its liberal mimicry . . . it is a great mistake to think that fascism only assumes the political forms of a dictatorship."[42] Although the ideological impetus of fascism came from right-wing and military circles, the liberal role was to harmonize the conflicts among those groups over what was the proper nature of Japan's body politic. The most emblematic example of this coexistence, Tosaka continued, was the "movement to clarify the national polity [*kokutai*]" (*Kokutai meichō undō*, 1935), which attempted to put an end to the disputes over the position of the emperor by declaring him above the constitution. Liberal (high) culture helped to structure the various myths and symbols of fascism, to make them respectable by grounding them in national history; fascist populism, thanks to its social rootedness, contributed to popularize the spiritualist solution that liberalism advocated in its quest to maintain the status quo. In this way, the politics and language of *nihonshugi* came to be articulated in a discourse on the emperor (*kōdōshugi*).[43] In short, the relationship between liberalism and fascism was not so much opportunistic as symbiotic.

Hasegawa's and Tosaka's writings were, perhaps, the two most sophisticated and insightful in a vast debate on fascism. For both, the methodological starting point was a comparative analysis that frequently referred to commonalities with Italy and Germany. Yet Hasegawa, and more so Tosaka, also felt constrained by the Italian model of fascism because it did not help to understand why, in Japan, fascism was able to coexist with parliamentarian institutions and liberal ideology. Hasegawa employed his comparative analysis to draw out patterns peculiar to Japan, but Tosaka was not satisfied with this conclusion. By tying fascism to capitalist crisis, he pushed the comparison into a theory of global fascism, connecting fascism in Japan with its manifestations elsewhere. "Japanism is a Japanese variety [*isshu*] of fascism. Unless it is regarded in this way, it is not possible to understand it comprehensively as a link [*ikkan*] of an international phenomenon."[44]

Fascism under Fire

It was this connection with Fascist Italy and, after 1933, with Nazi Germany, that those whom Yoshino, Hasegawa, and Tosaka singled out as fascists—or fellow travelers of fascism—worked hard to sever. In the first half of the 1930s everyone saw the signs of fascism; yet no one identified with it. The controversy that swirled around Baron Hiranuma Kiichirō was a case in point. Hiranuma had been a high-ranking bureaucrat in the Ministry of Justice, where he established a reputation for his anticommunism, a disposition that he backed up by strengthening the Special Higher Police. After being elevated to the peerage, he turned to politics and became a leading spokesman of the Right. He had founded the National Foundation Society (Kokuhonsha), a group that included military and industrial elites as well as high-level civil servants, and that rejected foreign ideologies, calling instead for a politics based on Japan's "national polity" (*kokutai*). This pedigree explains why the press singled him out as a fascist. In June 1932, Hiranuma felt compelled to reply to the latest accusation launched at him by the Marxist economist Ishihama Tomoyuki. Issuing a public announcement in the periodical *Kaizō*, Hiranuma declared that his "reformist movement" (*kakushin undō*) shared nothing with that of Mussolini: "Our nation is the nation of one sovereign and all the people [*ikkun banmin*], which means that all the people assist the nation with the imperial family at its center, paying their duty to achieve the supreme goal of the state, loving the life of the Japanese people [*Yamato minzoku*] and, especially, loving the great life of the state, for whose eternal, great life they are prepared to sacrifice their own lives." Incredibly, for Hiranuma, these values had nothing in common with those of fascism, which "arose from the national sentiment [*kokujō*] of a foreign country."[45] But, as Hiranuma's exculpation reveals—and as Tosaka had recognized—the logic of fascism was such that it eschewed global comparisons and links by concealing itself in the existing political process and nationalism.

The more fascism was discussed as a universal concept, the more Japanese fascists rejected it by retreating into national particularism. The nationalistic Right was in the throes of what has been called a "revolt against the West"—the notion that Japan had been contaminated by foreign ideas and habits and needed to restore its true national spirit.[46] The fixation with national uniqueness permeated all fields. From economics to politics and culture, intellectuals and activists on the Right assumed that there was a distinct Japanese way of solving the problems of modernity. This position also shaped their debates on fascism. Fascism, too,

"Fassho Show," with a pun on the word *fassho* (fascism), immediately reminiscent of *fasshon* (fashion). The models include Baron Hiranuma Kiichirō, sitting on a deck chair; General Ugaki Kazushige, who was seen as close to rebellious elements in the army; and, creeping onto the platform, the then prime minister, Saitō Makoto.

(Image courtesy of Yomiuri shinbun, *June 11, 1934.)*

being foreign, they denied its applicability to Japan. In this sense, Japanese fascism had its enemies not just in liberalism and socialism, as Tosaka argued, but also constructed a fictitious one in Italian Fascism.

Ironically, when fascism flourished, it was difficult to be a fascist. That an association with fascism could hardly yield political dividends is evident from the few Japanese who identified with this ideology. When Shimoi Harukichi returned to Japan in early 1933, his first impulse was to pursue his activities in Japan under the flag of Italian Fascism. As he boasted to a journalist upon his arrival, "having been an adviser to the Japanese Embassy in Rome, our government will now want to ask me, an expert on Italy [*Itaria tsū*], about conditions there."[47] Within six weeks of his arrival, he published four volumes on Fascist corporatism.[48] But he miscalculated. Just as official Japan shunned the favors of someone who had become a domestic nuisance, or a learned public preferred academic studies on corporatism, so the Right had misgivings about Shimoi's conviction that Fascist Italy's national spirit mirrored that of Imperial Japan. The strategy Shimoi had devised in the 1920s no longer worked.

Although he remained attached to Fascism, even Shimoi realized that it was advantageous to revise his reputation as Mussolini's best Japanese friend. Toning down his outspoken fondness for Fascism, he embraced the language and tactics characteristic of the Japanese Right. For example, he urged Japanese to form a "greater union [*dai kessoku*] for the upcoming Shōwa Restoration."[49] In this effort, Shimoi began to navigate the precarious waters of the Japanese Right. Capitalizing on his past as an educator, he reached out to teachers of the military, such as Banzai Ichirō, who between 1926 and 1932 was an instructor at the General Staff College, later a member of the Army General Staff, then a functionary for the Education Inspector General, or Ushijima Mitsune, head of the Education Section at the Army Engineer School.[50] He flirted with agrarianism (*nōhonshugi*), an ideology that championed rural communalism as an antidote to both capitalism and communism.[51] Although his exact involvement in agrarianist movements is difficult to establish, he served as the director of the agrarian sheet *Agriculture and Forestry Newspaper* (*Nōrin shinbun*) for which he traveled throughout Japan and its empire (on at least one occasion, he visited Korea and Manchuria). Interspersed with these endeavors were contacts with the ever more rabidly nationalistic Tokutomi Sohō, as well as a friendship with the doyens of the radical Right, Tōyama Mitsuru and Uchida Ryōhei.

Shimoi's attempt to promote fascism by infiltrating homegrown associations is best visible in his collaboration with the sect Ōmoto. Founded in 1892, this "new religion" was related to Shinto practices and was originally dedicated to "improving the world" through spiritual teachings.[52] In the 1930s, under the leadership of Deguchi Onisaburō, Ōmoto embarked on a secular project to reform Japan along right-wing lines, becoming one of the largest associations of its kind. The imposing size of the sect—in 1935 it had 1,990 local branches, 9,000 missionaries, and a membership of one to three million—attracted to its midst various right-wing exponents, including Tōyama Mitsuru and Uchida Ryōhei. As shown by Nancy K. Stalker, the sect's success owed much to Deguchi's "charismatic leadership" and his skilled use of modern mass media.[53] That a so-called new religion was entrusted to a charismatic leader was nothing new, but Deguchi departed from his predecessors by using print media, exhibitions, and film to spread the organization's message. Most crucially for the sect's right-wing activities, in 1933 Deguchi founded a political wing, the Shōwa Shinseikai (Shōwa Holy Association). The organization was launched with great fanfare the following year at a ceremony held at the renowned Kudan Army Hall in central Tokyo, and which saw the attendance of right-wing leaders, but also official authorities such as the home minister, the ministers of education, agriculture, and forestry, as well as fourteen Diet members, the speaker of the House of Representatives, major military figures, and academics. Clearly, the aim was to create a major force capable of absorbing the many strands of the Right.[54]

During the two years of its existence Shimoi was the Shinseikai's "chief of staff" (*sanbōchō*), a position that he used to introduce Italian Fascist practices to the movement, even though he refrained from openly declaring them as such. Shimoi's Fascist skills were ideally suited to transform Ōmoto into a political organization with a mass base. He was the association's public voice and promoted it by

Members of the Shōwa Shinseikai in paramilitary formation, ca. 1933. Reviewing them, at the far end, are Deguchi Onisaburō and, standing on his right, Shimoi Harukichi.

(Photo courtesy of Kuribayashi Machiko, Tokyo.)

producing films and accompanying Deguchi from Hokkaidō to Taipei.[55] He adjusted Fascist choreography to the Shinseikai. During the Ōmoto trial, the prosecutor asked a defendant whether it was true that, "when they visited their branches a flag bearer would be at the head of the march holding the leader's flag," and whether it was really the case that "Shinseikai members would lead or follow Deguchi's car as escorts." The defendant answered that "yes, those were Shimoi's instructions," adding that he himself had "marched before and behind" Deguchi's car, having been told by Shimoi not "to worry—I did the same in Italy."[56] Italian Fascist undertones are evident in the military drills, as well as in the vocabulary Shimoi employed. Speaking of the mission of the Shōwa Shinseikai, Shimoi declared that a small number of people could formulate the policies to reform the state, but that, to achieve the ultimate goal of a "union" (*kessoku*, that is, a *fascio*) it was necessary to mobilize all "the people" (*kokumin*) to forge order, discipline, and righteousness. The Shōwa Shinseikai, he argued, "is a movement that strives to achieve the great unity of the nation [*kokumin no daidō danketsu*] . . . and justice [*seigi*]."[57]

Shimoi's efforts, however, came to little. Members of the Shinseikai were suspicious of Fascism and Nazism, and it is likely that their mistrust extended to Shimoi. Even though he was careful to avoid overt references to Italian Fascism, he was at pains to shed his reputation as a staunch sympathizer of Mussolini. Some members of the Shinseikai even openly attacked Fascism. One contributor to a Shinseikai publication put it bluntly, charging that, for all its nationalistic boasting, Italian Fascism had failed to come to terms with finance capitalism—indeed, Fascism was but the "naked figure of capitalism."[58] Even more detrimental to his plans was the official repression of the sect. In 1935, alerted by the Shinseikai's size and its subversive potential, government authorities crushed Ōmoto altogether, arresting its key leaders, including Deguchi. Despite his high-level position, Shimoi was able to avoid incarceration, perhaps because, like his associate Uchida Ryōhei, he turned his back on Ōmoto.[59] Still, his cooperation with Deguchi and the Shinseikai demonstrates how difficult it was to be a Fascist at the time of fascism.

Just how controversial the concept of fascism had become emerged in 1932, when a prominent writer of popular fiction publicly embraced the term. Early that year, Naoki Sanjūgo, the young critic and novelist after whom one of Japan's most prestigious literary awards is named, stirred the literary world when he announced that, "from 1932 until 1933, I will be a fascist."[60] He was seconded by a number of other writers of popular fiction, many specializing in historical samurai fiction—they thus earned the sobriquet "literary warriors" (*bunshi*)—and that included Yoshikawa Eiji, author of the epic samurai novel *Musashi*; Mikami Otokichi; writer and editor Kikuchi Kan; and the poet Satō Haruo.[61] Other aspiring writers jumped on the bandwagon, founding the short-lived Japanese Fascist League (Nihon Fassho Renmei), a literary group with its own publication.[62]

How did Naoki come to this declaration? Naoki was a writer of popular fiction (*taishū bungaku*) who opposed the influential literary movement known as "proletarian literature." Associated with the socialist or communist Left, proletarian writers and critics such as Kobayashi Takiji, Nakano Shigeharu, and Aono Suekichi published works for social purposes, generally emphasizing the conditions of the working class. Naoki and other young writers invoked "fascism" to provoke this literary current: they found in fascism's nationalism and anti-Marxism a possibility of breaking away from proletarian aesthetics. The tone of the fascist declaration was deliberately polemical. "One, two, three . . . here begins my struggle against the Left. Come on! If you come close I'll cut you down! How does it feel? Scary . . . ?"[63] Naoki's own political stance was ambiguous. Clearly, he intended his assertions to be inflammatory. But it also became known that he sought to forge connections with army officials.[64]

Regardless of Naoki's true intentions, his declaration sparked a public debate on fascist literature (*bungei*) that involved some of Japan's most prominent writers and intellectuals. *Shinchō*, a leading journal of contemporary affairs and culture, held a number of roundtables (*zadankai*), inviting participants to comment on the question raised by Naoki, namely whether fascist literature was possible—or desirable—in Japan.[65] Most participants in the debate considered fascism a real political problem but doubted that it could generate its own literature. The literary and social critic Nii Itaru attacked Iwasaki Junko, a translator of modern Italian literature and cofounder of the Japanese Fascist League, on the grounds that even Italian Fascism had failed to create a distinctive form of literature. In Japan, Nii argued, fascism showed no sign of having its own "theory of literature." It was a mere fad, and a rather different one from the Marxist trend that had gripped Japan a decade earlier. In the 1920s it was possible to delineate a broad movement of "Marx-boys and Engels-girls," while to date there was no sign of "Fascist [*fassho*] boys or girls."[66] Maedakō Hiroichirō, the Marxist critic who in 1928 had composed a satirical play on Mussolini, also remarked that in those days "most artists [*bundanjin*] throw this curious [*myōna*] word at other people, or have it thrown at them by other people." But, he bemoaned, the tone was that of gossip, not of a serious discussion on the essence of fascism, an assessment that was echoed by his fellow critic Ōya Sōichi.[67]

The controversy sparked by Naoki revealed not only the polemical qualities of the concept of fascism, but also the fact that many writers were searching for an aesthetics that articulated a new nationalism without sounding foreign or, more precisely, fascist. When Naoki retracted the declaration at a roundtable in 1934, he argued that fascism, because it was a "transitional force characteristic of the crisis of old politics," could not generate its own literature. Rather, it was from Japan's "national essence" (*kokusui*) or from the "ancestral land" (*sokoku*) that a "national work" (*minzokuteki sakuhin*) would be born. Hayashi Fusao, a writer and critic who had recently renounced Marxism, joined him, asserting that he, too, felt the "desire to re-examine Japan, but this had nothing to do with fascist literature"; another participant in the discussion put it most explicitly when he argued that this new national work had to arise spontaneously out of the "patriotic spirit."[68] As argued by Alan Tansman, fascist aesthetics in Japan had to be felt, not theorized and articulated by a self-styled avant-garde.[69]

Fascists against Fascism

As they faced fascism, right-wing ideologues also confronted a dilemma. On one side, they believed in the peculiar national spirit that had the emperor at its center. No other country, the argument ran, could boast a link of blood to the imperial family. On the other side, they realized that it was difficult to sustain unequivocal distinctions between how they understood the "national polity" (*kokutai*) and how Fascists and Nazis asserted the essence of Italian and German nationalism. They conceded that fascism was an improvement over socialism and liberalism but hesitated to embrace the idea that this modern ideology could rival the timeless essence of the *kokutai*.

Rather than simply disavowing fascism, however, many right-wing intellectuals sought ways to come to terms with the fascist worldview. Their core preoccupation was not so much with Fascism or Nazism, despite finding much to fault in these ideologies, but with the idea that fascism was universal, and therefore potentially also Japanese. Their debates resulted in what can be called a fascist critique of fascism: an admission of commensurability with Fascist Italy and Nazi Germany but qualified by the assertion that Japan's way to a new order was superior. As Naoki Sakai has claimed, the "Japanese fascist formation was at the same time obsessively exclusionary and open, particularistic in respect to the national spirit but universalistic in integrating groups of different ethnic, regional, gender, and class origins."[70] Italian Fascism, and German Nazism too, could be subsumed. In fact, the right-wing debates on fascism do not just reveal uneasiness with an ideology that uncomfortably mirrored their own; there was also plenty of intellectual fervor invested in the formulation of strategies to assimilate fascism. Indeed, the discourse and policies of the new order that characterized the mid- and late 1930s were articulated in relation to fascism. By 1937, these attempts led the Japanese Right to substitute for the global meaning of fascism what they saw as a truly universal concept—"Japan" and its *kokutai*.

The impulse to separate fascism from Japan while recognizing it as an ideology of historical significance led Japanese intellectuals to formulate a number of responses. The moral philosopher Sugimori Kōjirō (1881–1961) stands out for his attempt to reconcile fascism and liberalism. A graduate of Waseda University, Sugimori had studied abroad, financed by the Ministry of Education, spending the six years (1913–1919) in Germany and England. There he developed an antipositivist bent, expressed in his 1918 book *The Principles of the Moral Empire*. After the Great War, he surmised, the world would relinquish the materialism that had caused the conflict and, instead, embrace an ethical and religious spirit. "Moral and theological reforms" would restore the "individual as the center of the Whole" and promote social harmony.[71] Yet, as he confronted the social conflict of the 1920s, Sugimori lost his faith that transcendental change could be achieved through a moral transformation of the individual alone. It was necessary, he found, to draw on the force of the state to harmonize the struggle between labor and capital. With these concerns in mind, he turned to the study of fascism.

A Japanese Mussolini or Hitler? Maybe not.

(Photo courtesy of Yomiuri shinbun, *April 20, 1933.)*

In 1933, Sugimori published a two-part critique of fascism in the journal *Shakai seisaku jihō* (Social Policy Report), the mouthpiece of the Concordia Association (Kyōchōkai), a half-private, half-official association that aimed to devise policies to harmonize relations between labor and capital. Sugimori understood fascism in three ways—as "reinforced [*saikyōka*] nationalism," "controlled [*tōsei*] economy," and "dictatorship." He admired the kind of nationalism championed by Mussolini because, to his mind, it presented a remarkable innovative improvement over the nationalism that was common before World War I. As developments in Italy demonstrated, this new nationalism had succeeded in mobilizing the people and fomenting "a decisive action" against communism.[72]

While he heralded Italian Fascism as a bold experiment in national rejuvenation, Sugimori did not believe, as was widely claimed by Mussolini's regime and its supporters, that Fascism constituted a third way between communism and liberalism. As he saw it, Fascism merely crushed liberalism through its wielding of state power. Probably in response to Mussolini's assertion that the state was everything, Sugimori mounted a philosophical defense of the individual. "The assumption," Sugimori wrote, "that human beings have no personal interests [*shieki*] or should have none, and that instead, a higher economic organization towers over them, is a vacuous construction. Personal interest ought to be recognized." Fascism, through its politics of spectacle and coercion, denied the individual his place in state and society. In Japan, by contrast, a peculiar relationship between the individual and the state had developed in the form of the national polity. The bond between the emperor and his subjects was benevolent, voluntary, and did not require an excessive use of violence. The state and the individual coexisted in harmony. He concluded that "fascism, in the case of Italy, is incomplete . . . a simplistic totalitarianism, no more than an illusion based on a deficient consciousness."[73]

The implication of this argument was that Japan—not Fascist Italy—represented the real model of a third way. Sugimori argued that Japanese ought to consolidate their polity by drawing eclectically from fascism to "amend" it. As liberalism stressed individualism, so fascism emphasized "communalism"; liberalism was reformist, fascism somewhat revolutionary; liberalism represented the bourgeoisie, fascism the proletariat. "For what we have in common [with Italy], we need to embrace totalitarian, communalist, dictatorial methods; for what concerns our own peculiarities, [we need] the method of liberalism. This will be a way to rejuvenate liberalism, while at the same time a method to adopt fascism."[74] The Japanese *kokutai*, it seemed to Sugimori, could achieve the necessary balance between fascism and other ideologies.

Many right-wing thinkers and activists were less sanguine about the possibility of dealing with fascism on an ad hoc basis. Defining the *kokutai* based on a distinction from fascism troubled them. As far as they were concerned, the superiority of the Japanese way was such that it did not just build on fascism but effectively superseded this foreign ideology. Validating the relationship between the Japanese people and the emperor meant to recognize that what fascism preached—the forging of national communities by bringing the people and the state together—had been part of Japan's national culture since antiquity. But because fascism unsettled long-held assumptions about the *kokutai*, the correct answer to the problem of fascism, they contended, had to come from within the Japanese tradition. There was little agreement, however, on what constituted this tradition. While all right-wingers shared a vague idea of revitalizing the nation by restoring power to the emperor, they fought bitterly over the means to achieve this goal.

Japan's right-wing movement eschews easy generalizations. It was vast in size—according to one account, some 750 groups were operating in Japan and its empire by 1936.[75] The groups could be either military or civilian, or a mixture, and differing constituencies often led to factionalism.[76] Ideologically, thinkers theorized about different avenues toward reform. Agrarianists (*nōhonshugisha*) championed farmers and the countryside; Japanists (*nihonshugisha*) called for a general spiritual revolution from below, at the hands of impassioned patriots; national socialists (*kokkashakaishugisha*) advocated state reform from above as the first step toward national reform.[77] In these disputes, fascism played an important role. Representing a foreign force of national revival, it helped to integrate the various currents of the Japanese Right, demonstrating that, ultimately, for rightists the problem was not fascism but their own political identity.

The centrality of fascism to the redefinition of the Japanese Right from the early to the mid-1930s can be seen in the theoretical debates between the Japanists and the national socialists.[78] From the late 1920s, these currents expressed a mixture of condemnation and admiration for Italian Fascism, as is evident from the writings of their exponents, Kita Reikichi, a leader in the Japanist camp and the brother of the more famous activist Kita Ikki, as well as Takabatake Motoyuki, the theorist and founder of national socialism.[79] In line with the mainstream view of the 1920s, they dismissed fascism as an Italian form of nationalism, serving primarily the necessities of Italy. Both mistrusted the general Japanese enthusiasm for Mussolini that had erupted in 1928. Kita argued that, only in the case that a domestic reformist movement failed to happen, "contrary to our liking we will have to long for the miraculous appearance of a Japanese Mussolini." That same year, Takabatake published a collection of essays in which he attacked Mussolini and Italian Fascism. He thundered that Fascism was "non-thought thought" (*mushisō no shisō*) because its claim to have overcome capitalism was a fraud: its economic policies were the result of a compromise that pleased the "capitalist class."[80] If there was a "thought" animating Mussolini, it was limited to an obsession with action.

It is striking that the rhetoric of the radical Right could be the most outspokenly denunciatory of fascism throughout the ideological spectrum. The derogatory use of the term "fascism" is evident in the way national socialists and Japanists condemned each other. In their polemics they frequently associated their rival with a particularly distasteful facet of Italian fascism. Takabatake accused the Japanist legal scholar Ninagawa Arata of single-mindedly heralding Mussolini's "heroism" (*eiyūshugi*), while remaining silent on his unconvincing industrial policies.[81] Just like the Duce, Takabatake continued, Japanists spoke the rhetoric of patriotism but in reality were little more than "the running dogs of the power of the established class, their puppets."[82] For their part, Japanists attacked the national socialists for being socialists in disguise. For Kita Reikichi, "if communism is the tiger in front of the gate, national socialism is the wolf inside the yard."[83] Mimicking Italian Fascism, which, in Kita's view, contained strong socialist elements, the state socialists had created "an original form of Japanese fascism"—in reality little more than "made-in-Japan [*wasei*] Bolshevism."[84]

Yet Japanists and national socialists were attracted to a specific goal of Fascism, that of forging a strong national community by reconnecting the people and the state. Both concurred in praising Fascist "rule" (*shihai*). As someone who believed in the necessity for the people to self-mobilize for the nation, Kita spoke fondly of Mussolini for having instilled this idea in Italians. As a result, he claimed that Italians had replaced "inefficiency, selfishness, and disorder with efficiency, discipline, and law and order."[85] By contrast, Takabatake expressed interest in the way Mussolini had revitalized the role of the state. Takabatake mistrusted individuals, arguing that the state was a prerequisite for taming their natural selfishness. In this regard, he concluded that, when it came to the "subject of rule [*shihai no shutai*], it is easier for a small number of able men to improve efficiency."[86] For Takabatake, an efficient state would engineer the spontaneous support of the people because it healed the social wounds caused by capitalism.

Kita and Takabatake were not alone in applauding fascism's merits as a community-building ideology. A large number of Japanist and national socialist ideologues became aware that they shared with fascism the goal of molding the people and the state into an organic totality. In 1927 Mussolini sloganeered that in his regime "everything [was] in the state, nothing outside the state, nothing against the state," later referring to these principles as "totalitarianism." The term was to have a long and often controversial life, being picked up by postwar political scientists as well as historians to describe a range of political systems that were not of the liberal capitalist kind, especially those of Nazi Germany and the Soviet Union.[87] Yet, as Fuke Takahiro has shown, there was a Japanese precedent for "totalitarianism."[88] In 1918 the philosopher and naval officer Kanokogi Kazunobu used the term *zentaishugi* to define a "transcendental state" that was premised on Japan's "unbroken line of imperial succession for ages eternal" (*bansei ikkei*) and, ultimately, represented by the union of the emperor and his subjects. Like Mussolini's *stato totalitario*, so Kanokogi's *zentaishugi* had positive connotations in that it referred not so much to the atomization of the individual in the face of a repressive state, the characteristic ascribed to totalitarianism by postwar theorists, but, to the contrary, to a harmonious union of the nation with the state.[89]

Kanokogi's idea of "totality" was revived in the 1930s, both by himself and by fellow right-wing ideologues, at about the same time that Mussolini developed his brand of totalitarianism. Japanists and national socialists recognized the commonalities, even if often with reservations. Nakatani Takeyo, a political scientist educated at Tokyo Imperial University, Japanist activist, and disciple of Kanokogi, acclaimed the reforms enacted by the Fascist minister for education, the philosopher Giovanni Gentile. In his view, Gentile had successfully remodeled Italian schools in such a way that children's minds were developed not only through "abstract knowledge" but also through "real action" (*jissai no kōdō*). Under such impulses, he believed, children's "personalities" were forged and their "moral character" tempered.[90] Fascist education was "thoroughly nationalistic and Italian culture-centered," one that "our own educators must take into consideration."[91] Education was an integral part of what he called the "fascist view of the state" (*kokka kan*), which fostered "action-centered nationalism" and, ultimately, rebuilt the "totality" (*zentai*) of the nation. This undertaking characterized both Italian and German fascisms, so that, he advised, "it is clear what the essence and direction of Japanese fascism ought to be."[92]

Totalitarianism was also central to the logic that led national socialists to mitigate their severe stance on fascism. After the death of Takabatake in 1928, their new leaders, especially Tsukui Tatsuo (1901–1989) and the ex-communist Akamatsu Katsumarō, began to stress the need to incorporate a broad, popular movement into their plans for state reform. This about-face on the role of mobilizing the masses led to a reevaluation of Italian Fascism. Tsukui backtracked on the assertion of his mentor, Takabatake, that Fascism was "non-thought thought," asserting that Fascism possessed "a highly suggestive theoretical content": it opposed Western liberalism and individualism with "totalitarianism" (*zentaishugi*). Citing the legal innovations carried out by Alfredo Rocco, the theorist of Italian corporatism, Tsukui examined the Fascist attempt to unite Italians and their state. The Italian experiment, however, had a flaw. Because it was carried out from above without involving the people, the Italian version was "totalitariansim of the Fascist Party"—that is, it was fabricated and rhetorical. Unlike this Italian artifice, Japanese totalitarianism would be organic, because the people and state had been linked for three thousand years in "will" and "blood." "In the case of Japan and the Japanese, totalitarianism is for the first time not just reckless talk but an embodiment of reality."[93]

It is possible to make two observations about the debate between Japanists and national socialists. First, as they evaluated the qualities of Japan's ideology in relation to Fascism, they came to a rapprochement. To be sure, they would not coalesce into a united front of the Right, as personal and ideological animosities lingered. But they did reach an unspoken compromise on the quest for a politics of totality. They agreed that what Japan needed was a way to strengthen the country by bringing the people and the state together, and, they concurred, this operation required simultaneously a mobilization from below and a reorganization of the institutions. Second, while they recognized the commonality of interest with Fascism, they were immovable on the superiority of the Japanese way and therefore proceeded to formulate Japan's totality in a political language that was unaffected by foreign thought. The rhetoric they advanced was that of the "imperial rule" (*kō*). This concept was conveniently vague. It spoke to those who emphasized that rule (*shihai*) was about forging a new subjectivity through a spiritual link between the emperor and his subjects but also to those who saw it as a problem of sovereignty, at the heart of which lay the question of how the state mediated the emperor's will. Not surprisingly, terms invoking the "imperial" proliferated in the right-wing language of the 1930s. This mood beame clear to Nakatani Takeyo when, in 1932, he published an article in which he reviewed recent debates on "reformist" thought. "In the end," he wrote, "one cannot avoid arriving at the holy ground of the imperial way"; the trend of times was "from fascism to the imperial way [*kōdōshugi*]."[94] As Tosaka Jun perceptively remarked in those years, the imperial way was nothing but a travesty of Japanese fascism.[95]

The significance of the right-wing discourse on fascism lies in what it reveals about the quest for Japanese political reform provoked by a clash of two ideologies that were at the same time conflicting and overlapping. Japanese ideologues accepted the premises of their European counterparts—that Fascism and Nazism were a push beyond liberalism and communism—but refused to recognize any fundamental connection to them. In other words, they were animated more by the desire to fight the fascist link than by fascism per se. Negating the concept but not its ideological elements, they articulated a fascist critique of fascism whose key claim to authority rested on the centrality of the emperor and the national polity (*kokutai*) in Japanese political life.

The sediments of right-wing antifascism settled in one of the decade's most defining documents, the *Cardinal Principles of Our National Polity* (*Kokutai no hongi*). Published in 1937 by the Ministry of Education, the pamphlet strove to establish the orthodoxy of the term *kokutai* by reconciling the decade-long disputes over its true meaning. The literary scholar Alan Tansman has rightly pointed to the tract's aesthetically charged language that "br[ought] readers to a sublime, fascist moment in which they might feel themselves to be one with their emperor and their brethren."[96] These aesthetics gave the text rhetorical consistency. Yet, in the context of the debates on fascism, it also becomes apparent that the *Cardinal Principles* reproduced the ideological conflicts over the *kokutai*. Its grandiloquent, religious overtones barely concealed its nature as a compromise—a number of intellectuals and bureaucrats had participated in its compilation—or the ongoing tensions over the association with fascism. Even though the authors of the tract recognized the emergence of "totalitarianism," "Fascism," and "Nazism" as proof that "the deadlock of individualism has led alike to a season of ideological and social confusion and crisis," it nonetheless relegated them to the category of Western ideologies and, as such, incompatible with Japan. Elsewhere, the text reneged on the disavowal of fascism. Invoking Japan's capacity to synthesize foreign elements, it expressed the confidence that also fascism, the latest emanation of Western thought, would be assimilated and "refined" in Japan. In yet another passage, the authors stated they believed that fascism could be selectively managed. To find a way out of the evils caused by individualism, they argued, it would not do either to reject Western ideas wholesale or to "mechanically exclude Occidental cultures."[97]

Fascism, in other words, was in one way or another comparable—but not compatible—with the *kokutai*, even though this was never meant to be more than tacitly understood. Nowhere was this state of affairs expressed more vividly than in a fictional dialogue imagined by the right-wing journalist and writer Murobuse Kōshin.

> A: I said that Fascism is not for export—these are not my words, but Mussolini's.
>
> B: Does that mean it cannot be applied to Japan?
>
> A: I'm not saying that it can be applied, or that it cannot be applied.
>
> B: So, neither?
>
> A: That both are correct is closer to what I'm thinking.
>
> B: What does that mean?
>
> A: It comes down to how fascism emerges—it doesn't really matter what you call it.
>
> B: So?
>
> A: So it's fine to call it fascism; it's also fine not to call it that. Perhaps it's better not to call it that. In that sense, let me announce that I'm not a fascist.[98]

The uneasy relationship between fascism and imperial politics generated a fake confusion that, in turn, dissimulated the fascist link.

4

IMPERIAL CONVERGENCE: THE ITALO-ETHIOPIAN WAR AND JAPANESE WORLD-ORDER THINKING, 1935–1936

> **To the blacksmith's astonishment, [that day] he had no customers whatsoever. This was because of the news from overseas in the morning and evening papers, as well as the radio broadcasts—everyone's mind was on that faraway African country, Ethiopia.**
>
> —"Shōbai te ni tsukanu kajiya san," *Yomiuri shinbun*, 28 September 1935

In the mid-1930s the debates on fascism entered a new phase.[1] The catalyst for the shift was Fascist Italy's attempt to carve out an empire in East Africa. The invasion of Ethiopia began in October 1935 and, after a short but brutal war, terminated in Mussolini's proclamation of an Italian empire in May 1936. While the Fascist leadership had invaded largely out of concerns with its domestic politics—the Duce's desire to boost his regime's popularity by making Italy into a great power—the significance of the war was in how it shook the political, economic, and ideological foundations that underpinned the post–World War I order.[2] Its institutional embodiment, the League of Nations, appeared not only unable to live up to the goal of maintaining peace among member nations, which included Italy and Ethiopia; some of the more scathing analysts attacked the League for bending to the influence of two Great Powers, Great Britain and France. Economically, the conflict further undermined faith in free trade, already shaken by the Great Depression, and strengthened calls to consolidate imperial self-sufficiency.[3] Discrediting liberal internationalism, the Italo-Ethiopian War paved the way for a rethinking of global politics, unwittingly giving fascism and imperialist dimension. No longer just signifying national rebirth, anticommunism, or virile leadership, fascism was now tied to the reform of the theory and practice of international politics.

Empire and Imperialism

The shift from an internationalist to a regionalist foreign policy had been in the making for some time, and the Italo-Ethiopian War accelerated this process.[4] In 1931 the Kwantung Army had invaded Manchuria and, the following year, proclaimed the establishment of the Japanese puppet state of Manchukuo. Army and civilian leaders hailed the new state as the cornerstone of Japan's new role in Asia. Manchukuo represented both a slap in the face to the open-door policy in China and, in the Pan-Asianist rhetoric dear to right-wing ideologues, a place where Chinese, Koreans, Manchus, Mongols, and Chinese would live in harmony.[5] Fascist Italy's war confirmed to these onlookers that the path they had trodden in Manchuria was the right one. The League looked frail, its diplomacy powerless in the face of the determination of an imperial power. For Japanese ideologues, economists, and politicians international relations were nearing a turning point.

The Italo-Ethiopian War catalyzed the crisis in international affairs with Japan's own imperial fervor and, in doing so, raised the question of the relationship between Imperial Japan and Fascist Italy. If, in hindsight, it is easy to notice the parallels between Rome and Tokyo's imperialist goals, in 1935 Japanese observers debated intensely over the commonalities between Fascist Italy's schemes in East Africa and Japan's visions for East Asia. The crux of the matter was Italy's place among the Western powers. On one side, they condemned the Italian invasion because it bore all the hallmarks of old-fashioned European imperialism, with its brutal subjugation of "colored races" to "white" rule.[6] It is therefore not surprising that large numbers of Japanese activists and ordinary people protested against Mussolini's invasion, participating in an antiwar movement which, in the second half of 1935, saw demonstrators taking to the streets in cities as far apart as London, New York, Beijing, and Calcutta.[7] On the other side, there were those who regarded Mussolini's rash act as symptomatic of the desire of "have-not" countries, such as Japan and Italy, to overturn the much-reviled Anglo-Saxon domination of the world. The Darwinian argument that colonies represented a nation's wealth and "lifeline" had gained prominence during the Great Depression, even though it was of older date. Most interesting was the almost simultaneous call for a colonial redistribution by pre–World War nationalists in Italy, such as Enrico Corradini and the poet Giovanni Pascoli, and, after the Great War, by the young Prince Konoe Fumimaro, who chastised the Versailles Peace Conference, which he had attended, for failing to adequately compensate Japan with colonies.[8]

The Italo-Ethiopian War, then, posed a dilemma to Japanese officials and foreign-policy pundits. They faced the problem of denying Italian imperialism on the grounds of Western world hegemony while supporting Italy to oppose the empires of the Great Powers in Africa and, indirectly, in Asia. The resolution of these disputes occurred gradually as a result of the geopolitical shift that the war itself had created. Although, during the early stages of the war, dismay over the Italian invasion dominated the Japanese discourse, from late 1935 it became apparent that sympathy for Ethiopia had moved toward understanding for Fascist Italy on the ground that the conflict, while objectionable in principle, could hasten in practice the overthrow of the League of Nations and weaken the European powers, especially Britain. The Italo-Ethiopian War led journalists, intellectuals, and politicians to discuss international questions relating to economic autarky, international organizations, and imperial politics and, in so doing, they inadvertently formulated the first articulation of the ideological links between Japan and Italy (as well as Germany), almost half a decade before the Tripartite Pact.

Anti-Italian Sentiment

Like the Manchurian Incident, the Ethiopian war was a media event. Indeed, the media apparatus and popular mobilization that emerged after 1931 also set the tone for the debates on the war in Ethiopia. Through a variety of outlets—radio, newspapers, pamphlets, movies, and well-publicized study groups—ideologues, journalists, and bureaucrats took a lead in discussing the Italian invasion, causing much sensation among the population in the attempt to influence government policy.[9] A September 1935 *Yomiuri* editorial illustrated the effort to align national interest with popular opinion, lamenting the "great necessity" that the "authorities pay attention to the domestic mood by investigating the rights and wrongs of the people's perspective on foreign policy, while we have to dedicate ourselves to move public opinion in the right and proper direction."[10] On their part, officials were all too aware that the Italian invasion was a matter of great public interest. In December 1935 the Japanese foreign minister, Hirota Kōki, cautioned his ambassador to Paris that the Italian-Ethiopian conflict was not just a matter of international affairs: "because our disposition towards the conflict has attracted significant attention among the public, it will be necessary to exercise utmost care."[11]

The popular mood was decidedly anti-Italian, to the point where the government had to struggle to keep public passions under control. In July 1935 Japanese hostility toward Italy erupted in a diplomatic rift quickly named by the press "the Sugimura affair," after Sugimura Yōtarō, the ambassador in Rome. The high-profile diplomat—he had been under-secretary general of the League, was a member of the International Olympic Committee, and a keen swimmer and judo wrestler—had not weighed his words carefully enough in a meeting with Mussolini, thus giving the Italian regime the opportunity to misquote him by asserting that Japan had little interest in Ethiopia. Relations between the two countries quickly deteriorated. In Italy, the "anti-Japanese movement" was so violent that two hundred policemen had to be deployed around the Japanese Embassy.[12] The anti-Japanese rhetoric, in turn, provoked a hostile reaction to Italy in Japan. Diplomatic commentators chastised Fascist Italy's crude attitude. The Sugimura affair "makes us doubt Italy's gentlemanly refinement," commented one analyst. This kind of attitude, he argued, did not become a Great Power and proved that Italy was not on the level of Great Britain and the United States—or Japan.[13]

Mussolini's lack of diplomatic finesse may have compromised support for Italy's invasion, but more than anything what rallied Japanese to the Ethiopian cause was Italian violence. The disproportionate military capabilities of the modern Italian armies, whose weapons included poison gas, and of the poorly equipped Ethiopian troops horrified Japanese onlookers.[14] "Italy is going to hell; choosing to go to war might be a shortcut" was the invective of one Japanese in the *Yomiuri* column where readers expressed their political opinions in pithy one-line commentaries.[15] Nowhere was the exasperation with Italy expressed more forcefully than in attacks against Mussolini himself. Up to 1935 the Italian leader had cut a relatively positive figure in the Japanese press. There was, especially among conservatives and the radical right, a certain admiration for the Duce's quashing of the socialists and for his advocacy of a social order based on intransigent nationalism. Opponents of parliamentary democracy approved of his efficient, personal rule; educators styled him as an example of masculine virtuosity. But widespread skepticism remained about Mussolini's resort to—even glorification of—violence as a means to achieve his goals. Preferring persuasion to repression as a way to control dissent, Japanese elites retained latent misgivings about the domestic politics of Fascist Italy.[16]

The Italian invasion of Ethiopia revived the topic of the violent nature of Fascism and its leader, Benito Mussolini. In columns, articles, and even cartoons, Japanese condemned the Duce as a bloodthirsty, arrogant, and cruel dictator. Yamakawa Kikue, a socialist feminist, declared him a mafia "boss" (*oyabun*). Other sardonic comments included the pronouncement: "This unmanly Mussolini! Should we send him a raw carp liver from Japan?"[17] Even children had misgivings about the Italian hero. Edamatsu Hideyuki, a sixth-grader from Sumiyoshi, a township near Osaka, declared that "when I see Mussolini in a photograph, I like him a lot as a hero but, to think that he bullies weak Ethiopia like that, I don't like that at all! [*iyadanaa*]." In Japan, he explained, it is "manly" for the strong to

Mussolini portrayed as a demon devouring an innocent cat that represents Ethiopia. In the background, the leaders of the League of Nations look on squeamishly.

(From Yomiuri shinbun, *April 21, 1936.)*

help the weak, and the idea of the suffering of so many Ethiopian children moved little Hideyuki "to tears." "Doesn't Mussolini understand the sadness of a boy?"[18]

Anti-Italianism and sympathy for Ethiopia merged into a discourse on solidarity of "races of color" against "whites." As another one-liner put it, the "lions of Africa have become fireflies before the white man, soon they will be eaten."[19] The theory that the Ethiopian war fell into the history of conflict between the West and the rest of the world was particularly dear to right-wing ideologues. In their Pan-Asianist rhetoric they championed the cause of anticolonialism even as they advocated Japanese domination in Asia. Ethiopia received the support of the powerful Amur River Society (Kokuryūkai), led by Tōyama Mitsuru.[20] Widely recognized as the high priest of the Japanese Right, in June 1935 he founded the Friends of Ethiopia Group to lobby for the African country in what he regarded as the wider struggle to liberate the world from the yoke of "racial discrimination." Ethiopia, one member of the group declared, fell "victim to both Italian power and European domination." "Our Imperial Japan, given its intrinsic mission to overthrow racial inequality, and given the sympathy for those seriously weak people who trust in us, cannot overlook the fact that it is tied closely to this question."[21]

The Right's determination to harness and direct the wave of popular sentiment was noted by Italian officials. Guglielmo Scalise, the Italian military attaché in

Tokyo, deplored the number of speakers, orators, and writers who were "swarming a bit everywhere, brandishing the same arguments" and producing a "remarkable flowering of pamphlets" against Italy. The diplomat also observed that, to prove that their sentiments of friendship went beyond rhetoric, some right-wingers held fund-raising rallies in Tokyo wards and other cities, managing to gather sums that were "conspicuous."[22] Other radicals were willing to take sensational if clearly unrealistic steps. The daily *Yomiuri* reported that in Osaka a group of four pilot volunteers, led by the businessman and postwar fixer as well as philanthropist Sasakawa Ryōichi, declared their "ardent desire" to form a squadron and join the Ethiopian army, ready to "risk their lives for the races of color."[23] More plausibly and, for Italian officials, worryingly, there were also those who threatened Giacinto Auriti, the ambassador in Tokyo, in "anonymous letters with insults and death threats."[24]

The Role of the League of Nations

Anti-Italianism, however, was not the only sentiment generated by the Ethiopian war; it was neither the most prominent nor the most enduring response. Alienating though Mussolini's attitude was, the community of foreign-policy analysts increasingly vented their frustration at the League's incapacity to stop a renewed European imperial venture. They viewed the war in the context of a wider imperial competition among the Western Great Powers and Mussolini's aggression in Ethiopia as a reminder that, while Japan was battling for a new Asia liberated from Western colonialism, in Africa the old coordinates of violent, racist white-man's domination remained in place. And, in their mind, the League was complicit in the perpetuation of the imperial status quo.

In Japan, the conviction that post–World War I international relations were set on rules that favored the Western powers was of long standing. It began at Versailles in 1919, when Woodrow Wilson rejected Japan's proposal to add a racial equality clause to the Covenant of the League of Nations in response to Australia's objections.[25] The London Naval Treaty (1930), which allowed Great Britain and the United States to maintain a larger fleet than Japan, aroused the ire of those Japanese policymakers and military who advocated an expansion of Japanese naval power in Asia.[26] Subsequent events in East Asia raised the stakes. Both the League and the Great Powers condemned the Japanese invasion of Manchuria (1931) and refused to recognize the puppet state of Manchukuo (1933), an opposition that offended the revisionist groups in the Japanese government to the point that they withdrew Japan from the League that same year. As far as Matsuoka Yōsuke, the head of the Japanese delegation at Geneva, was concerned,

Mussolini trumps the Ethiopian emperor, Haile Selassie, in collusion with the French foreign minister, Pierre Laval, and the British foreign secretary, Samuel Hoare. The cartoon is mockingly titled "Superior and Inferior Races."

(From Yomiuri shinbun, *October 20, 1935.)*

urgent measures had to be taken lest Europe and America carried out their goal to "crucify" Japan.[27]

Thus, by the early 1930s, while a number of older pro-British liberals in Japan still defended Wilsonian internationalism, a younger crowd of "go-fast imperialists" voiced their contempt for the ideas and institutions that underpinned the world order set up after World War I—and the war in Ethiopia provided the latest platform for their cause.[28] They were made up of a loose grouping of intellectuals—academics, high-level bureaucrats, and journalists—who wrote in respected journals close to the bureaucratic and political establishment such as *Gaikō jihō* and *Kokusai chishiki*.[29] In these pages they debated the Ethiopian war as a turning point for Japanese foreign policy. The editors of *Gaikō*, for example, drew attention to the Sugimura affair not so much to criticize Fascist Italy but because they found it symptomatic of a deeper problem with the conduct of Japanese foreign policy: "Japanese diplomats are trapped aimlessly in old-fashioned ideas and, as a result, are incapable of grasping the national consciousness [*kokuminteki ishiki*] of our new Japan."[30] Moved by the pressing concern with a revision of the international system set up at Versailles in 1919, these commentators regarded the Italo-Ethiopian War in light of their desire to press for what contemporaries called an "assertive foreign policy" (*kyōchō gaikō*) based on Realpolitik and aimed at upholding Japan's imperial interests in East Asia.

Many of them saw the Western handling of the Italo-Ethiopian War as duplicitous and found confirmation of their suspicions in the Hoare-Laval Pact of December 1935, in which Great Britain and France negotiated a deal with Fascist Italy at the expense of Ethiopia, a League member. Political commentators had expressed growing dismay with the attitude of the two European Great Powers, France and Britain, since early 1935. On January 7 the French foreign minister, Pierre Laval, had sealed an agreement with Mussolini as part of a diplomatic strategy aimed against Hitler's Germany. In return, France promised not to interfere with Italy's colonial ambitions in Africa.[31] This bilateral diplomacy proved to Matsuda Shōichi, a political scientist, that "in its relations with Italy, France had awakened to realistic politics."[32] According to him, France and Britain dealt with the crisis, not on the basis of the internationalism of 1919, but out of their own imperialist interests. "If we truly want to keep the League of Nations as the sanctuary of peace," he continued, "it is necessary to advance with the true principles of the League. It is not right to mislead the world and make use of the League opportunistically."[33] Hori Makoto, another political scientist, put it more bluntly. "While France has appointed itself as the most loyal follower of the spirit of the League, by supporting Italy's aggressive policies, it is trying to destroy this very spirit."[34]

The spirit of internationalism of the League, Japanese commentators contended, had done little to dispel the Darwinian logic that animated the foreign policy of the Great Powers, especially that of Britain. London's interests were such that, "on one side it proclaims frontally the superiority of the League and rallies together all small countries, on the other it moves its fleet and shows its resolve: it prepares for both peace and war."[35] Britain epitomized the Western desire to maintain the international status quo. For this reason Kano Kizō, a specialist in German geopolitics, welcomed the Italo-Ethiopian War, hoping that the conflict would "finally lay bare [the fact] that the League is a prop of British foreign policy." He was convinced that Italian saber rattling proved that "the strong" always find a reason to oppress the weak. "Just as in Aesop, when the wolf eats the lamb, the act of eating is the result of a decision taken from the beginning, which precedes the pretext for conflict. The Italian-Ethiopian conflict is just like that."[36] Italy's aims were reprehensible, but no more so than British hypocrisy.

The tensions of Wilsonian internationalism—the yawning gap between the ideals of the League and the practice of the Powers—was reflected in international law. For Tachi Sakutarō, an expert in international law, the League's legal framework was not only sluggish, but its covenant could not address a conflict such as the Ethiopian war satisfactorily. For example, Article 10 guaranteed the territorial integrity of member nations and therefore should have protected Ethiopia from Italian aggression. Italy, however, declared that Ethiopia threatened the Italian colony of Eritrea and invoked the right of self-defense.[37] Ashida Hitoshi, a diplomat-turned-politician (and future postwar prime minister), concluded that these conflicting arguments illustrated that the legal means at the disposal of the League to dissuade or punish a renegade state were limited. Enforcing the legal powers of the League was altogether a different matter. Article 16, he argued, gave the League the power to issue sanctions, but both Britain and France were unwilling to resort to a full embargo and continued to permit imports of coal and oil: "probably no country is thinking of using military force" to stop Italy, Ashida surmised in November 1935.[38]

In the eyes of these commentators, the League was convulsing in its death throes. It lacked a legal basis to enforce its ideals, suffered from a political deficiency consisting of the non-membership of the United States, and was struggling to survive the moral vicissitudes emerging from imperial power games. These problems, one political scientist put it, had reduced the League of Nations to a "European League."[39] Even the liberal journalist Baba Tsunego insisted that the idealism of the 1920s was dead. The nature of "Realpolitik," he explained dryly, was such that it "lacks any connection to ethics," concluding that in international relations there was "no god and no Buddha."[40]

The Italo-Ethiopian War generated not so much gloom as a widespread sense of relief, hardening the Japanese resolve to build a new world order on the ruins of the League. By mid-December 1935 foreign affairs journals registered their satisfaction with the year that was about to come to a close, concluding that Japanese, at last, had stood up to the League and corroborated their imperial consciousness. At home, the vestiges of 1920s constitutional democracy (*minponshugi*) were fading. The "movement for the clarification of the national polity [*kokutai*]" had defined exactly what that mystic entity meant, recasting the legal principle that the emperor was not subject to the Constitution, but transcended it.[41] Internationally, the Ethiopian war had undercut what legitimacy the League had left, promising a revision of the world order. "Domestically, the national consciousness [*kokumin ishiki*] has been perfected; abroad, the worldview of our nation has been corrected; in our international life we have gained tremendous confidence." With this newly found vigor and a foreign policy based on the "self" (*ji*)—self-sufficiency (*jishu*), autonomy (*jiritsu*), and confidence (*jishin*)—Japan could right the wrongs of the current world order, a task that required it to become "the leader of Asia."[42] Convinced that they faced the political and moral collapse of liberal internationalism, a growing number of Japanese political analysts believed that the moment had come to push ahead with neo-imperial visions by consolidating—and perhaps extending—the project started in Manchuria in 1931.

Political Economy

This prospect did not stop at a muscular foreign policy; it also meant reforming East Asia's political economy. While foreign-policy pundits ruminated about the possibilities of a colonial redistribution, business groups, industrialists, and government bureaucrats sensed that the moment had come to replace the remnants of free trade—and, hence, Western influence in Asia—with a regional economy centered on Japan. To thwart future crises of capitalism such as the Great Depression, in the early 1930s governments around the world turned toward protectionism and a tighter integration of the metropolitan and colonial economies. Japanese economists and businessmen regarded this transition as inevitable but at the same time felt uneasy about it.[43]

On the one hand, they regarded Japan as being at the forefront of the trend toward a "managed economy." At home, corporatism, a tighter cooperation between government and big business, promised to solve tensions between labor and capital and to guarantee social harmony.[44] In the empire, particularly in Manchuria, a young generation of technocrats (the so-called reform bureaucrats), in conjunction with military leaders, right-wing ideologues, and industrial conglomerates (*zaibatsu*), worked on a "rationalized," planned economy that would provide Japan with natural resources and Asia with a model for industrial "development."[45] On the other hand, they worried about Japan's increasingly uncertain foreign markets. After the Great Depression the Japanese economy had recovered fast. Exports of consumer goods such as cotton and rayon surged; military demand for steel and munitions increased; and new industrial conglomerates such as Nissan, Nichitsu, and Riken expanded the chemical and technology sectors. Companies, however, faced increasingly tight import restrictions in places like the United States, but also India and the Middle East. To secure their country's economic survival, then, economists, businessmen, and planners sought to extend Japanese access to Asian markets.[46] In this context, they came to see the Ethiopian war as opening an avenue toward bridging the gap between Japan's innovative economic thinking and its old problem of lacking access to resources and markets: the rising tensions in Europe would weaken the Great Powers' grip over their colonies in Asia.

The result was that the Ethiopian war brought together reformist thinking in both foreign affairs and political economy, inducing many economists to believe that a reconstruction of capitalism in an expanded empire was nearing. Indeed, what emerges from the reactions of the business community is just how marginal the idea of free trade on a world scale had become. Few businessmen were anxious about the possibility that the Italo-Ethiopian War might close Western markets to Japanese trade. Only the relatively marginal community that envisaged

Africa as an untapped trading frontier raised some concerns about the effects of the war. In these quarters Africa, and Ethiopia in particular, was thought of as a market for Japanese goods and as a place from which to import raw materials and agricultural produce. In fact, in the decade preceding the conflict, trade relations between Japan and Ethiopia had intensified, with Japanese firms exporting large amounts of cotton fabrics, rayon, pottery, and glassware to the African kingdom.[47] The two countries had signed a Friendship and Trade Agreement in 1928, and in the early 1930s further private and government initiatives got under way. In November 1931 the business newspaper *Chūgai shōgyō shinpō* (predecessor of the postwar financial daily *Nihon keizai shinbun*) reported on conditions in Ethiopia, pointing out that as "[Ethiopia] is venturing out onto the international stage, one can foresee that this will be a remarkable customer country for [our] exports."[48] According to the *Cape Times*, in the first half of 1934 Japanese products in Ethiopia outsold those of Western countries: Japan exported goods of the value of 8.5 million francs, compared to Britain's 3.2 million and Italy's tiny 240 thousand.[49] At the same time, the country was rich in lucrative export products, such as animal furs, coffee, beeswax, ivory, and musk. "As Japan receives treatment of most favored nation," the article concluded, "and given that there is a strong demand for Japanese products and that the climate is not too bad, those who are well-informed are increasingly making this new friend of Japan the object of their attention."[50] For these businessmen, the war, and even more so an Italian victory, meant being cut off from Africa.

But most industrialists and businessmen discussed the Italo-Ethiopian War with aplomb. Indeed, the prospect of a wartime economy created much cheer. "Europe's instability is East Asia's stability. When Europe darkens, Japan brightens up."[51] With such confidence the finance and banking journalist Katsuta Teiji (1893–1952) welcomed the possibility that Japanese goods would flow into those markets cut off from their European suppliers, as had happened during World War I. *Daiyamondo* (Diamond), the foremost popular business magazine, hurriedly published a guide about the war's influence on the stock market.[52] With a war raging in East Africa and, potentially, in the Mediterranean, Western merchant ships would likely be recalled to their home countries. "At one time foreign merchant ships in Asia had reached six hundred thousand tons; recently the figure is closer to one hundred thousand." Japan's shipping industry would reap great profits from this situation. The same was true of the spinning industry (should the Suez Canal be closed, British competition would all but disappear); the shipbuilding industry (which would benefit indirectly); and machinery (exported to markets in Asia but also Britain, Germany, and the United States).[53] More than any other, the ailing Japanese rayon business would find respite by taking over the Italian market share. As one reader bluntly put it, "traders in rayon are those who, deep in their hearts, hope most fervently that the war will expand."[54] Investors agreed that the war's impact on the stock market was likely to be minor. In November, Kajiwara Nakaji, former head of the Tokyo Stock Exchange, wrote that the situation was stable and that, unless the war degenerated into a second European-wide conflict, there was no reason for investors to fret; his advice was to "keep calm and keep buying."[55]

The wartime economy could boost big business for another reason. As the leaders of Japan's great firms saw it, a renewed period of destabilization would likely weaken the presence of Western capital in Asia and, crucially, do away with their competition. To discuss how to manage Japan's future hegemonic position in the region a number of corporate heavyweights gathered for a roundtable talk organized by the daily *Ōsaka Asahi shinbun*. They felt exhilarant. Yokota Tsukuri, managing director at Nomura Securities, declared that since the Meiji Restoration of 1868 Japan had not witnessed such a "blissful" period. The collaboration between the military and the bureaucracy was "far less self-interested" than party cabinets; Japan's position in East Asia had become "firm"; the alliance with Manchukuo had laid the groundwork for a "great fervor." Yokota, in other words, saw the Ethiopian crisis through the lens of Japan's "action" in Manchuria. Ethiopia continued that project, confirming the conviction that the world economy had reached a turning point. "Politically and economically, we have the essential elements ready, and although we are currently still in a preparatory period, it is clear that we are following the road to advancement."[56]

"Advancement" meant, first of all, no going back to the economics of the 1920s. A return "to the time of the prewar economy when trade was comparatively free is an illusion," argued Matsui Haruo (1891–1966), one of the "reformist bureaucrats" who had been active in Manchuria and who, in 1937, would become a member of the Planning Agency (Kikakuin).[57] But these arguments were not limited to technocrats like Matsui. Individuals with a long-standing liberal pedigree also hailed the Ethiopian war as a momentous event, revisiting their established convictions in favor of new solutions to the crisis of capitalism. On October 7, Katsuta Teiji, the finance and banking expert, welcomed the outbreak of hostilities between Italy and Ethiopia. The war was the natural result of the "impasse of European liberalism" and gave a chance to move beyond its strictures. "Thinking in terms of the interruption of the distribution economy [*ryūtsū keizai*], of the coming of a bloc economy, of the reoccurrence of wars for the redistribution of colonies, of a clean slate of the inequalities of capitalism, the Italo-Ethiopian War appears to be the first step toward a new century in the history of humanity." As Japanese capitalism was expanding "left and right" and as Japan was asserting its position as the "champion [*ōsha*] of East Asia," this was a "period of soul-searching."[58] The Ethiopian crisis dealt a double blow to both political and economic internationalism, signaling a global turn toward the kind of imperial economy that Japan had spearheaded in Manchuria.

The convergence of political and economic reformism in the mid-1930s gave the Italo-Ethiopian War a significance that it would not have had only a few years earlier. As Iida Seizō, an economist at Sumitomo Bank and, later, at Nomura Securities, explained, what distinguished the world economy in 1935 from that of World War I was the "stage of capitalism." World War I was a struggle for the balance of power; Ethiopia was fundamentally about imperial powers trying to secure resources.[59] In other words, the world economy would henceforth no longer be global and competitive but regional and regulated. It was this geopolitical framework that Matsui had in mind when he advocated a "bloc economy" based on a "new free trade."[60] The creation of self-contained, regional blocs entailed a conjoined action on two fronts. Politically, Japan had to redraw the parameters of an expanded sphere of interest in East Asia; and, economically, it was necessary to "rationalize" the use of resources. Taking this step, it seemed to Katsuta Teiji, was the "ironclad rule of capitalism."[61]

Economists and bureaucrats increasingly referred to these policies as "development." In September 1935 the aging (and soon-to-be assassinated) finance minister and sometime champion of the gold standard, Takahashi Korekiyo, bent to the winds of economic change. No longer expecting national growth through trade, the veteran minister now called on state intervention to secure Japan and Asia's "development."

> As far as our investments and cultural projects in North China are concerned, Britain, the United States, and all other countries are too troubled by the conflict between Italy and Ethiopia to call much attention to them. But, should the conflict be settled, it is clear that Western capital will necessarily flow toward North China . . . we are not yet prepared for [such] investments and this is not only a problem of prestige for Japan, the leader of East Asia—it is also a serious problem in terms of Japan's future development. Therefore from now on we ought to start considering the future prospects of North China, and instruct all ministries to make arrangements accordingly.[62]

The Italo-Ethiopian War prompted Japanese businessmen and bureaucrats to rethink the possibilities for capitalism in one empire. As they saw it, free trade had not to be abolished but reconfigured spatially within the boundaries of an expanded Japanese imperial polity. At the same time, some form of collaboration between state and capital was required to harmonize the economy. The "greatest impact of the Italo-Ethiopian War," wrote Takeuchi Kenji (1895–1978), a scholar of Adam Smith and David Ricardo, was that it had become increasingly necessary to establish a "fundamental plan for heavy industry and, especially, the steel industry." Like many bureaucrats, politicians, and journalists, he was beaming with optimism: "our country's political position has become very bright indeed."[63]

Toward a Reconciliation with Fascist Italy

Thus the Italo-Ethiopian War generated conflicting responses in Japan. On one side, it led to a popular anticolonialism that was expressed in widespread hostility toward Fascist Italy's aggression of an African country. On the other, it revived Japanese imperialism by emboldening those politicians, ideologues, and bureaucrats who were waiting for the moment to consolidate Japan's "independent foreign policy" and to extend the idea of a regional economic bloc to the rest of Asia. These contradictions in Japan's stance on world affairs did not escape Nogami Yaeko, the liberal feminist writer and activist. She had read an article by Bernard Shaw in which the British intellectual took the press of his country to task for antagonizing Italy but remaining silent on Britain's own imperialism. Sardonically, Shaw had called attention to the hypocrisy of those who drew all too clear distinctions between Britain's and Italy's methods of bringing civilization to the colonized. In turn, Nogami questioned the lack of self-criticism among Japanese intellectuals. "If in Japan we had an old man [*oji*] who spoke frankly in this way," Nogami wrote, "the general populace [*ippan taishū*] who, in the past two or three years, has had a bloated belly would feel relieved as if after an enema."[64]

Nogami's pointed critique raises the question of how various Japanese intellectuals and policymakers reconciled the contradiction between opposing Italian imperialism in Africa while pleading for Japan to build a new order in Asia. Several commentators found no inconsistency at all, resolving the paradox with arguments about national exceptionalism. Japanese were ethically equipped to "feel" the plight of the colonized people and then to lead them out of subjugation. "This is probably because of Japan's bushido," wrote the liberal intellectual Baba Tsunego, referring to that chivalrous attitude of the strong toward the weak that the Christian internationalist Nitobe Inazō had identified as the unwritten morality underlying Japanese social conduct. For Baba, bushido not only had a domestic meaning; it had an international applicability. Its moral code not only could harmonize Japanese society but could be exported to other countries as a way to resolve the tensions plaguing the contemporary world.[65] Tsurumi Yūsuke, another liberal internationalist, contended that Japanese values represented the apogee of civilizational progress. In his book on the Italo-Ethiopian War, *Ethiopia: Crucible of Misfortune* (1935), he argued that

> A superannuated Europe is resorting to its last strengths in the effort to hold on to its throne of world domination. Greece collapsed, Rome collapsed, the Han dynasty collapsed, the Mughal empire collapsed, Napoleon collapsed. Times change, nations [*minzoku*] rise and decline. A man's life does not reach one hundred years; how can a nation flourish for one thousand? Unless we make coexistence and coprosperity the ideal of humanity, we cannot tolerate that on this earth the monopoly of one people and one race [*hito minzoku, isshuzoku*] be powerful for eternity.[66]

The idea that in its foreign policy Japan was following a moral mission legitimized a clear-cut distinction between Italian aims in Africa and Japan's project in Asia. Kanezaki Ken, an advocate of Japanese expansion in North China, contrasted Italy's imperial aims with what he saw as Japan's moral mission. "The development of the Japanese nation [*minzoku*] is not about a persistent imperialism and expansionism, as Westerners believe. It is an expansion based on a pure sense of justice for the world. The Japanese people have a strong sense of justice [*seigi*] and resent injustice [*fugi*]."[67] Legal scholars also went to great lengths to distinguish between the two empires. Ashida Hitoshi, for example, maintained that the Italian invasion of Ethiopia was a "conflict"(*funsō*); the Japanese invasion of Manchuria was no more than an "incident" (*jihen*). In his mind, Japan "supported the independence of Manchuria" whereas Italy "destroyed an independent state."[68] This reasoning found its most extreme expression among some sections of the radical Right. The activist Kita Reikichi, for example, developed an argument in support of Japan's expansion based on Pan-Asianist fraternity, co-opting the language of sympathy with Ethiopia for a self-serving justification of Japanese empire.[69] He denounced Italy's "insane declaration" to subjugate "blacks," and called on Japan to work for "world justice" by embracing "racial equality as the basis of international affairs." Yet this criticism of Italian imperialism had nothing to do with Japan's hegemony over Asia. "Ruling over China, Japan should give grand spiritual encouragement to Ethiopia from the principle of a racial levelers' movement [*jinshu suihei undō*]."[70]

And yet, in the long run, arguments that drew all too neat distinctions between the Japanese and Italian empires gave way to a more conciliatory, even sympathetic, disposition toward Fascist Italy. By December 1935, the shift was palpable. Guglielmo Scalise, the military attaché in Tokyo, reported that "large swathes of public opinion are perhaps still sympathizing with Ethiopia, but among them there are various currents that work in our favor, and these currents are already setting foot in the milieus that direct politics and the various activities in the country, in particular the military and navy."[71] By late 1935, disillusionment with the League of Nations had eclipsed frustration with Italy, repositioning the Ethiopian conflict in a wider imperialist struggle that made many Japanese reconsider their priorities—and allegiances. In Japan's imperial schemes Italy may have counted for little, but more than Ethiopia. As this realization germinated, the Italo-Ethiopian War ceased to be a conflict between the forces for and against Western domination of the world and took on the connotations of an ideological war between resurgent nations such as Japan and Italy and the decadent liberal Great Powers. Imperial Japan's fascist tendencies overlapped with Fascist Italy's imperial policies; the commonalities were too obvious to be whisked away, even though this was often admitted only between the lines.

From the beginning, popular outrage against Italy was largely genuine but support for Ethiopia was qualified. Sympathy for the plight of Africans had never been uniform, being more pronounced among ordinary Japanese than among the political and intellectual elites, whose racialized views of Africans often paralleled those of their Western counterparts. Ethiopia entered public consciousness at a time in which there were firmly set hierarchies in the Japanese view of the world. If, as Stefan Tanaka has shown, China became categorized as a backward neighbor, no better treatment was to be expected for Ethiopia.[72] Sympathetic though they might have been, some commentators could not conceal their condescension, if not plain racism, toward Ethiopians. This was the attitude of an old liberal like the writer and journalist Masamune Hakuchō (1879–1962); in 1935, together with the writers Shimazaki Tōson and Tokuda Shūsei, he had just founded PEN Japan. "As a country, Ethiopia is ancient, but it seems that in terms of cultural production it has nothing to be proud of in this world. So, from that perspective, even if it is destroyed, we can feel relieved. Let it have its cultural institutions rebuilt by a conqueror and, from that point, it will create its own literature as a country."[73] The physiologist Uramoto Secchō questioned the value of the Ethiopian "race." "It appears that, as individuals and in their physical strength, Ethiopians hold sway over the rest of the world in running and in combat, but, when it comes to racial spirit [*jinshu kihaku*] . . . they're worth zero."[74] Taken on its own terms, outside the context of Italian aggression, Ethiopia no longer appeared a defenseless victim, but a backward place with an interesting, but inferior, civilization.

This Darwinian logic touched a nerve, as even some right-wingers wavered in their support for Ethiopia. Increasingly interpreting the Italo-Ethiopian War as an episode in the struggle for world hegemony between "have" and "have-not" countries, they aligned the interests of Japan with those of Italy and Germany against those of Great Britain, France, the United States, and the Soviet Union.

In the words of Mutō Naoyoshi, a little-known Pan-Asianist, the Italo-Ethiopian War's significance was that it illustrated the "historically inevitable and grave mission for countries whose development has been obstructed by a small and narrow territory." In this struggle for life or death, Mutō continued, the "highest principle is necessity." And, in his view, British interests interfered with the evolutionary needs of emerging countries. "Italy looking for a way into Ethiopia; Britain thrusting its nose into this matter. What difference can one see in the positions of Japan and Italy?"[75]

Other right-wingers outspokenly defended the cause of Fascist Italy on racial grounds. Shimoi Harukichi rallied a number of fellow travelers for what the Italian military attaché called a "thorough operation in favor of Italy." The group, named the Society for the Study of International Affairs (Kokusai Jijō Kenkyūkai), toured the country to give talks on the African war, presenting Italy's perspective to industrialists at Tokyo's Rotary Club, the Osaka Chamber of Commerce, intellectuals, students at Waseda University, military officers and, on one occasion, some one hundred Diet representatives. They churned out numerous pamphlets that countered the concept of racial war. One, for example, argued that Japanese had nothing in common with Ethiopians: "we are not a race of color," as this term (*yūshoku jinshu*) only denoted blacks. To argue otherwise would be "racial prejudice."[76]

Just like public sympathy for Ethiopia was, after all, relative, so economic and political elites were often ambivalent about their hostility to Fascist Italy. To be sure, the Italo-Ethiopian War was inconvenient to the Japanese government. Fearing that the conflict might have repercussions on Japan's hold of Manchukuo, it assumed a wait-and-see stance in the hope that the war would come to a quick end.[77] To make the situation even more sensitive, the war came at a time when domestic politics were in disarray due to the wave of right-wing terrorism. Many politicians would have preferred it if Italy had stayed in its place lest it destabilize international and domestic politics at a sensitive moment.

At the same time, they were pragmatic enough to see chances arising from the tribulations of the League and the weakening of the Royal Navy in Asia. This may also explain the behind-the-scene support for Italy of at least some elements in the Japanese army. In December 1935, Guglielmo Scalise, the Italian military attaché, cabled that "one colonel Kondo, belonging to the nationalist faction of General Araki and doing propaganda for us, has donated one hundred inflatable mattresses for a field hospital and written a highly noble letter expressing his admiration and best wishes for the Head of Government [Mussolini] and the Italian people."[78] He had also heard rumors that the industrial conglomerates Mitsui and Mitsubishi "might be prepared to supply our troops in East Africa should the Suez Canal be closed."[79]

If the rift between Fascist Italy and Imperial Japan was more superficial than it appeared at first sight, it was also because Italy's position in the Japanese divide between East and West was ambiguous. Italy's grab for empire in Africa fitted squarely into the Pan-Asianist narrative of a civilizational conflict between an imperialist West and the anticolonial movement led by Japan. But Mussolini's hostility toward the League and the Great Powers cast a different light on Fascist Italy, one that recalled Japan's own international ambitions. There were those who asserted that, in all the talk about sentiments and feeling, Fascist passions also deserved respect. For the diplomat, politician, and industrialist Kajima Morinosuke, the attack on Ethiopia was not a random act of violence but derived from fascism's realistic understanding of human nature, the nation, and foreign policy. No doubt, Kajima admitted, violence was an integral element of fascism; and Mussolini was an "extreme imperialist." But, he continued, the Duce's attitude was not unwarranted. He had used violence to quell the socialists at home, but had thereby established domestic stability. It was the same in foreign policy: he was making war to prepare for peace. This approach might seem irrational to Anglo-Saxons and to those Japanese who, "fixated with today's rationalist civilization, cannot in the least understand Fascism's wildly excited attitude." Italians, Kajima averred, had a passionate national spirit and saw things differently, and, in his view, rightly so. For "when men decide their actions, it is not so much reason [*risei*] but sentiment [*kanjō*] that gets the better of them."[80]

The result was that by late 1935 foreign-policy commentators could be heard thinking aloud about siding with Italy's cause. An editorial in *Gaikō jihō* declared that Japanese public opinion had demonstrated "an excess of sympathy with the Ethiopians" and a "cold attitude towards the position of Italy . . . which is not a view that we always support." As the editors saw it, Italy had, after all, been a "victim" of the Powers, who had prevented this imperial latecomer from acquiring territories in Africa and the Balkans that were necessary for its economic and political survival. Thus the invasion of Ethiopia was of "great significance" to the entire world and taught one "concrete, real lesson": "unless one determines a new principle for the redistribution of territory for emerging peoples [*shikō minzoku*] who have culture and energy to develop, the world's unrest will never stabilize."[81] More radical, right-wing ideologues, such as Murobuse Kōshin, welcomed this instability. The "deep symbolic meaning" of the Italo-Ethiopian War, he wrote in December 1936, was the imminent collapse of Western hegemony, a crisis for which Japan had to ready itself. "To war! To war! We can say with confidence that 1936 was the year that moved us toward the Second World War. Blood is throbbing, the spirit is in trepidation, reason has stopped working. We are on the eve of the spectacle of a second world war."[82]

Thus, the significance of the Italo-Ethiopian War lies in the way in which it intensified the crisis of the international system by synthesizing revisionist thinking in foreign affairs, economics, and empire. For Japanese public intellectuals, the Italian aggression on an African state caused moral consternation by demonstrating the error of the Great Powers rejecting Japan's appeal to include a racial equality clause in the Covenant of the League of Nations. The reaction of the League to the Italian invasion smacked not only of hypocrisy but also of the self-serving influence of Great Britain and France, two colonial powers that staunchly opposed Japan's call for an expanded sphere of interest in Asia. Such demands had become more strident with the search for a solution to the crisis of capitalism after the Great Depression. They were also wedded to the belief that Japan was morally empowered to liberate Asia from Western imperialism, an idea that was reinforced by the model of Manchukuo as a nominally independent state and that would find its most philosophical expression in the wartime writings of thinkers related to the Kyoto School.[83]

Yet, just as the Italo-Ethiopian War disclosed that liberal internationalism was shot through with imperial ambitions, so the conflict revealed the hypocrisy of Japan's professed anti-imperialism.[84] Sympathy for Ethiopia, based on Pan-Asian notions of racial equality, generally masked paternalism, which in turn concealed an imperial project of its own. Indeed, the Italo-Ethiopian War radicalized Japan's imperial fervor, consolidating the moral ground trodden in Manchuria. In the end, the primacy of empire laid bare Imperial Japan's commonality of interest with Fascist Italy. Caught between the Great Power status quo and Italian-induced instability, Japanese elites compromised with Fascist Italy. As Giacinto Auriti perceptibly reported to Rome, officials in Tokyo saw in Ethiopia a weakening of the British position in the Japanese sphere of interest. In the event of a "European war," Auriti assumed with prescience, "it is quite probable that Japan will ally with one or the other of the belligerents, but against Britain rather than allied to it."[85] Even hard-nosed believers in the singularity of Manchuria admitted that opposition to the League of Nations and the yearning for autarky pushed Italy and Japan toward similarly articulated imperial goals in Africa and Asia. As the interwar economist Karl Polanyi would later put it, Italy and Japan, as well as Germany, were "in a position to recognize the hidden shortcomings of the nineteenth-century order, and to employ this knowledge to speed the destruction of that order."[86]

Ultimately, the Italian war in Ethiopia sparked the realization that Japan, Italy, and Germany were ideologically linked by the desire to revise Wilson's national self-determination into what can be called imperial self-determination. Japanese visionaries noticed this coming together of global fascism but remained skeptical about the extent to which the three countries would cooperate. One pundit prognosticated an alliance among the countries but, although the three powers aimed at a "revolutionary" overturning of the status quo, doubted that they would form a "compact group": unlike the clans that had fought in the twelfth-century Genpei war, they would be "internally divided."[87] It was these conflicting forces toward integration and disaggregation that would be put to the test as Japan, Italy, and Germany gravitated toward an alliance in the late 1930s.

Thus, as they debated the Italo-Ethiopian War, Japanese also had to come to terms with the connections between the imperial politics of Japan, Fascist Italy, and, in due time, the Third Reich. In November 1935, Prince Konoe Fumimaro, soon to become prime minister, spoke of an "international New Deal" that would guarantee the "three great nations of Italy, Germany, and Japan" the expansion necessary for their "survival."[88] But ideologues and policymakers were remarkably aware of the irony that the imperial aspirations they shared with the European fascist powers also set clear limits to their collaboration. As Mark Mazower has pointed out, Japan, Italy, and Germany's hostility toward international institutions and diplomacy facilitated a "banding together" even as it undermined a coordinated policy. The point of all three empires was, after all, to remain politically and economically autonomous units.[89]

5

FASCISM IN WORLD HISTORY, 1937–1943

The threatening arrival in Uraga of the black ships is a dream of a long time ago. The white vessels from Italy have come to Yokohama to bring friendship.

—*Yomiuri shinbun*, April 19, 1938.

On July 30, 1940, Japan, Italy, and Germany entered into a formal political alliance by signing the Tripartite Pact. In this document, the three countries demanded that "all nations of the world be given each its own proper place" and stipulated that Japan, Italy, and Germany would "stand by and co-operate with one another in regard to their efforts in Greater East Asia and the regions of Europe respectively wherein it is their prime purpose to establish and maintain a new order of things."[1]

These somewhat vague terms exhibited a certain distrust for the European fascist powers in the higher echelons of the Japanese government. The military were divided over whether to attack the Soviets in unison with the Wehrmacht; the diplomatic corps was plagued by factional rivalry between advocates of further negotiations with the United States and declared sympathizers of the Axis, such as Foreign Minister Matsuoka Yōsuke; and senior court officials, especially the last *genrō*, Saionji Kimmochi, maintained a certain pro-British stance.[2] The road toward the Tripartite Pact had been tortuous. In many ways the alliance was a pragmatic, perhaps even reluctant, diplomatic move by three countries that sought to avoid isolation.[3]

Ideologically, however, the import of Japan's relationship with Fascist Italy and Nazi Germany was deep, because the Axis alliance came to intersect with Japanese visions of a new order at home and in Asia. In 1937, when the Japanese army launched an all-out attack on China, preparations for a state of total war were stepped up, with the Diet passing the National Mobilization Law (Kokka Sōdōinhō, 1938), just as Araki Sadao, the militant education minister, launched a "spiritual mobilization" campaign. Further political reforms followed in 1940. Prime Minister Konoe Fumimaro masterminded the New Political Order Movement (Shintaisei Undō), which culminated in the abolition of political parties and their merger into a single body, the Imperial Rule Assistance Association (Taisei Yokusankai).[4] Reforms at home mirrored ambitious plans abroad. The war in China, initially labeled as a "holy war," was integral to what Konoe called, in November 1938, a new order in East Asia, a vision of Japanese regional hegemony, which found its most brazen formulation in the declaration of the Greater East Asia Co-Prosperity Sphere (Daitōa Kyōeiken) in June 1940.[5] By then, the radicalization of politics at home and abroad solidified the common ground between Imperial Japan, Fascist Italy, and Nazi Germany.

The Tripartite Pact may have amounted to little in terms of diplomatic coordination, but it mattered as an ideological document that signaled the coming together of the Japanese, Italian, and German new orders since the late 1930s. In Japan, it heightened the sense among some of Japan's leading politicians, intellectuals, bureaucrats, and military men that they had reached a world-historical moment. They felt that an unprecedented opportunity had arrived to replace the international system set up at Versailles and, for many of them more important, to move into an altogether new stage in world history, with new hegemons working to overcome modernity itself.[6] In the drive toward this goal Italy and Germany were partners of a kind. In Konoe's words, delivered to the emperor in July 1940, the world faced a "great turning point" (*ichidai tenkanki*), and as Japan moved toward a "new world order" it was necessary to "seek intimate relations" with Germany and Italy, which were fighting for the same cause. It was "senseless" to rely on these two countries or "work as if we were their agents." Yet, "when it comes to growing out of the old world order, replacing the existing Anglo-American rule and establishing a new order, the Empire's stance is completely in unison with the interests of Germany and Italy."[7]

In 1940–41 the prospect of an Axis victory over the liberal powers raised the question of how Japan would negotiate world hegemony with its European partners. Though it was all very well for ideologues to acknowledge the commonalities with Italy and Germany, the knottier question was the extent to which Japan could reconcile its vision of the new order with that of its European partners. As they saw it, what both linked and divided their countries was national history. Arguments could be made that Japan, Italy, and Germany were nations whose rise signaled the overturn of Anglo-American liberalism and materialism. But could Fascist Italy and Nazi Germany really be disentangled from the "West?" Sharing a belief in national uniqueness was a paradox that set the limits to the collaboration—both diplomatic and ideological—among the three countries and their new orders, but it did not stop ideologues from attempting to reconcile their national histories. The result was a debate about the historical nature of Italy and Germany with the aim of assessing their place in world history and, by extension, their relationship to Japan. For the Japanese mission in Asia the Alliance opened up new possibilities even as it revived old complications.

Celebrating Fascist Italy

Japan's descent into total war ushered in profound changes to Japanese politics and society. The police apparatus increased its surveillance of the press and ordinary citizens, often with brutality. Labor laws mobilized men, women, and even children into compulsory factory work in industries that were crucial to the war effort. Consumer goods progressively vanished from stores; food became scarce.[8] And yet, as Ken Ruoff has demonstrated, in wartime Japan privations coexisted with celebrations. The state kept its citizens informed not only of major military exploits—first in China, then in the Pacific—but, in keeping with the heightened sense of history, poured vast resources into cultural events, in particular the 1940 festivities around the 2,600th anniversary of the mythical founding of Japan.[9] Promoted by government institutions and supported by civil groups, a celebratory mood often pervaded public life in what was designated as an epoch-making moment.

Fascist Italy and Nazi Germany were integrated into these performances. The half-decade stretching from 1937 to 1943 represented a new phase in the relations between the three countries, a period in which the fascist powers enjoyed unprecedented exposure in the journalistic, academic, and official debates.[10] Starting with Italy's joining of the Anti-Comintern Pact in November 1937, sealed the previous year by Japan and Germany, the government began to stage commemorative events to celebrate the important dates in the Axis calendar—anniversaries of pacts or military victories—but also to honor individuals and representatives of these countries. Through these campaigns, Japanese officialdom sought to conjure a cordial image of Italy and Germany. Kawai Tatsuo, the head of the Foreign Ministry Information Section (Gaimushō Jōhōbu) and postwar ambassador to Australia, expressed the official stance when Italy joined the Anti-Comintern Pact, asserting that it was "a natural outcome for people [*kokumin*] with a spiritual proximity to get close and seek one another" and that, as this friendship grew, they would advance "world civilization and peace."[11]

In the case of Italy, it is remarkable how fast official and public discourse shifted from one of apprehension and hostility during the invasion of Ethiopia to one of support and sympathy in the years after 1937. Tacit realignment had, in fact, started even earlier. On May 9, 1936, only four days after Italian forces had entered the

Ethiopian capital, a functionary of the Japanese Embassy in Rome paid a visit to the Italian Foreign Ministry. He "expressed congratulations for the surrender of Addis Ababa," the ministry recorded, "adding that the congratulations of the Japanese Government ought to be considered among those truly sincere."[12] The enthusiastic Japanese official may have overstated the case, as a substantial pro-British faction in the foreign ministry opposed an alliance with Italy. Nonetheless, as argued by the diplomatic historian Valdo Ferretti, the Japanese Foreign Ministry spearheaded a conciliatory policy toward Italy, proceeding to improve relations with Rome through a rapid series of diplomatic agreements.[13] On November 18, 1936, Japan became the first power to recognize the Italian annexation of Ethiopia and downgraded its embassy there to the rank of a consulate. The Italians reciprocated somewhat belatedly, as it took some time to disengage from its China-centered foreign policy in East Asia.[14] But the following year, in November 1937, Italy joined Japan and Germany in the Anti-Comintern Pact and recognized Manchukuo. In March 1939 Italy and Japan signed a cultural pact and, on September 27, 1940, the Tripartite Pact.

Determined not to let the pacts be dead letters, the Japanese government, in coordination with Fascist authorities, devised a series of strategies to introduce Italy to the Japanese public. But top-down propaganda alone cannot fully account for the variety of responses to the alliance with Italy.[15] Despite the undoubtedly official nature of these initiatives, patriotic associations, newspaper editors, industrialists, artists, as well as private individuals celebrated the alliance with Fascist Italy, revealing how the interest in the ally included actors who had played a key role in mobilizing Japanese society since the Manchurian Incident of 1931.[16]

The celebration of the Anti-Comintern Pact offers an insight into the participation of individuals, as well as into the interplay between city, prefectural, and central government levels, in the construction of a friendly image of Fascist Italy. The ceremonial was held at the Kōrakuen stadium in Tokyo in front of a large crowd of officials and ordinary Japanese who had been mobilized to show appreciation for the new diplomatic partner. The most fervent admirers contributed to the festivities by offering gifts to Mussolini. Miyamoto Kinpachi, a violin maker from Denenchōfu, in the suburbs of Tokyo, presented Mussolini with a violin—"I heard," he wrote in the note to the Duce, "that in what little leisure time official duties allow you, you play the violin."[17] Gotō Tadanao, the head of the Amama paper-manufacturing company in Shizuoka Prefecture, commemorated the first anniversary of the Anti-Comintern Pact by sending Mussolini a painting of Mount Fuji—"wrapped in beautiful paper," as the Italian Embassy specified.[18] The Women's Patriotic League (Dai-Nihon Rengō Fujinkai) and the Young Girls' Youth Movement (Dai-Nihon Rengō Joshi Seinendan), honored the anticommunist alliance by sending gifts to Mussolini and Hitler. In January 1938 Ambassador

"Springtime for the Anti-Comintern Pact." Produced in January 1938, this poster displays three young women each holding a *hagoita*, a wooden paddle used to play *hanetsuki*, a game similar to badminton, during the New Year. Pictures on the bats portray the leaders of the Axis countries, Adolf Hitler, Konoe Fumimaro, and Benito Mussolini.

(Courtesy of Kyōdō News.)

Auriti formally accepted the Women's League's "pure Japan-style 'Yamato doll' that expressed the faith of its twenty million members."[19] Later, in June 1939, the city of Kawasaki dedicated a cherry tree to Benito Mussolini and his brother Arnaldo—poor weather conditions had a negative effect on the turnout, though youth associations and school students were made to attend.

A high point in the celebrations of Fascist Italy was reached during a visit to Japan by an official delegation of the National Fascist Party, comprising some two dozen Fascists and headed by the ex-diplomat Giacomo Paulucci de' Calboli as well as the writer and amateur Orientalist Pietro Silvio Rivetta. Officials took great care to make the visit, the most high-profile by Fascist representatives to date, into a memorable one, for both the guests and the hosts. On March 22, 1938, the party sailed into Nagasaki for a one-month sojourn, during which the Italians toured Japan's major cities as well Manchuria. The tour was highly publicized. The media kept a close eye on the journeying Fascist delegation, reporting on their activities and meetings with local and government notables. The impressive number of gifts for Mussolini that the travelling party collected from these

The "Benito Mussolini Cherry," auspiciously planted with Shinto rites despite the adverse weather. Kawasaki, November 30, 1939.

(Photo courtesy of ASMAE.)

encounters indicates the extent to which authorities and local elites took the alliance seriously. Yonai Mitsumasa, the navy minister, donated a precious suit of samurai armor, complete with bow, arrows, and sword. The city of Fukuoka also gave a sword, and Kure a lacquered pen. Tsuda Shingō, the head of the Kanegafuchi Spinning Company in Kobe, contributed an "enormous and precious carpet," and Shirai Matsujirō, director of the Osaka Bunraku Theatre Company, a "three-hundred year old puppet." From Arita, a rural township in Saga Prefecture famous for its pottery, came a "splendid porcelain plate," while in Tokyo the mayor added a "large stone lantern"; in Manchukuo, Emperor Puyi gave a "marvellous skin of a tiger, a rare exemplar for its size and value."[20]

Ordinary Japanese were also drawn into the festivities. The delegation included a film crew from Italy's documentary and cinematographic center, the Istituto Luce. The footage they shot during the tour of Japan, Korea, and Manchukuo reveals the extent to which Japanese authorities mobilized the population for the occasion.[21] The delegation was paraded through Kamakura, posing in front of the Great Buddha. In Nara, the ancient capital, de' Calboli addressed a vast crowd at a gathering held on the grounds of one of the city's temples. As they passed through Osaka, the Italians drove through streets lined with their national flags and were hailed by a sea of bystanders, some of whom demanded autographs. Socializing with the Italian visitors was common during the many receptions held in their honor in the various cities they visited. The media did their part. The delegation was advertised in newspapers and on radio. Businesses chimed in. Purchasing space for commercials, Kirin beer toasted the Fascist visitors, as did the department store Mitsukoshi.[22] Some Japanese joined the festive spirit by sending lyrical effusions to the daily *Yomiuri shinbun*.

> Welcome, delegation from our faraway friend Italy, be our guest in this bright spring[23]
>
> The empire of the rising sun and Fascist Italy are fraternizing, the flowers are in bloom, and the birds sing.[24]
>
> Regretting to part with the cherry blossoms in bloom, their mission of prosperity accomplished, the Fascist friends have left the capital.[25]

With the Anti-Comintern Pact, the Right, too, fell in line with the official embrace of Fascist Italy. Tōyama Mitsuru took the occasion to backtrack on the anti-Italian sentiments he had championed at the time of the Ethiopian crisis. According to the journalist who interviewed him, Tōyama now "supported wholeheartedly the rapprochement between Italy and Japan . . . participating enthusiastically in pro-Italian demonstrations." Tōyama added that he was a personal admirer of Mussolini and that he was convinced that "the moment of renovation has inexorably arrived; the hour has come for Italy, Japan, and Germany to hurry and bond with one other to consolidate their union."[26]

In what could be called a form of new-order tourism, some right-wingers and admirers of the Axis found it worthwhile journeying to Rome to extend to the dictator their personal compliments, as well as those of the institutions they

Members of the Mission of the Fascist Party, surrounded by entertainers, at a reception in their honor. Their leader, Paolucci de' Calboli, sits in the middle. Place unknown, 1938.

(Photo courtesy of Kuribayashi Machiko, Tokyo.)

represented. Hatoyama Ichirō, a leading figure in one of the two largest political parties, the Seiyūkai, and postwar prime minister, traveled to Rome and Berlin in November 1937. There he was granted an audience with both dictators. He was particularly impressed by Mussolini, enthusing about "the effective national capacity under the Fascist regime" and praising the "great moral force" of Italians.[27] Nakano Seigō, now a right-wing Diet representative and outspoken pro-Axis advocate, followed in Hatoyama's steps when he visited Mussolini and Hitler the following week.[28] According to Auriti, Nakano, close to Tōyama Mitsuru, apologized for his past support of the Ethiopian cause—"he spontaneously acknowledged the mistake and said, 'I feel ashamed about it.'"[29] On his return to Tokyo, Nakano reported about Fascist Italy at a meeting of the Army General Staff also attended by Imperial Prince Chichibu, the emperor's younger brother, who had a reputation for possessing right-wing sympathies.[30] Auriti was informed that "Nakano's communiqué deeply impressed the military" and, no doubt with some exaggeration, said that "all are by now convinced that the only country in the world on which Japan can rely is Italy."[31] Another right-wing activist, the Osaka industrialist and head of the Greater Japan Justice Association (Dai-Nippon Seigi Dan), Sakai Eizō, also visited Mussolini. It was his second journey to Rome (he had met

Mussolini in 1923). This time he expressed his conviction that Japan and Italy had joined hands to fight international communism, thanking Mussolini for "accepting my proposal for a perennial collaboration between fascism and the Greater Japan Justice Association of which I am the president."[32]

Resurrecting the Heroic Narrative of Fascism

All these initiatives had an important consequence. In celebrating Italy, the government and sympathetic voices in the public also redefined the meaning of fascism. In the 1920s fascism was closely associated with its country of origin, and Japanese manifested a high degree of interest in what appeared to be an innovative and radical form of nationalism. Starting in the early 1930s, with the rise to power of the radical Right across Europe, the term assumed global connotations. At this time the Right lionized Italian Fascism for its patriotic politics even as several ideologues had misgivings about the commensurability of fascism and their own "reformist" politics. But after the Italian-Ethiopian war and, more so, in conjunction with the Anti-Comintern Pact, intellectuals, politicians, and writers reevaluated fascism, averring that Japan had more in common with Italy and Germany than they had been willing to admit only a few years earlier. In a discursive shift, ideologues resurrected the heroic right-wing narrative of fascism of the early 1930s, according it an official status. Although Fascism referred specifically to Italy's regime and ideology, it was nonetheless intimately linked to Japan's new order, becoming an integral ideological component of the Axis alliance.

The task of defining the official meaning of the alliance was taken up by a government-sanctioned institution, the Itaria No Tomo No Kai (Society of the Friends of Italy). Established in May 1938, the Itaria No Tomo No Kai was a direct product of the rapprochement between Japan and Italy following the Anti-Comintern Pact (its Italian twin was the Società Amici del Giappone, Society of the Friends of Japan). While its founder, one Ishida Tatsuo, was a private individual of means with an interest in Italy, the membership quickly expanded to include a mixture of "reformist bureaucrats," right-wing activists, academics, writers, and intellectuals, all of whom contributed to the Society's mission to "unite the pro-Axis opinion leaders, striving to make a clean sweep of our country's liberalists and to take active measures to build a new Japan."[33]

Until late 1940 the Itaria No Tomo No Kai largely relied on Italian funding. In the 1930s Italy's propaganda in Japan had been decidedly ad hoc, with one official remarking that the most "efficient and strenuous asserters of the Fascist fatherland" were the priests of the Catholic Salesian Mission in rural Miyazaki

Prefecture.[34] In 1938, however, the regime sent a new cultural attaché, the pugnacious Mirko Ardemagni, an ex-journalist and "first-hour" Fascist, to step up the spread of information.[35] Under Ardemagni's aegis, the Society channeled its energies into the organization of talks and behind-the-scenes lobbying, especially in military quarters. To do so, Ardemagni sought the help of the old pro-Italy hand, Shimoi Harukichi, and other Fascist sympathizers. These men traveled around the country distributing pamphlets drafted by the cultural attaché and held talks at the major universities, corporations, and other public venues. To spread knowledge of Italian, they set up language courses, priding themselves as being the only institution outside universities to do so.[36]

The second phase of the Itaria No Tomo No Kai began after the Tripartite Pact (September 1940) and was characterized by a marked involvement of the Japanese government.[37] In late 1940 the Foreign Ministry and the Cabinet Information Board, the institution in charge of coordinating propaganda among various ministries, began funding the Itaria No Tomo No Kai, promoting it as the government's unofficial voice on Fascist Italy. As a sign of the unity of mind that existed between Rome and Tokyo, little changed in the functioning and mission of the Society with the exception that the new backing allowed for the publication of a monthly, *Itaria* (Italy), in May 1941. Throughout the two and a half years of its lifetime, this journal enlisted a variety of contributors, ranging from the diplomatic architects of the alliance, Foreign Minister Matsuoka Yōsuke, and the ex-ambassador to Italy, Shiratori Toshio, to Pan-Asianists such as Ōkawa Shūmei and Kanokogi Masanobu, and to public intellectuals and writers including Hasegawa Nyozekan and Satō Haruo. This diverse group gave an aura of respectability to the journal and its mission to "introduce Italy, promote friendship between Italy and Japan, and promote the pro-Axis argument [*ronkyaku*]."[38] *Itaria* never achieved a mass circulation, but its emphasis on contemporary Italian politics, Fascist ideology, and relations between the Axis Powers, makes it valuable as a source for examining the orthodox view of Fascism in wartime Japan.

The goal was to make the most obvious shortcoming of the alliance, the unwillingness among the three nations to coordinate foreign and military policies, into a strength: Japan and Italy, as well as Germany, were bound together not so much by old-fashioned international law as by ideological commonality and feeling. "We love Italy," declared the journalist Tokutomi Sohō, proclaiming that the "Tripartite Pact is solid like a rock, and rises to the sky like Mount Fuji."[39] Emphasizing a uniformity of war aims (the destruction of international communism and Anglo-Saxon world hegemony), political commentators wrote about the parallel wars that each Axis country had undertaken independently. In the words of Shiratori Toshio, who was also the president of the Itaria No Tomo No Kai, "the

A poster invoking "Tripartite friendship" on the occasion of the New Year in January 1941, shortly after the signing of the Tripartite Pact.

(Image courtesy of Getty Images.)

conclusion of the Tripartite Pact once again makes clear the 'federative but reciprocal character' (*sōgo renmeisei*) that exists between the wars in Asia and in Europe." Shiratori argued that the three countries were linked to one another by the regional political structures they were putting in place in their respective spheres of influence. "Japan will go beyond the Japan-Manchuria-China bloc and build a Greater East Asia Co-Prosperity Sphere . . . while Germany and Italy will create a vast region that includes Europe and Africa." He dismissed lack of coordination as a minor matter. It was "natural" that, "in their objective to form a new world order, Japan, Germany, and Italy should collaborate on the basis that each attacks the objective that it chooses." Moreover, the global effort of the Axis Powers, Shiratori continued, should not be confused with the aggressive wars of the past. The aim of the Axis was to overturn the "liberal civilization" of Anglo-America, which would lead to the triumph of "human culture" and the "renovation of the world."[40]

Academics and social scientists made a more methodical appraisal of Italy, frequently championing Fascism's legal and political achievements. The Waseda legal scholar Wada Kojirō (1902–1954), for example, upheld Mussolini's doctrine of the state. Wada saw the "totalitarian state" as a remarkable development in political theory and practice. It replaced liberalism and Marxism with an idea of leadership embodied in Mussolini and made it possible to "spiritually unify" Italians.[41] The economist and social scientist with a bent for political philosophy, Ueda Tatsunosuke (1892–1956), praised Italy's corporatism as a way to mend the class struggle generated by capitalism. Corporatism, Ueda explained, mobilized "all the forces of the state . . . spiritually, politically, and economically." It stood at the heart of the domestic and international new order. Amounting to a "leadership principle" equal to Japan's "ideal of 'all the world under one roof,' " corporatism was a model of the new "supervision and management" of the world.[42]

Referring to commonalities between Japan and Italy was another way to underscore the alliance. Ueda had pointed to similarities emerging from economic reforms, but some contributors pointed out the cultural resemblances between the two countries. The literary critic Kamei Katsuichirō (1907–1966) explained the spiritual proximity between Japan and Italy on the grounds of the natural and geographic environment of the two countries. In an article entitled "A Dream for Italy" Kamei lyrically theorized that a nation (*minzoku*) blessed by the seas has a natural tendency to long for "things far away." It was an inclination that he described as a "nation's youth [*seishun*]" that was born from "the infinite élan vital of the ocean." "Japan in the Pacific, Italy in the Mediterranean—they have been such nations since antiquity."[43] Kamei was echoed by Kiyosawa Kiyoshi, a journalist and public intellectual schooled at the University of Washington. Kiyosawa's self-identification as a liberal did not keep him from expressing a sense of familiarity with Fascist Italy.[44] When he visited Italy in 1937, Kiyosawa was struck by how natural it was for a Japanese to feel accustomed to the local culture. It was an impression that could not be expressed in "theories" but only on the level of "feelings"—there was something about ancient cultures with a common history of adopting foreign elements. He also noted that Japan and Italy were distinct from the Anglo-Saxon world in one further respect. During his sojourn in Italy, he was surprised to notice that "the toilets were Japan-style, and whenever I saw one, I felt it as such a Japanese thing."[45]

Itaria took advantage of commemorations that were significant for the Axis or Italy. One occasion presented itself when in August 1941 Mussolini's son, Bruno, a keen aviator, died as the result of a botched landing. Saitō Mōkichi, a prominent poet and sometime psychiatrist, devoted a few lyric lines to him in a poem entitled "Immortal" (*Fumetsu*).

> Leonardo, Michelangelo were immortal, and so are you Bruno Mussolini.
> A symbol of bravery, you took command—thinking of you my heart aches.
> You dropped bombs over Ethiopia, France, Greece, Yugoslavia.
> The frontlines in Greece could not take your young life.
> Your youthful blood stains the grass in the outskirts of Pisa like deep-pink plum blossoms.
> You devoted yourself to your ancestral land, our ally Italy.
> You make the heart of your father and your ancestral land throb.
> Hearing your country Italy gather and cry, I, too, weep.[46]

The Italian Past in the Japanese Present

In these expressions of sympathy for Italy, writers may have been currying favor with the government, but their enthusiastic participation cannot be categorized entirely under the rubric of propaganda. This point becomes all the more obvious in the deep—if contested—way in which eminent historians and philosophers began debating about the significance of the Tripartite alliance in the course of world history. In their view, the magnitude of the present rested on the belief that the new order in East Asia, and by extension a new world order, would come about through Japan's pursuit of its historical mission. If in this endeavor Japan had tied itself to two European powers, the resulting question was about the extent to which Fascist Italy and Nazi Germany were animated by a similar drive to fulfill their own histories. How, then, did the pasts of Italy and Germany compare to that of

Japan? And how could one fit these countries into the cosmology of Japan's world history?

At stake in the debate over the Axis was therefore not only the issue of national uniqueness; the alliance with the fascist countries also complicated the relationship between Japan and Western civilization. Harry Harootunian has shown how Japanese modernist intellectuals critiqued the social unevenness brought about by capitalism, lamenting that it was the result of the influence of Western modernity. They sought to overcome this condition by imagining communities that would be harmonious and found the solution in putatively timeless cultural practices such as religion, the aesthetics of the folk, and premodern customs. In so doing, they counterposed (Japanese) culture to (Western) civilization.[47] But they were not alone in proposing these theories. As Benjamin Martin has argued, in the late 1930s Italian and German intellectuals discussed very similar possibilities. They reviled civilization as liberal, Anglo-Saxon, and universal; and they praised culture (*cultura* and *Kultur*) as spiritual, national, and authentic. Just like an Italian–German cultural alliance would define the meaning of the new order in Europe, so the Japanese spirit would reform the face of Asia.[48] In this way, from a Japanese perspective Fascist Italy and Nazi Germany became uncomfortable cultural allies, pursuing the same goals yet unsettling the notion of Japanese national peculiarity along with drawing a rigid distinction between East and West.

An important forum for the discussion of the relevance of the Italian past to Japan's present was the journal *Nichi-I bunka kenkyū* (Studies in Japanese and Italian Culture). Appearing monthly between May 1940 and March 1944, the journal was tasked with promoting Italian culture to a Japanese readership. It inherited this mission from its parent organization, the Nichi-I kyōkai (Japan-Italy Association), founded in July 1940 for the same purpose.[49] Unlike the Itaria No Tomo No Kai, whose associates were often right-wingers who exposed the political valence of the Axis, the Nichi-I kyōkai and its publication attracted an educated, mainstream membership that set out to discuss the merits of the Italian cultural tradition—*italianità* or, as the Fascist regime was fond of calling it, *romanità* (Romanness). Hitherto limited to a handful of specialists and connoisseurs, Italian culture was to become more broadly known in Japan and promoted through the right channels (Italian officials made a fuss that the "masterpieces of Italian art are introduced to the Japanese public through cheap French and German books; and the task of illustrating *romanità* in all its aspects is carried out exclusively by Germans").[50]

In 1993, reminiscing about their work in the journal, a group of contributors to *Nichi-I bunka kenkyū* stressed that the periodical—and the Association—were exquisitely cultural. One old member pointed out that the leading figures, academics such as the legal scholar Tanaka Kōtarō; the art historian Dan Inō, who in the early 1920s had spent time in Naples in the company of Shimoi Harukichi; the Renaissance specialist Yashiro Yukio; and the painter and scholar Wada Eisaku, were "liberals" (*jiyūshugisha*). They were "men of culture" (*bunkatekina hito*), adding that the Association had no room for "economics and politics."[51] Indeed, in its short life, *Nichi-I bunka kenkyū* attracted a remarkable range of young and talented scholars of Italian culture who covered topics such as classics, medieval philosophy, and the Renaissance. Unlike *Itaria*, Fascist theoretics was not its main theme. Yet, the group's comprehension of Italian culture was far from disconnected from politics. *Romanità*, for example, was integral to Fascist ideology, from the symbolism of the fasces to the Roman salute, and from the cult of Rome as a foundational myth of Italy to the desire to re-create a Mediterranean empire.[52] More crucial, however, was the consciously presentist goal adopted by the journal's contributors. Quoting the philosopher Benedetto Croce's adage that "all history is contemporary history," Dan Inō noted that Italy's rich history "clearly necessitates a new, contemporary interpretation . . . from our scholars we expect an original [*dokuji*] interpretation."[53] Japanese humanists may not have discussed politics, but they raised issues of culture that were eminently political in the context of Japan's new order in East Asia.

Perhaps the most central—and contested—topic discussed in the pages of *Nichi-I bunka kenkyū* was the Renaissance. This age, which conjured up an idea of rebirth in the arts, civic life, and science, carried a powerful allegorical meaning at a time when Japanese intellectuals were outlining plans for a resurgence of their own culture. Just as painters such as Michelangelo, the scientist Galileo Galilei, or the political philosopher Niccolò Machiavelli, displayed a keen self-consciousness about how to advance their fields, so contemporary Japanese intellectuals felt that they were engaged in a reflection on their present condition.

As far as its historical meaning was concerned, the Italian Renaissance was crucial for Japanese intellectuals for two reasons. It was part of what some contemporaries in Italy called the "Italian tradition," a glorious moment whose inheritance belonged to the greatness of Italian national history. But how could the Italian tradition be compared to that of Japan? Moreover, at the same time that it validated the Italian past, the Renaissance was also implicated in the development of European culture. In particular, what role had the Renaissance played in the development of capitalism, socialism, and liberal democracy, the features of Western civilization that many Japanese had increasingly come to criticize? Was the Renaissance at the origin of these divisive political and philosophical currents, or, to the contrary, had it sought to create a society in which citizens and state formed a coherent totality? The stakes were high. The interpretation of the Renaissance was directly tied to the nature of the relations between Italy and Japan, East and West, and more broadly, to the position of Japan in world history.

Far from having a unified view, *Nichi-I bunka kenkyū* reflected a variety of positions on the Renaissance. One loose group was made up of scholars of Western history (*seiyōshi*) who cast a positive light on the Renaissance. These academics argued that because the Renaissance had unified science and spirit into a harmonious whole, it had to be regarded as a genuine turning point in history, both for Italy and Europe. For Ōrui Noboru (1884–1975), a pioneering scholar of the classics and the Renaissance, the culturally unifying force of the Renaissance was visible in the way in which it strove toward the "completion of humanity [*ningensei no kansei*]." Ōrui argued that the "man of the Renaissance" should be seen not only as an artist or idealist but as a "multifaceted" individual rooted in "actuality" (*genjitsu*). He mastered politics as well as the arts, merging them, as Machiavelli had done. Combining the "ideal" and "reality" created the characteristic "great harmony of the total." The spirit of the Renaissance, Ōrui concluded, was not merely a brief outburst in the fifteenth century but a "force alive in eternity."[54] The cultural historian Kamo Giichi (1899–1977) presented an argument on the harmonizing capacity of the Renaissance from the perspective of the history of science. Kamo argued that, during the Renaissance, science was not divorced from the "spirit," as was the case in modern times. The "idea of harmony" between parts of the totality distinguished the Renaissance, but it also was a necessary principle whenever "a new era begins." On such occasions, the "feeling of the self [*jiko kanjō*] spontaneously extends to feeling of the state [*kokka kanjō*]"—this alignment was visible also in the "new Renaissance" of Japan.[55]

Other scholars stressed the centrality of Italian culture to European civilization. Italy could not match the German, French, and British lead in military, financial, or colonial power, but it trumped its European neighbors by virtue of having given (and continuing to give) the continent its cultural identity. Contributors elevated Italy to the status of the mother of European high culture, pointing out the Italian achievements in a variety of areas. Niizeki Ryōzō (1889–1979), a distinguished scholar of German and classical theater, argued that Italian theater stood at the heart of modern drama. The theater of the Renaissance, he argued, had absorbed the theories of Rome and Greece and reworked them for modern purposes. Italian Renaissance theorists, Niizeki continued, defined the principles of acting, character structure, and even the architecture of theaters and then spread them to the rest of Europe.[56]

Nishiwaki Junzaburō, writer, critic and, after the war, nominee for the Nobel Prize in Literature in 1958, painted the significance of Italian culture in broader strokes. For him, Italy had held firm to the essence of Roman culture throughout the period of decadence that followed the collapse of the Roman Empire. The Christian Church, he argued, remained the repository of the Roman "spirit." From the early medieval period, through Dante, the Renaissance, and all the way up to the twentieth century, "men of culture" had traveled to and learned from Italy. Nishiwaki was a linguistic prodigy—he read German, French, and English and had written his dissertation in Latin—and made it clear that, for him, Italy stood at the top. "Be it from the perspective of the Middle Ages or the early modern period, it is clear that Italy has been the cultural epicenter of Western Europe." Even today, he claimed, analyzing Italian culture was crucial to understanding Europe. Nishiwaki claimed that he had intensely studied German, French, and English literature, but it was through reading Italian literature that it was possible to "historically know the truth [*jijitsu*] of the culture of the Europeans."[57]

These scholars were neither sympathetic to Italian Fascism nor spokesmen of Japan's new order; indeed, the opposite could be the case, as when Hani Gorō, the Marxist historian, published an article on Leonardo da Vinci that subtly criticized contemporary politics.[58] Ironically, however, they painted an image of the Renaissance that suited both Italian and Japanese wartime rhetoric. By positing that the Renaissance represented a high point in European culture, they replicated the claims of some Italian and German intellectuals, who regarded humanism as a foundation for a new cultural order in Europe.[59] But by stressing that, as a movement, the Renaissance was characterized by a capacity to absorb ancient and diverse cultural traditions and mold them into a harmonious totality, they also came close to likening its significance to the peculiarity that new-order ideologues ascribed to Japanese culture—namely its ability to synthesize the civilizations of East and West. Consciously or not, they created both links and parallels between Italian and Japanese history.

This universalist interpretation of the Renaissance, along with its implications for Japanese history, ran up against the resistance of a group of thinkers and writers associated with the Kyoto School of Philosophy, the Japan Romantic Group, and the Literary Society.[60] In July 1942, exponents from this group met in Tokyo for a symposium on the theme of "overcoming the modern." As the meeting coincided with Japan's military conquest in Southeast Asia and the Pacific, these thinkers discussed the meaning of this "world-historical" moment and what Japan's role in pushing history to the next stage should be. The goal was to redeem Japan from the pernicious influence of Western civilization, which they equated with modernity, and to revive the pure spirit of Japan in the construction of a new, ethical, world. Because the Renaissance occupied a key role in the history of Western civilization, it is not surprising that these scholars felt the need to criticize it as the intellectual movement that was at the root of modern social conflict and moral decay. In their view, the Renaissance had failed to maintain the unified order of things of antiquity by separating the spiritual from the material, thus giving rise to the evils of modernity.

These intellectuals had expressed such views in *Nichi-I bunka kenkyū* even before the symposium. In March 1942, the literary critic Kobayashi Hideo, one of the more militant members of the Kyoto School, published an article entitled "The Legacy of Ancient Rome," in which he examined the role of the Renaissance in the transformation of Roman thought from antiquity to the present.[61] Kobayashi admired ancient Rome. The Romans had created civilization by developing law and "imperial thought." The combination of these principles created a "unified state" and invested power in the sovereign, the emperor. His rule (*shihai*) extended over a vast empire; and, crucially for Kobayashi, it was a benevolent rule. The Romans, he claimed, had "joined the concept of world peace with the thought of empire." Even after the collapse of the Roman Empire, its spirit did not fade. Charlemagne, the Holy Roman Empire, Napoleon—all proceeded in attempts to "restore" (*saikō*) the Roman Empire. The same attempt was also visible in the war aims of Fascist Italy and Nazi Germany, two countries that earned his respect: "It would be a great mistake to think that the expansionary movement of our Axis partners Italy and Germany are merely an act of aggression. Both have built a unified state under a new system, and there can be no doubt that their goal is to seek the happiness and prosperity of their own peoples and, ultimately, world peace."[62]

And yet, though he saw a direct continuity between the principles established by the ancient Romans and those of Mussolini and Hitler, Kobayashi did not go so far as to equate the Roman tradition with the East Asian one borne by Japan. Japanese history was pure and unbroken in the imperial lineage; Western history was hybrid, because Roman civilization had been corrupted by Greek culture, which was the origin of notions of individual rights and democracy. The Greek cities, he pointed out, were at constant war, without one being able to dominate another. The survival of Greek thought and practices brought about the collapse of the Roman Empire and the disunity of Europe ever after. Worse, this condition lay at the root of the development of "liberal thought" and "trade competition."[63] Greek thought, therefore, stood in antithesis to Roman, and the history of the West demonstrated a continuous struggle between the two. Because the Renaissance valorized Greek as well as Roman traditions, Kobayashi disapproved of this movement, but, implicitly, he also rejected the claim that a European order under the Nazi–Fascist aegis could stand up to that of Japan in Asia.

In the same spirit was an article, written for the same issue of *Nichi-I bunka kenkyū*, by another intellectual who would participate in the symposium on "overcoming modernity," the Catholic theologian Yoshimitsu Yoshihiko. A scholar of medieval theology, he bemoaned the fact that modernity had lost the religious spirit that had characterized ancient times. Seeing in the Renaissance the movement that had separated faith and science, he instead valorized the Middle Ages, a time in which everyday life, untarnished by materialism, still retained a sense of spiritual totality. In his article, Yoshimitsu examined the influence of the medieval philosopher Saint Thomas Aquinas on Dante's *Divine Comedy*, arguing that the poet's masterwork had been conceived as a work of theology. In Yoshimitsu's view, there was a religious nucleus in Dante, a "belief" (he used the Italian word *credo*) that had its origin in Aquinas. Yoshimitsu's argument was not merely academic, for his aim was to devise an interpretation of Dante for "us today." He therefore advanced the thesis that the condition of metaphysical turmoil that afflicted modern man called out for a turn back to religion and poetry—precisely what he saw as the essence of Dante's work.[64]

Kobayashi and Yoshimitsu refrained from openly criticizing the Renaissance in the pages of *Nichi-I bunka kenkyū*. But months later, at the symposium, Yoshimitsu was less reticent. "The so-called modern European culture with which we have come in contact is actually a culture that has lost sight of God," he thundered. "This loss," he continued, "results in the Renaissance's inability to concretely revive classical humanity in its true sense." As he saw it, the faults of the Renaissance extended all the way up to the modern period. But what about Japan? Through the introduction of Western thought in the late nineteenth century Japan was also affected, but not in the same way as the West. Whereas in the West the problem was a constitutive one, Japan had kept the pure spirit of antiquity until its encounter with the West. Even when the Western influence made itself felt, Japanese maintained more of the ancient traditions than the West had done. What the West lacked was the unbroken lineage of the imperial family.[65]

The divergent positions on the Renaissance held by historians of the West and members of the Overcoming Modernity group represented a conflict over the symmetry between Eastern and Western civilization. For the historians of the West, the Renaissance contained a unified core where the spiritual and material components of Western civilization coexisted in harmony. On these grounds, they accorded the West a status equal to that of Eastern civilization. In contrast, the Kyoto philosophers denied that the two civilizations could be put on the same plane: Western thought tended by nature toward conflict and fragmentation. The historians of the West were relativists, arguing that Japan and Italy were equals in their own cultural spheres; the Overcoming Modernity group believed in cultural hierarchies, and, in their view, Japan's culture towered over that of the West, even where it carried the spirit of Italian history. As a consequence, they saw Fascism as a botched Western attempt to overcome Western modernity.

This view of history had direct implications for the understanding of the alliance with Italy and Germany. In a second seminar held in July 1942 by the Overcoming Modernity group, called "The World-Historical Position and Japan" (*Sekaishiteki tachiba to Nihon*), the philosophers Kosaka Masaaki, Nishitani Keiji, Kōyama Iwao, and a historian of the West, Suzuki Shigetaka, fleshed out the relation between Japan and its Axis partners.[66] They argued that there was a clear "link" (*tsunagari*) between the "right to life" of Japan, Italy, and Germany. This commonality sprang from being latecomers to the nation-state form and the imperial game. Far from being an impediment, this condition had forged a peculiar relationship between the nation (*minzoku*) and the state, one animated by "moral energy" (*moralische Energie*). Persisting to the present, this national characteristic explained the consistent "concentration into oneself" (*jiko shūchū*), making Japan, Italy, and Germany into "leading countries" to push the world into a new order.[67] Yet even though the group acknowledged the common Axis intent for a spatial rearrangement of the world, they averred that an irreconcilable gap existed in terms of the temporal meaning of Japan's undertaking. Germany and Italy acted out of a need to reinforce themselves as nations, a project that dated to the nineteenth century. Japan, in contrast, was animated by a morality that had sprung from its "world-historical consciousness."[68] In the case of Germany, Kōsaka concluded, the new world order was an "extension of world history"; in Japan it was "the call from within history."[69]

Overcoming Internationalism

Just as intellectuals found that the past harbored differences between the Axis countries, so they realized that, after a putative victory, the future interaction of these countries presented its share of obstacles. By announcing the creation of a Greater East Asian Co-Prosperity Sphere in August 1940, the Japanese government charted the outline of an Asia under Japanese hegemony, but in so doing it also opened itself to the need to define the future relations with the new orders being set up in Europe. As Prime Minister Tōjō Hideki later put it, "it is truly an unprecedentedly grand undertaking that our Empire should, by adding these regions, establish everlasting peace in greater East Asia based on a new conception, which will mark a new epoch in the annals of mankind, and proceed to construct a new world order along with our allies and friendly Powers in Europe."[70] Conscious that Japan could not bring about a new world order by itself, intellectuals and academics turned to formulating the moral and legal principles that would replace liberal international law. With regional blocs being a common feature of Axis geopolitical thinking, they were confronted with the problem of how these spheres would cooperate.

Japanese visions of the interaction between Japan, Italy, and Germany rested on two contending conceptions of Asian regionalism.[71] The first stream of thought was an outgrowth of Pan-Asianism. Its proponents, such as General Ishiwara Kanji and the publicist and activist Shimonaka Yasaburō, emphasized Japan's "kingly way" (*ōdō*) as the embodiment of an Eastern ethics (*jingi dōtoku*) that would challenge Western oppression and form the basis of an Asian union.[72] The second current sought to devise scientific criteria for an Asian "community" (*kyōdōtai*). It was promoted within the Shōwa Research Association (Shōwa Kenkyūkai), a think tank close to Konoe Fumimaro, by such intellectual exponents as the philosopher Miki Kiyoshi and social scientist Rōyama Masamichi. Miki devised the concept of "cooperativism" (*kyōdōshugi*) in which he outlined the principles for a bloc economy in East Asia that would overcome the contradictions of capitalism by stressing the claims of the collectivity over those of the individual.[73] Rōyama, who was dissatisfied with the culturalist arguments of Pan-Asianism, developed geopolitics, especially those of Karl Haushofer, to redefine the political and economic framework of an Asian "*Grossraum*."[74] Despite their distinct emphases, both the Pan-Asianist vision and that promoted by the Shōwa Research Association informed Konoe's declaration of the new order in East Asia (1938) and, subsequently, the Greater East Asia Co-Prosperity Sphere—after all, they had an important common ground because they both opposed a world order based on liberal internationalism. But it was an altogether different matter to square these visions with those of Fascist Italy and Nazi Germany, even though these powers shared their antagonism toward internationalism.

The quest for an ideological common ground was strewn with obstacles. Like their counterparts in Italy and Germany, Japanese writers discerned an "ideological kinship" between their new orders in their rejection of international law.[75] Rōyama, for example, stated that the new order in East Asia was but "one link" (*ikkan*) of a "new world order"; Italy and Germany were working on the same project in their spheres in the Mediterranean and in central Europe.[76] But the problem of how these countries would interact was complex, because it was not clear what norms would replace international law and underpin the future interactions between the Axis Powers. Pan-Asianists believed in a fundamental—and rigid—separation between Eastern and Western ethics. How could they embrace Fascist Italy and Nazi Germany as equal partners? Also, social scientists like Rōyama faced a theoretical challenge. If each bloc constituted a finite, self-sufficient unit, there would no longer be a need for these spheres to interact, not least because doing so smacked of old-style internationalism. So, paradoxically, for some Japanese foreign-policy pundits, the fact that Fascist Italy was an unlikely partner in the traditional (balance of power) understanding of diplomatic alliances only made it a more plausible member in a vision of international affairs where imperial blocs would work together on an ad hoc basis.

Many Japanese writers and theorists integrated the relationship with the Axis into their discussion of the new order in East Asia. The bureaucrat, postwar construction entrepreneur, and diplomatic historian Kajima Morinosuke (1896–1975) and Fujisawa Chikao (1893–1962), an ideologue and right-wing Japanist activist, deserve particular attention for their attempts to overcome internationalism by reconciling the new orders in Asia and Europe. After World War I both had been committed supporters of the League of Nations, but by the early 1930s they became disenchanted and began to search for ways to reform internationalism. In those years they came to regard Fascist Italy and Nazi Germany as two inspiring competitors of the Anglo-American world order. In the late 1930s Kajima and Fujisawa took on positions in government think tanks devoted to producing ideas and policies for the Japanese new order. Fujisawa worked for the Kokumin Seishin Bunka Kenkyūjo (Research Institute for the National Spirit and Culture), an organ affiliated with the Ministry of Education, and taught at the Asia-oriented Daitō Bunka Academy. Kajima headed the high-level Imperial Rule Assistance Association Research Institute (Taisei Yokusankai Chōsakyoku Chō). It was in these positions that both men began to publish widely in academic and current affairs journals, theorizing about continental blocs in a dialogue with ideas promoted by intellectuals such as the Nazi legal theorist Carl Schmitt and Count Richard Nikolaus Eijiro von Coudenhove-Kalergi, the founder of the federalist Pan-European Union. Relating the theories of these thinkers to the Japanese pronouncements about Asian reform, they reached a loose consent on the moral and legal principles for a new world order based on imperial blocs. Thus an analysis of their writings provides clear pictures of an attempt to solve the contradictions inherent in fascism and of a Japanese conception of postwar international relations in a world dominated by the Axis Powers.

Kajima's move from early 1920s internationalism to wartime support of fascist blocs occurred gradually. A graduate of the Faculty of Law at Tokyo Imperial University (1920), he entered the Foreign Ministry, serving in Berlin, where he encountered Coudenhove-Kalergi. The Austrian aristocrat (whose mother was Japanese) left a deep impression on the young bureaucrat. He was much taken with Coudenhove-Kalergi's *Pan-Europa*, published the year after his arrival in 1923, in which the count espoused the conviction to forge European unity on the basis of liberal democracy and a federation of states.[77] Upon meeting Coudenhove-Kalergi, Kajima was seemingly urged to promote an East Asian Union on the same model. Indeed, Kajima later recalled that "I advocated Pan-Asia from Berlin."[78] In the 1930s, even as he quit his career in the Foreign Ministry to devote himself to his father's construction business, Kajima remained an establishment figure with close ties to policy circles while also making a name for himself as a commentator in foreign affairs—a combination that prompted Tosaka Jun, the Marxist critic, to ask sardonically, "Why must foreign-policy theorists [*gaikō rironka*] always sound so like diplomats [*gaikōkanteki*]?"[79]

Japan's seizure of Manchuria swung Kajima further toward regionalism. As Mitani Taichirō has argued, this event led many intellectuals and bureaucrats such as Kajima and Rōyama to try to reform internationalism in a regionalist key. They argued that an East Asian Federation (Tōa renmei) would be a more effective "institution for peace" than the existing League of Nations, but did not reject internationalism outright: even as Japan occupied a special role in the setup of an East Asian Federation, it would abide by the principle of international cooperation.[80] For Kajima, the same was true for Europe. "The question is not," he contended, " 'the League of Nations or Pan-Europa?' but 'the League of Nations in accordance with Pan-Europa.' " Moving away from the old League "centralism" to a "continental federalism" (*tairikuteki renbōshugi*) would, in the long run, pave the way to a "United States of the World."[81]

Even the Anti-Comintern Pact with Germany, and later Italy, did not shake Kajima's faith in regional federalism. Quite the opposite was the case. Unlike his mentor Kalergi, who rejected the Nazis as chauvinist nationalists, Kajima regarded the pact as a celebration of his ideas. The pact, Kajima argued, sprang from the desire to contain the spread of communism and advance the members' mutual interest in reforming the international system. It was not, he stressed, directed at the Soviet Union or toward other nations. As an effort at "international collaboration," the pact did not "see Britain, France, and the United States in a hostile way," as the signatories strove to "maintain relations of friendship with all countries," to which membership in the pact presumably stood open.[82] His position was perhaps expressed in clearer words by the international lawyer Takayanagi Kenzō, who hoped that the "Berlin–Rome–Tokyo Axis . . . which has been so much abused in the West, may gradually develop into the London–Paris–Berlin–Rome–Tokyo–Washington–Moscow Axis."[83]

With the outbreak of the war in Europe, Kajima dropped the last vestiges of internationalism. In June 1940 German military power overran France and, along with it, Coudenhove-Kalergi's (and his own) lofty vision of voluntaristic federations. The following month Kajima announced that Hitler's Germany (and, to a lesser extent, Mussolini's Italy) constituted the practical and theoretical vanguard of a new Pan-Europa, as well as a model for Pan-Asia. The new world order rested, after all, on power politics. Kajima now discounted Coudenhove-Kalergi's vision of "federated Europe" on the basis that liberalism and democracy were an "utter impossibility" and that the count's Constitution of Europe had become "scrap paper." "Just as Napoleon unified Europe," Kajima observed, "the idea to unify Europe by force has emerged, and it is precisely force that Hitler is using to unify Europe."[84] He supported the Tripartite Pact on the basis that Germany and Italy were to become the "focal points" in Europe, while Japan would pursue the same role in Asia. For that reason Kajima urged Japan's leaders to take action. The time of the "coexistence of small nations" had passed, he explained. The future would give birth to larger political and economic units, and for this reason the Greater East Asia Co-Prosperity Sphere would be "the basis to see through the future of international affairs, and therefore we have to give the peoples of Greater Asia our earnest support."[85] By now, Kajima's federalism was designating the loose alliance between Imperial Japan, Fascist Italy, and Nazi Germany.

Fujisawa Chikao took a different road to imperial blocs. Where Kajima pushed federalism into regional autarky, Fujisawa attempted to reform international law through the national ethics of "kingly way" (*ōdō*). Like Kajima, in his youth Fujisawa also possessed the credentials of a highly educated internationalist. He graduated from the Law Faculty of Tokyo Imperial University in 1917 and then joined the Ministry of Agriculture and Commerce (Nōshōmushō). A polyglot, he acquired fluency in French, English, German, Dutch, Russian, Spanish, and Italian—the "good young man," a journalist found out, had learnt Esperanto in "three or four days," before representing Japan at the 1920 Esperanto World Conference in Belgium.[86] In recognition of his academic prowess, the Ministry of Education granted him a scholarship to Germany, where he was awarded a doctorate in philosophy from the University of Berlin in 1923. After returning to Japan, however, Fujisawa turned his back to the West. As he shifted to the right, he began to attack the entire tradition of Western philosophy: "[Western] scientific philosophy now in vogue cannot attain the true nature of human knowledge and formulate an appropriate outlook on life. Occupied exclusively with the scrutiny of the trees, the adepts of modern epistemology are prone to lose sight of the existence of the forest. In accordance with our Oriental conception, the ultimate end of philosophy is to penetrate the secrets of the world."[87] Like many of his contemporaries on the right, Fujisawa condemned Western civilization for its materialism and individualism. To his mind, the answer to this condition, which he also observed in Japan, was to enact a political reform that was based on the ethics of a nation.

In the early 1930s Fujisawa was inspired by Italian Fascism and German Nazism because he believed that these movements were putting into practice the kind of moral and political renovation that he advocated. But he felt compelled to examine the compatibility between European fascisms and Japanese "national thought." Like the Japanese spirit, Fascist thought stood in opposition to Western materialism and its political expressions, whether liberalism, socialism, or democracy. It was a political philosophy in its own right. "The goal of fascism," Fujisawa wrote, "is a fundamental reform [*kakushin*] of political and moral [*dōtoku*] thought; [Fascism] is by no means a vulgar reactionary movement." He was convinced that legal changes in political and social institutions, such as corporatism and parliamentary reforms, constituted a significant national renewal, stating that "fascism should not be a monopoly of Italy, it is a global question."[88] At the same time, he cast doubts on Japan's need to learn from outside models. He declared that there was a fundamental "otherness" (*i*) between Fascism and Japan's "kingly way." *Ōdō* was totality. It encompassed a "religious morality" (heaven), "politics" (man [*hito*]), and "economics" (earth [*chi*]).[89] Fujisawa found Fascism, as well as Nazism, to be "incomplete" because these ideologies lacked the notion of "loyalty" (*chū*) that Japanese felt toward the emperor. As far as he was concerned, "our country is the origin of the *fascio*, and the more Western fascism develops, the more the imperial way will become a matter of interest for all humankind."[90] He concluded that, given its perfection, *ōdō*—not Fascism or Nazism—had to be exported. "Japanism" (*nihonshugi*), Fujisawa wrote, "must contribute concretely to the welfare and peace of humankind around the world."[91]

Fujisawa's condescension toward Fascism and Nazism did not stop him from enlisting them as worthy partners in a new world order. Regardless of the differing stages of spiritual evolution, the Japanese, Italian, and German new orders constituted an international "current of thought" that sprang "organically" from their domestic orders. Cooperation was the natural outcome. Indeed, it struck Fujisawa as a "strange enough historical destiny" that Japan, Italy, and Germany found themselves fighting under a similar "leadership principle."[92] This principle was the precedence of national culture over international law and universal, liberal civilization. Thus he argued that a shared notion of culture was at the root of the Anti-Comintern and Tripartite pacts. "Culture is politics and politics is culture," Fujisawa maintained.[93]

This reasoning had implications for the practice of international relations. The culturalist norms that underlay the expansion of Japan, Italy, and Germany would make empires—not nations—into the basic units of a new world order and, in turn, call for a reform of international law.[94] It was the jurist Carl Schmitt who, for Fujisawa, articulated the new principles of international law most incisively. In the interwar years Schmitt was well known among Japanese legal scholars and political scientists, and caused a debate for an article he wrote in April 1939 that outlined his vision of a new international order based on *Grossraum*.[95] Japanese scholars of international law, especially Yasui Kaoru (1907–1980), turned to this theory in 1942, after the declaration of the Greater East Asia Co-Prosperity Sphere, in the effort to elaborate an "East Asian international law" (*daitōa kokusai hō*) that would determine the laws and rules by which this area would form relations with Japan and the outside world.[96]

Yet for Japanese new world order ideologues, including Fujisawa, Schmitt represented only a sophisticated synthesis of the theories they had been developing for over a decade. True, their own formulations of a new world order bore the imprints of Carl Schmitt, but they had their origins in Pan-Asianism, the establishment of Manchukuo, and the great power politics with Western nations. For this reason Fujisawa praised Schmitt for showing that a territorial rearrangement by a "leader-nation" (*shidō minzoku*) would lead to that new "unit of international law, the great-region" (*dai chiiki*, the literal translation of *Grossraum*). But, he pointed out, Schmitt was merely stating the obvious, for Japanese had been stressing their "co-prosperity sphere" in Asia since at least the Manchurian Incident. Nevertheless, Fujisawa agreed with Schmitt's "fundamental principle of the new international law," namely the "principle of mutual respect of one another's great-region or co-prosperity sphere." For both Fujisawa and Schmitt, this meant that these regions would not "interfere" with each other and would "safeguard the divisions."[97]

Superseding the existing practice of international relations—and its premises in international law—was critical for all the Axis Powers. In Japan, as illustrated by the writings of Kajima and Fujisawa, a loose consent emerged on the notion of a greater East Asia, but it was not clear how the interaction between the Asian and European spheres would be managed. The autonomous yet collaborative nature of the new empires was intended to be a compromise between nationalism and a desire not to descend into provincialism. Yet not even the theoretical sophistication of Carl Schmitt and his Japanese acolytes could reconcile the contradictions of what Fujisawa saw as the "new international law" that would regulate the new world order. For all the talk of "mutual respect," the assumptions of Fujisawa, as well as those of Mussolini and Hitler, were that clear hierarchies existed not only within the various great-regions but also among themselves. As the philosopher Nishida Kitarō remarked in 1943 in an article entitled "The Principles of the New World Order," "not only the Anglo-Saxon powers will submit [to the Japanese *kokutai*], but also the Axis will come to the point of emulating it."[98] With "equality" written out of the mindset of the fascist new world order, it is not surprising that wartime collaboration among the Axis Powers was all but nonexistent. It was not only a matter of power politics or opportunism; the moral principles that Fujisawa outlined as the basis of the new world order made the idea of a "new internationalism" theoretically impossible.

Linked but incomparable—this was the often implicit understanding of the Axis among Japan's commentators. Despite its ambiguities, it was a powerful notion that pervaded Japanese politics and culture during the years of the alliance with Fascist Italy and Nazi Germany. The Tripartite Pact connected the war in Asia with the one in Europe, but the new world order was more than rhetoric about a joint war effort. As an ideological pronouncement, it was also a cultural order to which intellectuals, writers, and bureaucrats lent their support, even if often qualified. Regardless of their political stance, ordinary Japanese were also involved in the many festivities surrounding the Axis Alliance—and many simply referred to the Rome–Berlin–Tokyo relationship with the familial-sounding acronym RO-BER-TO. Nazi Germany may have rapidly outpaced its southern ally as the paramount military power in Europe, but Fascist Italy maintained an important place in the imaginary of Japan's new order in Asia, its classical—and imperial—heritage remaining a consistent point of reference for intellectuals. When, in April 1942, the architect Tange Kenzō sketched the Memorial of Greater East Asia, to be erected near Mount Fuji, he drafted a structure that combined elements of a Shintō shrine with the style of Michelangelo, placing it in a setting reminiscent of the Capitoline Hill, the sacred high ground in Rome.[99] The Italian past, it seemed, deserved a prominent place in Japan's future.

Epilogue

FASCISM AFTER THE NEW WORLD ORDER, 1943–1952

Our country was attacked by the fascist aggressor, Japan. The "Sons of Heaven" were promptly joined by their fascist partners of Germany and Italy.

—*Army Talk* (U.S. War Department, March 24, 1945)

Japanese nationalism is entirely unrelated to occidental forms of nationalism.

—*The Brocade Banner: The Story of Japanese Nationalism* (General Headquarters, Far East Command, Military Intelligence Section General Staff, September 23, 1946)

When, on December 11, 1941, Italy joined Japan and Germany in declaring war on the United States, Japanese military, political, and ideological elites knew their allies well. For almost two decades they had been part of a dialogue on what seemed to them to be the ideology and politics of the future: fascism. From the first appearance of the term in the 1920s, Japanese intellectuals and public figures time and again evoked fascism in their efforts to redefine Japanese politics. Social critics interpreted fascism as a particularly strong form of nationalist revival characteristic of Italy, but with lessons for Japan. Mussolini, in particular, was admired for his leadership and for his capacity to mobilize youth to strengthen his nation. In the early 1930s, Japanese observers examined fascism as a global alternative to socialism, liberalism, and democracy, probing the possibility of its applicability to Japan. And in the second half of that decade a consensus on fascism emerged according to which Japan, Italy, and Germany were linked in the ideological endeavor to forge a new world order even as they retained a nucleus of incomparability due to their national peculiarities.

In tracing the shared fascist experiences of Japan and Italy—from anticommunism, through domestic reform, to an international new world order—this book has shown not only that fascism was integral to interwar political and cultural thought, but also that it was the product of complex, and deeply fought, processes of global exchange. At the heart of the debate on fascism was the struggle over how to define and practice a "revolution-restoration" from the right. In the early 1920s, Italian Fascism and Benito Mussolini pioneered this attempt and bestowed upon it its own name, but in so doing they only set the terms of the debate, not provide a rigid model. Indeed, in many ways, the history of fascism since Fascism has been one of mistrust and denial—not only from the Left but also from the Right. Today, what amounts to Europe's largest fascist party, Greece's Golden Dawn, refutes the appellation "fascist" even as it heralds Mussolini and Hitler as heroes. For many interwar Japanese intellectuals, activists, and politicians, predominantly on the right or liberal, the problem was how to bring about fascism without fascism—this was the logic of global fascism, or what I have referred to as the "fascist critique of fascism." And yet, I argue, the contradictions between universal claims and particularistic (national) rationales unsettled fascism as a global ideology but did not prevent Japan from participating in the making of a world fascist consciousness.

After World War II, however, the connections between Japan, Italy, and Germany were broken, and the fascist flirtations forgotten or downplayed. Much as no postwar Japanese government ever officially denounced its alliance with Italy and Germany, so few historians made much of it. Both considered the past alliance with the Axis Powers a departure from Japan's political trajectory. The discourse on the European partners was dismissed as propaganda; the diplomatic pacts signed by the Axis Powers were made to appear inconsequential. This view relieved postwar Japanese of the need to reflect on such controversial matters as the links between the "Japanese ideology," as Tosaka Jun called the pronouncements on the "national polity" and the "kingly way," and Italian Fascism, as well as German Nazism. But it also helped to sideline the history of fascism into the history of a concept that, during the Cold War, liberal and conservative historians discounted as vague and meaningless.

The severance of the fascist link occurred in two phases that were determined by the course and outcome of World War II. The first turning point came in 1943. On July 10, Allied troops landed in Sicily, rapidly defeating Italian and German defenses. Facing an Anglo-American invasion, renegade Fascists deposed Mussolini, while King Victor Emmanuel III named an army general, Marshal Pietro Badoglio, prime minister. In Japan, these events caused much speculation about the future of the Axis. Shimoi Harukichi, still a trusted friend of Italy, tried to dispel fears that Badoglio might leave the alliance. Boasting that he was a good friend of the marshal, he explained that Badoglio was a man of the best Italian military tradition, reliable and trustworthy. He had proven in the Great War that he did not follow the "Western, calculating way" of making war, but fought "in a rather Japanese way" (*nihonjinrashiku*)."[1] Italy, Shimoi implied, might have shed Mussolini, but its martial valor and spiritual determination lived on in his successor, guaranteeing that the country would honor the pact with Japan and Germany.

Shimoi miscalculated. After a summer of uncertainty as to whether or not Italy would pursue the war and if so on which side, on September 8, 1943, Badoglio signed an armistice with the Allies. Italy was thus divided into two—the south, controlled by the Allies and forces loyal to Badoglio and the king, and the north, occupied by Nazi Germany but nominally an independent state headed by Mussolini and known as the Italian Social Republic. This anomalous state of affairs stirred Japanese into rescinding the alliance with Fascist Italy. The prime minister, General Tōjō Hideki, inveighed against the Italian half-capitulation, confiding that, politically speaking, he had always thought that Italy was the "black star" of the Axis (militarily, he welcomed the event, as it would give Hitler a free hand in Europe).[2] The media followed suit. Condemning Fascism as a fraud and Italy as a second-rank country, commentators called Badoglio a "traitor" and his decision to capitulate to the Allies a "contemptible step of [people] without confidence in their military power." His unconditional surrender violated the Tripartite Pact, an alliance that was meant to be "stronger than iron." It was an "act of disloyalty," as the undersecretary of the Foreign Ministry called it, that "not even heaven could forgive."[3] Japanese authorities considered the "betrayal" an offense to the "sacred international morality" that the three countries had promoted.

The relations between Imperial Japan and Italy degenerated. Shortly after September 8, Japanese authorities entered the Italian Embassy in Tokyo and arrested its Italian occupants. With the exception of Mirko Ardemagni and a handful of Fascist diehards, who swore allegiance to Mussolini's Social Republic, all other Italian subjects refused to do so. As a result they were sent to internment camps across Japan, where they endured harsh treatment and, according to one ex-prisoner, abuse worse than that to which Korean forced laborers were subjected by the Japanese. One of the favorite "amusements" of the head of the "concentration camp," a postwar Italian report stated, "was to force the Italian ambassador to compete with other officials for a bucket of water to do laundry, make a repulsive soup, or take a shower, initially just at biweekly intervals, then monthly."[4] In Italy, anti-Fascist partisans considered Japanese nationals enemies. In June 1944, a group of partisans attacked and killed the Japanese naval attaché, Rear-Admiral Tōyō Mistunobu, as he was traveling near Pistoia, in Tuscany.[5] And, on July 15, after Nazi Germany had surrendered but before the war in the Pacific had ended, Italy declared war on Japan, a gesture with little practical impact, but by which the Italians hoped to improve their condition in postwar negotiations.[6]

Thus Imperial Japan and Fascist Italy, declared friends since the late 1930s, ended World War II on a more ambiguous, even hostile, note. Although collaboration with Mussolini's Social Republic continued until the very end, the events

A camp housing Italian internees in Kemanai, Akita Prefecture, in the north of Japan.

(Photo courtesy of ASMAE.)

that took place in mid-1943 damaged the political relations between the two countries. The status of fascism suffered accordingly. Initially accorded a high status in the Japanese discourse about a new world order, now ideologues and politicians felt compelled to discredit fascism as the ideology of an unworthy ally. The breaking of the fascist link, then, began at the hands of Japanese at a time when they accused Italy of failing to live up to the ideals of Fascism itself.

The wartime distancing from Fascist Italy was reinforced after 1945. During the Occupation period (1945–1952), American and Western authorities dropped references to fascism and, with it, the links between the Axis Powers that they had regularly, even if somewhat hesitatingly, asserted before Japan's defeat in World War II. In 1937, for example, William Henry Chamberlin, the American historian and journalist, wrote that he doubted Japan had evolved into a "full-blooded dictatorship on the German or Italian model" but that, nevertheless, one could speak of a "semi-Fascist" state.[7] Hugh Byas, Chamberlin's fellow journalist and a Japanologist, commented on Japan's "Nazified bureaucrats" and regretted the Allied mistake of understating Japan as "Hitler's little yellow partner."[8] Even where Western commentators mentioned "nationalists" and "patriotic societies," they often did so in a comparative frame of mind. The leaders of Japan's military and right-wing societies, claimed the political scientist William C. Johnstone in January 1945, had "played a role in Japan similar to that of the Rosenbergs, Goebels [*sic*], Heines, von Killingers and Streichers in Germany."[9]

But the emerging alliance between Japan and the United States was premised on a rereading of Japanese history with fascism left out. This shift owed much to the American Cold War preoccupation of moving from the fight against fascism to the crusade against communism. Geopolitical considerations led Occupation authorities and academics—sociologists, historians, and anthropologists—to promote Japan as an Asian bastion against communism by emphasizing its successful modernization and dismissing the darker sides of its past as an aberration that could be remedied.[10] Dwelling on fascism as a central feature of Japanese history would have connected Japan's past to that of Italy, Germany, and perhaps other countries, and thus raised the uncomfortable question of fascism's role in solving the global crisis of liberal capitalism in the 1930s. For this reason, as argued by Harry Harootunian, postwar social science increasingly "banished" fascism as a useful historical paradigm, a trend that became evident also in the revisionist historiography on Germany and Italy in the 1960s and 1970s.[11] Japan, however, was the first country to be separated from fascism.[12]

In its stead, disciplines from law to history and sociology developed the tropes of "militarism" and "ultranationalism." In distancing Japan from Italy and Germany, these concepts created two advantages. Legally, the distinction supported the decision of the Supreme Commander of the Allied Powers (SCAP), General Douglas MacArthur, to retain the emperor, for it would have been far more difficult to legitimize the monarch's exemption from prosecution had greater commonality between Japan, Italy, and Germany been established (Mussolini was tried and executed by Italian partisans, and it would have been inconceivable that Hitler would not have faced a court had he not committed suicide).[13] As it turned out, the International Military Tribunal for the Far East used the categories of "militarists" and "ultranationalists" to define those labeled "Fascists" in Italy and "Nazis" in Germany to prosecute war criminals and purge unwanted individuals from holding office in the postwar state. After 1952, when the ban on "ultranationalists" was lifted, some of these figures, such as the two future prime ministers Hatoyama Ichirō and Kishi Nobusuke, who had had once spoken fondly of fascism and its leaders, recanted their past pronouncements or swept them under the carpet.[14]

But "militarism" and "ultranationalism" also had implications for the writing of the history of Japan. Rather than tackling the question of the global crisis of capitalism of the 1930s, these concepts singled out pathological elements in Japanese national history, often remnants of a premodern past, to explain the country's aggression in World War II. Japan, the narrative ran, had failed to fully modernize in Meiji, retaining a number of feudal traits that accounted for the behavior of the military and the passive attitude of the populace. "The feudal tradition," explained George Sansom, the British historian and diplomat as well as wartime adviser to the United States, created a "military class whose history had led them to believe in discipline and force, and whose conception of power was based upon a long tradition of feudal warfare in which victory meant the conquest of territory, and control over its inhabitants."[15]

The embrace of this view was not limited to Western historians. It was the liberal intellectual and political scientist Maruyama Masao who produced the most sophisticated analysis of ultranationalism in an essay he published in 1946. Maruyama used the concepts of "fascism" and "ultranationalism" almost interchangeably and did, in several instances, compare Imperial Japan and Nazi Germany. But he, too, emphasized national uniqueness, explaining that the key factor that pushed Japan toward the war and imperialism was an "all-pervasive psychological coercion," which stemmed from an internalized nationalism that prevented Japanese from acquiring a truly modern, individual, subjectivity. Ultimately, Maruyama relegated fascism to Italy and Germany.

Japanese Marxists revisited the concept of "emperor system fascism"; but theirs was an understanding of fascism that ignored many of the complexities and ambiguities that the term had carried in the 1930s. Continuing to argue that the emperor system retained a feudal character, these intellectuals sought to underline the contradiction between the idea of a democratic Japan and that of the continuing presence of the emperor, even in his constitutionally reduced role as the "symbol of the nation." Activists of the reborn Japanese Communist Party, concerned over the policies of the "reverse course" (1947–1952)—curtailing labor unions, the progressive reinstatement of the prewar elites, the "red purge"—saw a return of the specter of "fascism." As early as February 1946, the Communist Party warned of a "conservative-reactionary fascist front" that attempted to "crush the people's [*jinmin*] consciousness."[16] In August 1948 the "Committee for the Improvement of Livelihood" called for a "people's mass demonstration" (*jinmin taikai*) to protest against the "terroristic repression and fascism" of the government of Prime Minister Ashida Hitoshi.[17] While the organized Left was correct in detecting signs that the Occupation and the Japanese government were set to roll back several democratic reforms enacted immediately after 1945, the use of the term "fascism" smacked of the all-embracing Comintern definition, according to which all noncommunist forces were suspect of fascist leanings.

Thus, in the postwar period fascism, too, was "post." By now signifying little more than the politics of interwar Italy, fascism was banished not only in time but also in space, and Japan was the first case that fell to this logic. Fascism lost the sense of open-endedness that, as this book has shown, it possessed in the debates stretching from the mid-1920s to the wartime. The possibility that fascism might assume different forms or arise outside the "core countries," was discounted. Whereas, before the war, Japanese discussed fascism in terms of the attempt to overcome capitalist modernity, postwar social scientists saw the issue as one of incomplete modernization; if, in the 1930s, fascism was central to Japanese (and global) thinking, in the 1950s it became a peripheral problem of a select number of countries.

In many ways Shimoi Harukichi's postwar existence was symptomatic of the changed environment. Much like the ideology he had once advocated, he remained forgotten. Because his identity was so closely tied to Fascist Italy's fortunes, he risked imprisonment in 1943 at the hands of Japanese authorities and in 1945 by Allied tribunals. Shimoi eluded the former and escaped with an ordinary ban from public office from the latter, a probable indication that neither authority took him seriously. Shimoi fought on, if only to make a living. His wartime connections to Italian priests of Tokyo's St. Paul's congregation helped him to make some behind-the-scenes deals selling Japanese scrap metal.[18] Adjustment to the new, American, world order proved difficult. As he told the visiting (ex-Fascist) journalist Indro Montanelli in 1952, he was involved in a "Society for the Improvement of Eloquence," for, he was convinced, "Japanese are not capable of speaking. No one. Not the lawyers. Not the teachers. And least of all the Dietmen."[19] In a fashion echoing the spite for the German people expressed by Hitler—but also the social conservatism of the 1920s—Shimoi blamed the Japanese people:

> In Japan nothing is left: not even Japan, for what is the place in which we now live? A zoo full of monkeys who are copying the Americans. You buy a book: it's American. You read a newspaper: it's about news from New York. You turn on the radio: you'll hear the voice of a Negro baritone from Hollywood. You stroll in the streets: you'll find girls dressed as if they were in Chicago . . . a tradition of two hundred years is suffocating one of two thousand years.[20]

He returned to the study of Dante and reminisced fondly about the years he had spent in Naples. "Italy—one should have seen it in those days. There never was in the world a country more beautiful, more noble, more generous."[21] Embittered and nostalgic, he mourned fascism, an ideology that, in the pursuit of social and political order, had brought about violence and destruction.

Notes

INTRODUCTION

1. Antonio Gramsci, *Selections from the Prison Notebooks of Antonio Gramsci* (New York: International Publishers, 1971), 219–23.

2. *Yomiuri shinbun*, August 2, 1933.

3. György Lukács, *History and Class Consciousness: Studies in Marxist Dialectics* (Cambridge, MA: MIT Press, 1971), 83–86.

4. Benito Mussolini, "Fascism's Myth: The Nation," in *Fascism*, ed. Roger Griffin (Oxford: Oxford University Press, 1995 [1922]), 44.

5. See, most notably, the conservative historian Itō Takashi. Developing a parallel argument to the Italian revisionism of Renzo De Felice, Itō stated that the argument for fascism was an ideological tool of the Marxists, who attacked the national past in order to serve left-wing political goals in the present; Itō, "Shōwa seijishi kenkyū e no isshikaku," *Shisō*, no. 624 (1976). As noted by Sakai Tetsuya, Itō's revisionism paralleled a global turn against the concept of fascism. It was in these years that American scholarship attempted to shrug off fascism from Japan's past, claiming, in line with Itō, that it was a loose and Eurocentric concept that did not accurately describe the political reality of Japan. See, for example, Peter Duus and Daniel Okimoto, "Fascism and the History of Pre-War Japan: The Failure of a Concept," *Journal of Asian Studies* 39 (1979). Most English-language scholarship is derivative of this moment. Hence the historian of fascism Stanley G. Payne refers to "Japanese authoritarianism" (Payne, *A History of Fascism, 1914–1945* [Madison: University of Wisconsin Press, 1995], 335), while Robert O. Paxton, in his analysis of generic fascism, prefers "militarist expansionist dictatorship" (Paxton, *The Anatomy of Fascism* [London: Penguin, 2004], 199).

In recent years, however, a growing number of scholars have revisited the question of fascism in Japan through new methodological approaches, showing that the debate is far from over. Harry Harootunian has stressed the centrality of fascism in the cultural and philosophical production of the 1930s and 1940s; Harootunian, *Overcome by Modernity: History, Culture, and Community in Interwar Japan* (Princeton, NJ: Princeton University Press, 2000). Alan Tansman has uncovered a fascist aesthetic among several of Japan's foremost interwar writers; Tansman, *The Aesthetics of Japanese Fascism* (Berkeley: University of California Press, 2009). See also Alan Tansman, *The Culture of Japanese Fascism* (Durham, NC: Duke University Press, 2009). Two studies that have associated the political and institutional trends in interwar Japan with fascism include Janis Mimura, *Planning for Empire: Reform Bureaucrats and the Japanese Wartime State* (Ithaca, NY: Cornell University Press, 2011); and Suzaki Shinichi, *Nihon fashizumu to sono jidai: tennōsei, gunbu, sensō, minshū* (Tokyo: Ōtsuki Shoten, 1998). Rikki Kersten has criticized the Eurocentric bias in the historiography on Japanese fascism, pointedly capturing the tensions between particularism and universalism inherent in the study of fascism; Kersten, "Japan," in *The Oxford Handbook of Fascism*, ed. R. J. B. Bosworth (Oxford: Oxford University Press, 2009). Federico Finchelstein provides an innovative study of fascism outside Europe, investigating links between Argentina and Italy; Finchelstein, *Transatlantic Fascism: Ideology, Violence, and the Sacred in Argentina and Italy, 1919–1945* (Durham, NC: Duke University Press, 2010).

6. The Japanese debates on Italian Fascism have received scant attention, both in Japanese- and English-language scholarship. One exception is Fuke Takahiro, who has treated the subject in depth, showing how Fascism and Nazism stimulated a wide debate among Japanese right-wing ideologues and movements; Fuke, *Senkanki Nihon no shakai shisō: "Chōkokka" e no furontia* (Tokyo: Jinbun Shoin, 2010), esp. chapters 5, 6, and 8. Two further studies are Yamazaki Mitsuhiko, "Itaria fashizumu, sono Nihon ni okeru jūyō to hyōgen keitai," in *"Taishō" saikō*, ed. Seki Shizuo (Tokyo: Mineruba, 2007); Yamazaki Mitsuhiko, "'Fashisuto' Mussorini wa Nihon de ika egakareta ka: hyōgen bunka ni okeru seijiteki eiyūzō," *Ryūkoku Daigaku kokusai sentā kenkyū nenpō*, no. 15 (2006). See also Hori Makiyo, *Nishida Mitsugi to Nihon Fashizumu undō* (Tokyo: Iwanami, 2007), 8–18, 21–26. Valdo Ferretti has written on diplomatic relations between the two countries; Ferretti, *Il Giappone e la politica estera italiana* (Rome: Giuffrè, 1983).

7. Antonio Gramsci, *Quaderni del carcere*, 4 vols. (Turin: Einaudi, 2007), 3:16–19.

8. Maruyama Masao, "The Ideology and Dynamics of Japanese Fascism," and "Theory and Psychology of Ultra-Nationalism," both in *Thought and Behaviour in Modern Japanese Politics*, ed. Ivan Morris (Oxford: Oxford University Press, 1969). The terms "authoritarianism" and "militarism" have informed Ben-Ami Shillony, *Politics and Culture in Wartime Japan* (New York: Oxford University Press, 1981); Richard H. Mitchell, *Thought Control in Prewar Japan* (Ithaca, NY: Cornell University Press, 1976); Elise K. Tipton, *The Japanese Police State: The Tokkō in Interwar Japan* (Honolulu: University of Hawai'i Press, 1990). "Total war" has been put forth as a paradigm that describes a broader interwar trend applicable both to Japan and to liberal democracies. See, for example, the essays in Yasushi Yamanouchi, J. Victor Koschmann, and Ryūichi Narita, eds., *Total War and "Modernization"* (Ithaca, NY: Cornell University Press, 1998). Elaborating on the "total war" paradigm, Louise Young stresses the role of empire in forging social, economic, and cultural mobilization; Young, *Japan's Total Empire: Manchuria and the Culture of Wartime Imperialism* (Berkeley: University of California Press, 1999). After 1945, only Marxists held on to the term "fascism" to characterize prewar Japan, but typically in terms of a national history of backwardness, not of global connections. Marxists focused on the "emperor system" as the pivotal institutional and ideological site of "absolutism" and "fascism." See, for example, Inoue Kiyoshi, *Tennōsei zettaishugi no hatten* (Tokyo: Chūō Kōron, 1951); Hattori Shisō, *Tennōsei zettaishugi no kakuritsu* (Tokyo: Chūō Kōron, 1948).

9. Paxton, *Anatomy of Fascism*, 15.

10. Harry Harootunian, "Introduction: A Sense of an Ending and the Problem of Taishō," in *Japan in Crisis: Essays on Taishō Democracy*, ed. Bernard S. Silberman and Harry Harootunian (Princeton, NJ: Princeton University Press, 1974), 4.

11. For a discussion of the historiography on Taishō democracy and liberalism, see Andrew Gordon, *Labor and Imperial Democracy in Prewar Japan* (Berkeley: University of California Press, 1991), 5–9. Peter Duus has highlighted some of the tensions in prewar Japanese liberalism; see Duus, *Party Rivalry and Political Change in Taishō Japan* (Cambridge, MA: Harvard University Press, 1968); and "Liberal Intellectuals and Social Conflict in Taishō Japan," in *Conflict in Modern Japanese History*, ed. Tetsuo Najita and J. Victor Koschmann (Princeton, NJ: Princeton University Press, 1982). See also the essays in Harry Wray and Hilary Conroy, *Japan Examined: Perspectives on Modern Japanese history* (Honolulu: University of Hawai'i Press, 1983). More recently, Narita Ryūichi has stressed the interplay of empire and democratic politics in the Taishō period; Narita, *Taishō demokurashii*, vol. 4, *Shiriizu Nihon kingendaishi* (Tokyo: Iwanami, 2007).

12. *Asahi shinbun*, August 2, 1933.

13. Alan Tansman has pointed out the aesthetic logic that informed the "disavowal" of fascism in his provocative study of the culture of Japanese fascism. Tansman also shows that what he calls the "rhetoric of unspoken fascism" informed one of the key political texts

of the 1930s, the *Kokutai no hongi* (Principles of Our National Polity, 1937); Tansman, *Aesthetics of Japanese Fascism*, 19, 150–68.

14. Two studies that examine the impact of empire building on Japanese society, politics, and culture are Young, *Japan's Total Empire*, and Mimura, *Planning for Empire*.

15. Prasenjit Duara discusses Manchukuo in terms of overlapping discourses on nationalism, empire, and anti-imperialism; Duara, *Sovereignty and Authenticity: Manchukuo and the East Asian Modern* (Lanham, MD: Rowman & Littlefield, 2003).

1. MEDIATOR OF FASCISM: SHIMOI HARUKICHI, 1915–1928

1. Shimoi Harukichi, *Fassho undō* (Tokyo: Minyūsha, 1925), 39–40.

2. Ibid., 18–19.

3. Shimoi has often been indicated as a representative of a minor pro-Italian current in interwar Japanese politics; Hori Makiyo, *Nishida Mitsugi to Nihon Fashizumu Undō* (Tokyo: Iwanami, 2007), 13–14; Christopher W. A. Szpilman, "Fascist and Quasi-Fascist Ideas in Interwar Japan, 1918–1941," in *Japan in the Fascist Era*, ed. Bruce E. Reynolds (New York: Palgrave Macmillan, 2004), 97. A closer study of Shimoi's activities between Japan and Italy can be found in Fujioka Hiromi, "Shimoi Harukichi to Itaria, Fashizumu: Danunchio, Mussorini, Nihon," *Fukuoka Kokusai Daigaku kiyō* 25 (2012).

4. ACS, MI, Polizia Politica, fascicoli personali, pacco 654, 47, Shimoi Harukichi, Rome, October 9, 1931.

5. For an outline of various fascist movements around the world, see Stanley G. Payne, *A History of Fascism, 1914–1945* (Madison: University of Wisconsin Press, 1995), 329–54; Stein Ugelvik Larsen, *Fascism Outside Europe: The European Impulse against Domestic Conditions in the Diffusion of Global Fascism* (Boulder, CO: Social Science Monographs, 2001).

6. The rise of socialist and liberal activism is discussed in Peter Duus and Irwin Scheiner, "Socialism, Liberalism, and Marxism, 1901–1931," in *Modern Japanese Thought*, ed. Bob Tadashi Wakabayashi (Cambridge: Cambridge University Press, 1998). The tension arising between culture and politics in the 1920s is addressed in Harry Harootunian, "Introduction: A Sense of an Ending and the Problem of Taishō," in *Japan in Crisis: Essays on Taishō Democracy*, ed. Bernard Silberman and Harry Harootunian (Princeton, NJ: Princeton University Press, 1974).

7. Maida Minoru, "Itari no seikyoku (*jō*)," *Gaikō jihō* 493 (1925): 64–66.

8. Katayama Sen, "Fuwashizumu to Ōshū no genjō," *Kaizō* 5, no. 9 (1923): 72.

9. Ninagawa Arata, "Fuasichizumu no kōryū to rōdō sōgi no gentai," *Tōtaku geppō* 5, no. 1 (1924): 2. See also "Ikoku no saikin kakumei to sono kōka," *Gaikō jihō* 4, no. 1 (1923).

10. Early renderings for "Fascism" included *fuwasshizumu* and *fasshisutei*. See, for example, Fujii Tei, "Sekaiteki fuwasshizumu to Nihon no kensei," *Chūō kōron* 8 (1927).

11. Until the early twentieth century there were only limited contacts between Japan and Italy. After the Meiji Restoration, a small number of Italian artists were active in Japan, most notably the painters Antonio Fontanesi (1818–1882); Edoardo Chiossone (1833–1898), who painted the famous portrait of Emperor Meiji; and the sculptor Vincenzo Ragusa (1841–1927). See the essays in Adolfo Tamburello, ed., *Italia-Giappone, 450 anni*, 2 vols. (Naples: Istituto italiano per l'Africa e l'Oriente; Università degli Studi di Napoli "l'Orientale," 2003). Japanese travelers and missions to Europe in the late nineteenth century are the subject of W. G. Beasley, *Japan Encounters the Barbarian: Japanese Travellers in America and Europe, 1860–1873* (New Haven, CT: Yale University Press, 1995). See also Hirakawa Sukehiro, "Japan's Turn to the West," in *Modern Japanese Thought*, ed. Bob Tadashi Wakabayashi (Cambridge: Cambridge University Press, 1998), 54–69.

12. Victoria de Grazia argues that Fascism continued the nineteenth-century project of making national citizens; de Grazia, *How Fascism Ruled Women: Italy, 1922–1945* (Berkeley: University of California Press, 1992), 6–7.

13. The social meanings of "rising in the world" are the focus of Earl H. Kinmonth, *The Self-Made Man in Meiji Japanese Thought: From Samurai to Salary Man* (Berkeley: University of California Press, 1981).

14. Donald Roden, *Schooldays in Imperial Japan: A Study in the Culture of a Student Elite* (Berkeley: University of California Press, 1980), 157. For a discussion of the culture and thought of social mobility, see Carol Gluck, *Japan's Modern Myths: Ideology in the Late Meiji Period* (Princeton, NJ: Princeton University Press, 1985).

15. Fujioka, "Shimoi Harukichi to Itaria, Fashizumu," 53–54.

16. Roden, *Schooldays in Imperial Japan*, 10, 247. On conservatism in late Meiji, see also Kenneth Pyle, "Meiji Conservatism," in *Modern Japanese Thought*, ed. Bob Tadashi Wakabayashi (Cambridge: Cambridge University Press, 1999).

17. Jason Karlin has explored the student culture of late Meiji with a focus on the gendered aspects of the literature that these youths consumed; Karlin, "The Gender of Nationalism: Competing Masculinities in Meiji Japan," *Journal of Japanese Studies* 28, no. 1 (2002): 70–77.

18. For a discussion of the crisis of Meiji conservative morality in Taishō, see Harootunian, "Introduction," 18.

19. These themes were central in Iwaya's journal *Shōnen sekai* (Children's World). Harry Harootunian examines the "folk" as a representational strategy of communitarian life at a time of capitalist modernization; Harootunian, "Figuring the Folk: History, Poetics, and Representation," in *Mirror of Modernity*, ed. Stephen Vlastos (Berkeley: University of California Press, 1998).

20. Shimoi Harukichi, *Ohanashi no shikata* (Tokyo: Dōbunkan, 1926 [1917]), 1.

21. Ibid., 5.

22. *Yomiuri shinbun*, January 22, 1920.

23. For a study on the relationship between the Florentine modernists and Fascism, see Walter L. Adamson, "Modernism and Fascism: The Politics of Culture in Italy, 1903–1922," *American Historical Review* 95 (1990): 362.

24. Nicola D'Antuono, *Avventura intellettuale e tradizione culturale in Gherardo Marone* (Naples: Laveglia, 1984), 9–12.

25. Quoted in Adele Dei, *"La Diana" (1915–1917), saggio e antologia* (Rome: Bulzoni, 1981), 7.

26. An exposition of the Italian reception of Japanese culture is to be found in Flavia Arzeni, *L'immagine e il segno* (Bologna: Il Mulino, 1987), 41–49. See also Tamburello, *Italia-Giappone*, esp. vol. 1, sections 3–5, for studies on the contribution of Japanese culture to the development of Italian art and literature.

27. In the closest thing to a manifesto for *La Diana*, Lionello Fiumi declared that he wanted "neither past-ism, nor futurism, but presentism"; Fiumi, "Appello neoliberista," in *Opere poetiche*, ed. Beatrice Fiumi Magnani and Gianpaolo Marchi (Verona: Fiorini, 1994), 3–7.

28. Giuseppe Ungaretti, *Lettere dal fronte a Gherardo Marone, 1916–1918* (Milan: Mondadori, 1978), 81.

29. Giovanni Papini, "Lettres italiennes," *Mercure de France*, nos. 11–12 (1917): 151.

30. The episode is mentioned in the second edition of *Lirici giapponesi* by Marone himself. He felt flattered at being mistaken for Yosano Akiko and reminisced nostalgically about the days when he and Shimoi worked on the project; Shimoi Harukichi and Gherardo Marone, eds., *Lirici giapponesi* (Lanciano: G. Carabba, 1926).

31. Shimoi Harukichi and Gherardo Marone, eds., *Poesie giapponesi* (Naples: Riccardo Ricciardi Editore, 1917), 5–17.

32. Shimoi and Marone, *Lirici giapponesi*, Ungaretti to Marone, September 15, 1917. For Ungaretti's interest in Japanese poetry, see also Ungaretti, *Lettere dal fronte a Gherardo Marone*, 81. The extent to which Japanese poetry influenced Italian modernists is still disputed, but it cannot be denied that a number of poets avidly read the Japanese poetry published in *La Diana* and adopted the haiku's forms as their own. For example, "hermeticism" (*ermetismo*) was a current in poets including Ungaretti and Eugenio Montale, who came of age during the 1920s and 1930s and were loosely associated with *La Diana* in their early years. Marone had used the term "hermetic" in a comment about Maeda Suikei, a little-known poet: "He is an extraordinary poet precisely because he accumulates his vast intuition in a hermetic sobriety of expression"; Marone to Fiumi, undated letter, in Silvana Gallifuoco, ed., *Lettere di Lionello Fiumi* (Naples: Macchiaroli, 2003). On this topic, see also Suga Atsuko, "Ungaretti e la poesia giapponese," in *Atti del Convegno Internazionale su Giuseppe Ungaretti* (Urbino, 1979).

33. Antonio Gibelli has illustrated the ways in which World War I changed the worldview of soldiers; Gibelli, *L'officina della guerra e le trasformazioni del mondo mentale* (Turin: Bollati Boringhieri, 2007). For an account of the role of youth in World War I, as well as the representation of death and mourning following the conflict, see George L. Mosse, *Fallen Soldiers: Reshaping the Memory of the World Wars* (Oxford: Oxford University Press, 1990).

34. Ernst Jünger, *Storm of Steel* (London: Allen Lane, 2003). An account of the experience of World War I among youth can be found in Mosse, *Fallen Soldiers*, 53–69.

35. Shimoi Harukichi, *La guerra italiana* (Naples: Libreria della Diana, 1919), 19, 22, 32. Giuseppe De Lorenzo, a distinguished geologist, amateur scholar of Indian Buddhism, and since 1913 senator, vouched for Shimoi's commitment to Italy, declaring that he "has for more than three years dedicated all his energy to the study and understanding of our country"; ibid., 19.

36. Ibid., 32.

37. Ibid.

38. Ibid., 29.

39. Ibid., 44.

40. Ibid., 25.

41. Ibid., 46.

42. Ibid., 30.

43. For Shimoi's discussion of D'Annunzio's rule at Fiume, see Gabriele D'Annunzio, "Le pagine di D'Annunzio," in Shimoi, *La guerra italiana*, no page numbers provided. See also Michael Ledeen, *The First Duce: D'Annunzio at Fiume* (Baltimore, MD: Johns Hopkins University Press, 1977). For evidence of the lascivious behavior of D'Annunzio's men, see Claudia Salaris, *Alla festa della rivoluzione* (Bologna: Il Mulino, 2002), 12.

44. For a study of the role of aviators in the popular imaginary, see Robert Wohl, *The Spectacle of Flight: Aviation and the Western Imagination, 1920–1950* (New Haven, CT: Yale University Press, 2005).

45. Vito Salierno, "Il mancato volo di D'Annunzio in Giappone," in *Un capitolo di storia: Fiume e D'Annunzio, Atti del Convegno, Gardone Riviera, San Pelagio, 27–8, ottobre 1989*, ed. Elena Ledda and Guglielmo Salotti (Rome: Lucarini, 1991), 158.

46. By his own admission a "fanatic of aviation," the future Duce contacted the organizers, expressing his "intention to participate" and to "prepare me a plane." Letters Mussolini-Brezzi, October 9 and 20, 1919, in Guido Mattioli, *Mussolini aviatore e la sua opera per l'aviazione* (Rome: Casa Editrice Pinciana, 1936), 50–54.

47. KKK, 2A, 11-200, 1313-100, reel 26200, Cabinet Secretary to various ministries, September 12, 1919.

48. Ibid., Tanaka Giichi to Hara Kei, September 13, 1919.
49. Ibid.
50. Shimoi, *La guerra italiana.* D'Annunzio's autograph, Easter 1919.
51. SHPP, D'Annunzio to Shimoi, *Fiume d'Italia*, January 29, 1920.
52. AV, AP, 303l/2899.
53. The same was true in Italy, where he was invited to give talks and write articles about his experience at Fiume and on Japanese culture; *Yomiuri shinbun*, January 21–23, 1920.
54. *Asahi shinbun*, January 17, 1920.
55. *Yomiuri shinbun*, January 28, 1920.
56. *Asahi shinbun*, January 19, 1920.
57. *Yomiuri shinbun*, January 15, 1920.
58. Doi Bansui, "Su le orme dell'ippogrifo," trans. Shimoi Harukichi and Elpidio Jenco, *Sakura* 1, no. 2 (1920), 14–15.
59. Doi Bansui, "Tenba no michi ni: Gaburiere Danunchio o mukauru chōshi," *Chūō kōron* 35 (1920). The Italian translation appeared in *Sakura*, "Su le orme dell'ippogrifo."
60. *Asahi shinbun*, May 10, 1921. Shimoi's story was published in three installments, on May 7, 9, and 10.
61. The standard account of Mussolini's rise to power is Adrian Lyttelton, *The Seizure of Power: Fascism in Italy, 1919–1939* (London and New York: Routledge, 2004). For a study focusing on the role of Mussolini, see R. J. B. Bosworth, *Mussolini's Italy: Life under the Dictatorship 1915–1945* (New York: Allen Lane, 2005), 123–216. On the early Fascist squads, see also Mimmo Franzinelli, "Squadrism," in *The Oxford Handbook of Fascism*, ed. R. J. B. Bosworth (Oxford: Oxford University Press, 2009).
62. Tokutomi Rōka, *Nihon kara Nihon e*, vol. 13, *Rōka zenshū* (Tokyo: Shinchōsha, 1929), 192–200. Upon learning that D'Annunzio had called off the flight, Tokutomi, disappointed, refrained from sending the poem.
63. *Yomiuri shinbun*, July 12, 17, and 20, 1920.
64. Dan published two books about his journey to Italy and the Mediterranean. See Dan Inō, *Itaria bijutsu kikō* (Tokyo: Shunyōdō, 1922); Dan Inō, *Parunasu no junrei* (Tokyo: Ōmura, 1924).
65. Shimoi's writing about this collection of poetry earned him some repute in the scholarly world. The Dutch Japanologist (and later Fascist and Nazi sympathizer) Jan Lodeweijk Pierson regularly referred to "professor Shimoi's" interpretations of the Manyōshū. See, for example, J. L. Pierson, *The Manyōshū: Translated and Annotated*, vol. 1 (Leyden: Brill, 1929), 3, 112, 147.
66. Tsuda Shun, "Casupole giapponesi di campagna," *Sakura* 1, no. 4 (1920): 102.
67. Shimoi Harukichi, "Duello di poesia," *Sakura* 1, no. 1 (1920): 26–27.
68. Ibid.
69. "Fior di ciliegio," *Sakura* 1, nos. 1–2 (1920): 1.
70. Introduction to Yosano Akiko, *Onde del mare azzurro*, trans. Shimoi Harukichi and Elpidio Jenco (Naples: Sakura, 1920), 16.
71. An internal accounting document of the Oriental Institute at the University of Naples states that Shimoi "had resigned" in the 1919–1920 academic year, and there is no further reference to him at the university while he was residing in the city; AION, *Elenco delle proprietà immobili, Ispezioni ministeriali, Bilanci, Prospetto analitico del personale, 1919–20.*
72. GGSK, I, 3, 1, *Teikoku, mokuji.*
73. *Asahi shinbun*, May 9, 1921.
74. *Il Popolo d'Italia*, September 13, 1922. The newspaper named the three deputies as Masaki, Yuasa, and Sakurauchi.

75. Shimoi returned to Japan from December 1924 to May 1925, from October 1925 to February 1926, from May to November 1926, and from March to July 1927. For his reception in Japan, see *Asahi shinbun*, December 2, 5, 9, 12, and 18, 1924. Earlier, in 1921, he had sought to establish a Dante Museum (Casa di Dante) as a "bridge of poetry," but the attempt came to nothing; *Asahi shinbun*, May 10, 1921. See also Yosano, *Onde del mare azzurro*, 16.

76. AV, AG, XXVIII, 1, Shimoi Harukichi, June 6, 1924.

77. AV, AG, b. Shimoi Harukichi, nn. 26288–89, Telegram D'Annunzio–Shimoi, October 31, 1924. See also AV, AG, XXVIII, 1, Letter Shimoi to D'Annunzio, July 30, 1924.

78. Mussolini, March 1926, in an advertising pamphlet entitled *Itari gen shushō Mussorini shi no messeji narabini ryakuden* (Tokyo: Karupisu Seizō, 1926). The same message was reprinted in an advertisement in the newspaper *Asahi* ("Itari shushō Mussorini no messeji kuru: zen Nihon seinen danjo shokun e!," May 15, 1926). Military valor was one stereotype that Italians associated with Japan. Nitobe Inazō's *Bushido* (1900) was translated into Italian in 1917, though it had been read earlier in English.

79. ASMAE, 1919–1930, b. 1189 (4663) rapporti politici, Della Torre to Mussolini, Tokyo, May 16, 1926. Della Torre puts the number as "not inferior to ten thousand" while Shimoi claimed no less than 30,000 (ASMAE, AP, Giappone, 1919–1930, b. 1189, miscellanea, Shimoi–Mussolini, Rome, January 28, 1927). One Italian resident, however, declared the event a commercial farce and Shimoi an "ambitious charlatan and swindler"; ASMAE, 1919–1930, b. 1189 (4663) rapporti politici, Pastorelli to Mussolini, May 24, 1926.

80. *Yamane seishi kaihō*, August 15 and 19, 1926, 2.

81. ASMAE, 1919–1930, b. 1189, miscellanea, Shimoi–Mussolini, Rome, January 28, 1927.

82. Friends of dictators, though not always deriving benefit from that relationship, did usually gain renown. See, in the case of Hitler, the English aristocrat Lord Londonderry and his childhood friend August Kubizek: Ian Kershaw, *Making Friends with Hitler: Lord Londonderry, the Nazis, and the Road to War* (New York: Penguin, 2004); August Kubizek, *The Young Hitler I Knew* (London: Greenhill Books, 2006).

83. For a thesis according to which Fascism amounted to little more than Mussolini "invok[ing] symbolic means and forms that would excite emotions in the people," see Simonetta Falasca-Zamponi, *Fascist Spectacle: The Aesthetics of Power in Mussolini's Italy* (Berkeley: University of California Press, 1997).

84. Shimoi Harukichi, *Taisenchū no Itaria* (Tokyo: Shingidō, 1926), 11.

85. Fascism insisted on its youthful character even when, by the 1930s, many of its leaders had passed middle age. See Patrizia Dogliani, "Propaganda and Youth," in *The Oxford Handbook of Fascism*, ed. R. J. B. Bosworth (Oxford: Oxford University Press, 2009). The generational aspect of Italian Fascism is explored in Bruno Wanrooij, "The Rise and Fall of Italian Fascism as a Generational Revolt," *Journal of Contemporary History* 22 (1987). The regime founded various institutions to organize youth, such as the Opera Nazionale Balilla (ONB) and the Gruppi Universitari Fascisti (GUF).

86. Tokutomi Sohō in Kitamura Mitsuko, *Seinen to kindai: seinen to seinen o meguru gensetsu no keifugaku* (Yokokama-shi: Seori Shobō, 1998), 251.

87. David Ambaras, *Bad Youth: Juvenile Delinquency and the Politics of Everyday Life in Modern Japan* (Berkeley: University of California Press, 2006).

88. Kitamura, *Seinen to kindai*, 248.

89. The evocation of heroism and sacrifice was part of a larger culture of remembrance explored in Jay Winter, *Sites of Memory, Sites of Mourning: The Great War in European Cultural History* (Cambridge: Cambridge University Press, 1995).

90. Modris Eksteins, *Rites of Spring: The Great War and the Birth of the Modern Age* (Boston: Houghton Mifflin, 2000), 214.

91. George L. Mosse, "The Poet and the Exercise of Political Power: Gabriele D'Annunzio," in *Masses and Man: Nationalist and Fascist Perceptions of Reality* (Detroit: Wayne State University Press, 1987).

92. Shimoi, *Taisenchū no Itaria*, 11.

93. Ibid., 235.

94. For a study of mass culture in the 1920s, see Minami Hiroshi, *Taishō bunka* (Tokyo: Shinsōban, 1988), 269–380. See also the relevant sections in Minami's *Shōwa bunka* (Tokyo: Keisō Shobō, 1987).

95. *Yomiuri shinbun*, March 1, 1930. Shimoi Harukichi, *Fassho undō* and *Mussorini no shishiku* (Tokyo: Dai Nihon Yūbenkai Kōdansha, 1929). Other publications include Shimoi Harukichi, *Gyorai no se ni matagarite* (Tokyo: Shingidō, 1926), *Taisen ga unda Ikoku no niyūshi* (Tokyo: Teikoku bunka kyōkai, 1926), and *Fassho undō to Mussorini* (Tokyo: Bunmei Kyōkai, 1927).

96. ASMAE, AP, Giappone, 1919–1930, b. 1189, miscellanea, Shimoi–Mussolini, January 28, 1927. Shimoi, *Gyorai no se ni matagarite.*

97. Shimoi, *Fassho undō to Mussorini*, 45–47.

98. Ibid.

99. Ibid., 20–21, 106.

100. Ibid., 68–69.

101. Ohara Tatsuaki, in Shimoi, *Taisen ga unda Ikoku no niyūshi.*

102. ASMAE, AP, Giappone, 1919–1930, b. 1189, miscellanea, Shimoi–Mussolini, January 28, 1927.

103. Shimoi, *Fassho undō to Mussorini*, 26–27.

104. Sano Manabu, "Fashizumu ni tsuite no danpen," *Keizai ōrai* 11 (1927): 88–89.

105. ASMAE, AP, Giappone, 1919–30, b. 1189, (4663) rapporti politici, Della Torre to Mussolini, November 29, 1925.

106. ASMAE, AP, Giappone, 1919–1930, b. 1189, miscellanea, Shimoi–Mussolini, January 28, 1927.

107. Ibid.

108. ASMAE, AP, Giappone, b. 1889, 1925–28, f. commemorazione, Della Torre to Mussolini, February 23, 1928.

109. GGSK, I, 1, *Byakkōtai kinenhi kankei, dai ichi maki*, Yamakawa to Tanaka, February 1, 1928. Japanese foreign ministry officials passed a French translation to their Italian counterparts (ASMAE, AP, Giappone, b. 1889, 1925–28, f. commemorazione).

110. ASMAE, AP, Giappone, b. 1889, 1925–28, f. commemorazione, 138/68, Della Torre to Mussolini, March 3, 1928.

111. ASMAE, AP, Giappone, b. 1889, 1925–28, f. commemorazione, note "Biakko-Tai." The selected text read: "Rome always present in the spirit of the heroes with this millenarian column exalts the memory of the Byakkōtai—image of a Fascio—sixth year of the Fascist Era, 1928."

112. ASMAE, AP, Giappone, 1919–30, b. 1189, commemorazioni ed onoranze, 685/292 and 835/327, Aloisi to Mussolini, Tokyo, December 6, 1928.

113. ASMAE, AP, Giappone, 1919–30, b. 1189, commemorazioni ed onoranze, 835/327, appendix to Aloisi to Mussolini, Tokyo, December 6, 1928. Mussolini reciprocated Konoe's niceties: "In expressing my best wishes for the prosperity of the Japanese nation I am pleased that the event gave us the opportunity to confirm once again the ties of friendship that [have] exist[ed] for a long time between our two countries" (ibid., Mussolini to Konoe, December 5, 1928).

114. ASMAE, AP, Giappone, 1919–30, b. 1190, rapporti politici, letter Aloisi to Mussolini, Tokyo, July 12, 1929.

115. *Yomiuri shinbun*, November 26, 1929.

116. GGSK, I, 1, 7, *Byakkōtai*, Debuchi to Matsuda, February 28, 1928.

117. ASMAE, AP, Giappone, 1919–30, b. 1189, commemorazioni ed onoranze, 835/327, Aloisi to Mussolini, Tokyo, December 6, 1928.

118. Matsudaira himself was committed to advancing the cause of Aizu. Only three months before the *byakkōtai* commemoration, in September 1928, he wedded his daughter Setsuko to Prince Chichibu, the emperor's younger brother—clearly Matsudaira's key role in the Byakkōtai Committee was not coincidental.

119. ASMAE, AP, Giappone, 1919–30, b. 1189, commemorazioni ed onoranze, 685/292, appendix from Aloisi to Mussolini, October 6, 1928.

120. GGSK, I, 1, 7, *Byakkōtai*, Debuchi to Matsuda, February 28, 1928 and GSK, I, 1, 7, *Byakkōtai*, Matsuda to Tanaka Giichi, November 2, 1928. The ambassador also recalled a past embarrassing episode in Shimoi's private life—a scandal he had provoked years earlier in Naples when he "lived with another woman." Shimoi's conjugal immorality, though, was less outrageous in the eyes of the Italian ambassador. "If one considers," he wrote, "that until a few years ago concubinage was a legally recognized institution in Japan, if one considers that until one year ago there was a high court dignitary who appeared in public between his wife and concubine . . . it does not seem to me logic to inveigh against the poet guilty of having reevoked in his family life the customs of the daimyo and samurai"; ASMAE, AP, Giappone, 1919–30, b. 1189, commemorazioni, onoranze, 118/58, Della Torre to Mussolini, February 28, 1928.

121. ACS, SPD, CO, Shimoi Harukichi, note "Ministero degli Affari Esteri," Rome, December 26, 1927. Beltramelli's wife, Yoshiko Tetsu Beltramelli, who was Japanese, had studied music in Italy. After World War II Shimoi claimed that he had introduced Yoshiko to Beltramelli to repay him a favor: "Bring her to me," was Beltramelli's sexist remark, "I'll teach her how to sing"; Indro Montanelli, *L'impero bonsai, cronaca di un viaggio in Giappone, 1951–2* (Milan: Rizzoli, 2007), 168. For an assessment of Beltramelli's work see Luisa Passerini, *Mussolini immaginario* (Rome: Laterza, 1991).

2. THE MUSSOLINI BOOM, 1928–1931

1. Mizuno Hironori, "Fasshizumu to Nihon," *Keizai ōrai*, no. 11 (1927): 82. Mizuno does not mention the name of the newspaper that conducted the survey. The second was Bernard Shaw, with half the votes of the Italian leader.

2. Simonetta Falasca-Zamponi, *Fascist Spectacle: The Aesthetics of Power in Mussolini's Italy* (Berkeley: University of California Press, 1997), 50–55. For a study on the reception of Mussolini in the United States, see John P. Diggins, *Mussolini and Fascism: The View from America* (Princeton, NJ: Princeton University Press, 1972). Falasca-Zamponi also considers aspects of the Duce's image outside of Italy. For Japan, Yoshimura Michio concentrates on the political meanings of the Japanese debates about Mussolini; Yoshimura, "Shōwa shoki no shakai jōkyōka ni okeru Nihonjin no Mussorini zō," *Nihon rekishi*, no. 497 (1989). A more sophisticated reading of the various expressions of Japanese interest in Mussolini can be found in Fuke Takahiro, *Nihon fashizumu ronsō: Taisen zenya no shisōka tachi* (Tokyo: Kawade Bukkusu, 2012), 39–66.

3. Peter Duus, "Liberal Intellectuals and Social Conflict in Taishō Japan," in *Conflict in Modern Japanese History*, ed. Tetsuo Najita and J. Victor Koschmann (Princeton, NJ: Princeton University Press, 1982), 420–21.

4. Tetsuo Najita, *Japan: The Intellectual Foundations of Modern Japanese Politics* (Chicago: University of Chicago Press, 1974), 120–21.

5. Harry Harootunian, "Between Politics and Culture: Authority and the Ambiguities of Intellectual Choice in Imperial Japan," in *Japan in Crisis: Essays on Taishō Democracy*, ed. Bernard S. Silberman and Harry Harootunian (Princeton, NJ: Princeton University Press, 1974), 122–24.

6. I use "consent" in the sense that Antonio Gramsci understood it. How, Gramsci asked, could "legislators prepare the 'spontaneous' consent of the masses who must 'live' those directives, modifying their own habits, their own will, their own convictions to conform with those directives and with the objectives which they propose to achieve?"; Gramsci, *Selections from the Prison Notebooks* (New York: International Publishers, 1971), 266. The question of the "new individualism" in Taishō is raised in Harry Harootunian, "Introduction: A Sense of an Ending and the Problem of Taishō," in *Japan in Crisis: Essays on Taishō Democracy*, ed. Bernard Silberman and Harry Harootunian (Princeton, NJ: Princeton University Press, 1974), 12.

7. Tsurumi Yūsuke, *Eiyū taibō ron* (Tokyo: Dai Nihon Yūbenkai Kōdansha, 1928), 10.

8. The German terms employed by Weber were, in fact, "alltäglich" and "ausseralltäglich," literally "everyday" and "outside-everyday." English translations of them as "ordinary" and "extraordinary" fail to give the temporal sense of the original. See Max Weber, *Wirtschaft und Gesellschaft. Grundrisse der verstehenden Soziologie*, vol. 3, *Grundrisse der Sozialökonomik* (Tübingen, 1922), 140–47.

9. The formation of the myth of Mussolini has been examined in Renzo De Felice and Luigi Goglia, *Mussolini, il mito: Grandi opere* (Rome: Laterza, 1983). See also Falasca-Zamponi, *Fascist Spectacle*. For a study that de-emphasizes the purchase of Mussolini's myth on Italians, see R. J. B. Bosworth, *Mussolini's Italy: Life under the Dictatorship, 1915–1945* (New York: Allen Lane, 2005).

10. Tsurumi, *Eiyū taibō ron*, 5–8.

11. Tsurumi Yūsuke, *Ōbei tairiku yūki* (Tokyo: Dai Nihon Yūbenkai Kōdansha, 1933), 659–60, 662–63.

12. Ibid., 659–60.

13. Harootunian, "Between Politics and Culture," 140–41.

14. Nitobe Inazō, *Ijin gunzō* (Tokyo: Jitsugyō no Nihon sha, 1931), 87–90.

15. For a biographical sketch of Nakano, see Leslie Russell Oates, *Populist Nationalism in Prewar Japan: A Biography of Nakano Seigo* (Sydney: Allen & Unwin, 1985). Inomata Keitarō, a former member of Nakano's Tōhōkai (Eastern Society), has also produced a biography; Inomata, *Nakano Seigō* (Tokyo: Yoshikawa Kōbunkan, 1960).

16. Nakano Seigō, "Entakukei no Mussorini to yōchina rōnōtō," *Chūō kōron* 43, no. 5 (1928): 81–83.

17. Inahara Katsuji, "Mussorini kōtei ni naruka," *Gaikō jihō* 577, no. 12 (1928): 13. Another journalist, Shiotsu Seisaku, stated that the dictator "was trying to make Italy into a second Prussia"; Shiotsu, "Mussorini no kōka," *Kokusai chishiki* 8, no. 8 (1928): 60.

18. Inahara, "Mussorini kōtei ni naruka," 21.

19. Ibid., 19.

20. Uesugi Shinkichi, "Dōri to seigi no teki Mussorini ron," *Chūō kōron* 43, no. 2 (1928): 29–31, 39–40.

21. A discussion of reformism among Taishō politicians can be found in Sharon Minichiello, *Retreat from Reform: Patterns of Political Behavior in Interwar Japan* (Honolulu: University of Hawai'i Press, 1984), 1–6.

22. *Yomiuri shinbun*, April 20, 1933. Participants in this group conversation (*zadankai*) on Hitler, Mussolini, and patriotism (*aikokushin*) included the journalists Ōya Sōichi and Murobuse Kōshin and the actor and musical pundit Iba Takashi.

23. Ugaki Kazushige, *Ugaki Kazushige nikki*, 3 vols. (Tokyo: Misuzu Shobō, 1968–1971), 1:391, 414.

24. Jung-Sun N. Han has shown how liberal thinkers, especially Yoshino Sakuzō, rationalized the relationship between imperialism and liberalism; Han, *An Imperial Path to Modernity: Sakuzō and a New Liberal Order in East Asia, 1905–1937* (Cambridge, MA: Harvard University Press, 2012), 40–88. See also Jung-Sun N. Han, "Envisioning a Liberal Em-

pire in East Asia: Yoshino Sakuzō in Taishō Japan," *Journal of Japanese Studies* 33, no. 2 (2007).

25. Two studies that examine the complex relationship between Japanese internationalism and imperialism are Thomas W. Burkman, *Japan and the League of Nations: Empire and World Order, 1914–1938* (Honolulu: University of Hawai'i Press, 2008); Jessamyn R. Abel, "Warring Internationalisms: Multilateral Thinking in Japan, 1933–1964" (PhD diss., Columbia University, 2004). The military and political aspects of Japan's invasion of China are discussed in James B. Crowley, *Japan's Quest for Autonomy: National Security and Foreign Policy, 1930–1938* (Princeton, NJ: Princeton University Press, 1966).

26. Maida Minoru, "Itari no seikyoku," *Gaikō jihō* 493, 495 (1925): 34.

27. Nakahira Akira, "Mussorini no gaikō," *Gaikō jihō* 518, no. 7.1 (1926): 81–82. Anticipating Japan's wartime Asianist rhetoric, of which he would become a supporter, Nakahira added that "we must plan the construction of an Asian civilization. Our country needs a higher form of absolute supremacy—if Italy has the right to call for war based on industrial development, must we feel restraint in calling for the liberation of Asia based on principles of humanity and culture?"

28. Falasca-Zamponi, *Fascist Spectacle*, 45–47. The regime's policies, however, often met with indifference and even resistance. For a persuasive account that relativizes the extent to which Italian society succumbed to Fascist ideology and culture, see Bosworth, *Mussolini's Italy*.

29. Yoshida Yakuni, "Mussorini enzetsu no inshō," *Kaizō* 11, no. 3 (1929): 119–20.

30. Peter Duus has argued that Nagai's anti-imperialism more than his liberalism was at the heart of his drift toward "nationalism"; Duus, "Nagai Ryūtarō and the 'White Peril,' 1905–1944," *Journal of Asian Studies* 31, no. 1 (1971). Nagai is also the focus of Sharon Minichiello's study. Employing Itō Takashi's category of "reformism," she locates Nagai's turn to the right in the 1930s. But his flirtation with Mussolini suggests that his liberalism was already imbricated with fascist elements; Minichiello, *Retreat from Reform*, 94–96.

31. Nagai Ryūtarō, "Mussorini shushō no shojo enzetsu," *Yūben* 18, no. 1 (1927): 22. It was a wording that very likely paraphrased the title of a famous article written by the liberal scholar Yoshino Sakuzō in 1916, "On the Meaning of Constitutional Government and the Methods by Which It Can Be Perfected." Yoshino's statement read "kensei no hongi o toite sono yūshū no bi o sumasu" and was widely celebrated as a tribute to the nascent parliamentary democracy of the 1920s. Nagai's phrase was "dōryoku o kago shi sono yūshū no bi o togeshime."

32. Ibid.

33. Audiences with Mussolini, with a focus on German visitors, are the subject of Wolfgang Schieder, *Mythos Mussolini. Deutsche in Audienz beim Duce* (Munich: Oldenbourg Wissenschaftsverlag, 2013).

34. Until 1929 the audiences were held at the Quirinale or in Palazzo Chigi.

35. Okada Tadahiko, *Senpūri no Ōshū* (Tokyo: Teikoku Shoin, 1936), 339–42.

36. This thesis is expressed in Emilio Gentile, *The Sacralization of Politics in Fascist Italy* (Cambridge, MA: Harvard University Press, 1996).

37. Takaishi Shinjirō, "Ningen Mussorini to kataru," in *Itaria no inshō* (Tokyo: Itaria Tomo No Kai, 1943), 155–58.

38. Nagai Ryūtarō, "Uiruson kara Mussorini made," in *Yūkō kurabu kōenshū* (Tokyo: 1927), 14–15.

39. Ibid., 24.

40. Miriam Silverberg, "Constructing a New Cultural History of Prewar Japan," in *Japan in the World*, ed. Masao Miyoshi and H. C. Harootunian (Durham, NC: Duke University Press, 1993), 127.

41. As shown by Miriam Silverberg, other figures, too, had a similar function. In the early 1920s, for example, the media played a key role in popularizing the young Shōwa emperor; Silverberg, *Erotic Grotesque Nonsense: The Mass Culture of Japanese Modern Times* (Berkeley: University of California Press, 2009), 25–28.

42. This musical theater, evoking Broadway-style productions in its melodrama and choreography, opened in 1914 and within a few years had become a great popular success. Kishida Tatsuya was an important playwright in Takarazuka's early period. He had studied with Giovanni Vittorio Rosi, the Italian choreographer and a key figure in introducing Western opera to Japan in the 1910s. Kishida toured France and Italy before returning to Japan and producing his greatest hit, the revue "Mon Paris," in 1927 and the following year the "Revue Italiana." See also Jennifer Ellen Robertson, *Takarazuka: Sexual Politics and Popular Culture in Modern Japan* (Berkeley: University of California Press, 1998).

43. Tsubouchi Shōyō had adopted Shikō as his son only to repudiate him over disagreements about Shōyō's private life. Shōyō was also involved in the foundation of the musical theater Takarazuka. He had studied at Harvard and later became a professor at Waseda University.

44. James R. Brandon, "Mussolini in Kabuki: Notes and Translation," in *Japanese Theatre Transcultural: German and Italian Intertwinings*, ed. Stanca Scholz-Cionca and Andreas Regelsberger (Munich: Iudicium, 2011), 71. In this essay Brandon focuses on Osanai Kaoru and Ichikawa Sadanji. See also James R. Brandon, *Kabuki's Forgotten War, 1931–1945* (Honolulu: University of Hawai'i Press, 2009), 18–20.

45. Brandon, *Kabuki's Forgotten War*, 10–13. Another form was the "overnight pickle," a play that staged recent developments in the Russo-Japanese war, effectively being half-news half-entertainment.

46. Yamazaki Mitsuhiko, "'Fashisuto' Mussorini wa Nihon de ika egakareta ka: hyōgen bunka ni okeru seijiteki eiyūzō," *Ryūkoku daigaku kokusai sentā kenkyū nenpō*, no. 15 (2006): 207–10.

47. "Mussorini" alarmed Italian authorities, even in the sanitized version that appeared in Kaizō. Having asked Shimoi Harukichi to translate the entire play for Italian scrutiny, Roman officials protested that the piece was a "disgraceful attack on Italy, Mussolini, and Fascism." Yet the decision of the Japanese authorities to ban the play from public performance did little to alleviate Italian outrage. To their chagrin, the prohibition was issued, not because of the way it represented Mussolini, but for its talk of "revolutions, violence, and strikes . . . for its repercussions on domestic politics and the Japanese people"; ASMAE, AP, Giappone, 1919–30, b. 1189, pubblicazioni offensive, Guido Perris to Ezio Maria Gray, March 11, 1928. For a more detailed analysis of Maedakō's play, see Reto Hofmann, "The Fascist Reflection: Japan and Italy, 1919–1950" (PhD diss., Columbia University, 2010), 91–98.

48. Yamazaki, "'Fashisuto' Mussorini wa Nihon de ika egakareta ka," 208.

49. Osanai Kaoru and Ichikawa Sadanji, as quoted in Yamazaki Mitsuhiko, "Itaria fashizumu: sono Nihon ni okeru jūyō to hyōgen keitai," in *"Taishō" saikō*, ed. Seki Shizuo (Tokyo: Mineruba, 2007), 269–73.

50. Tsubouchi, in Yamazaki, "'Fashisuto' Mussorini wa Nihon de ika egakareta ka," 211.

51. Tsubouchi Shikō, "Mussorini," in *Nihon gikyoku zenshū. Gendai hen* (Tokyo: Shunyōdō, 1928–30), 500.

52. Ibid., 501.

53. Ibid., 485.

54. Ibid., 495–96.

55. Ibid., 504.

56. Luisa Passerini, *Mussolini immaginario* (Rome: Laterza, 1991), 154.

57. Nakagawa Shigeru, *Mussorini*, vol. 52, *Ijin denki bunkō* (Tokyo: Nihonsha, 1935).

58. Okumura Takeshi, *Kaiketsu Mussorini* (Osaka: Enomoto Shoten, 1928), and *Jidōsha ō Henri Fōdo* (Osaka: Enomoto Shoten, 1928).

59. Passerini, *Mussolini immaginario*, 42–61.

60. Giuseppe Prezzolini, *Fascism* (New York: E. P. Dutton, 1927); Luigi Villari, *The Awakening of Italy* (London and New York: Methuen, 1924); Pietro Gorgolini, *The Fascist Movement in Italian Life* (London: Unwin, 1923).

61. Luigi Sturzo, *Italy and Fascismo* (New York: Harcourt, 1926); Ivanoe Bonomi, *From Socialism to Fascism, a Study of Contemporary Italy* (London: M. Hopkinson, 1924); Guglielmo Ferrero, *Four Years of Fascism* (London: P. S. King, 1924).

62. The (unnamed) editor in Usuda Zan'un, *Wagahai wa Mussorini de aru* (Tokyo: Chūseidō, 1928), 337.

63. Sawada's *Mussorini* was published in 1928, 1936, and 1938; his *Hittora-den* in 1934, 1939, and 1940. Both found a postwar afterlife, being published again in 1983.

64. Sawada Ken, *Mussorini den* (Tokyo: Dai Nihon Yūbenkai Kōdansha, 1928), 1.

65. Ibid., 3.

66. Ibid., 4–5.

67. Ibid.

68. Usuda, *Wagahai wa Mussorini de aru*, 1–3.

69. Though probably Usuda was unaware of the fact, Mussolini was fond of cats—one exemplar would often sit on his desk—and at least once compared himself to one: "Have you ever watched a cat while it studies its prey and then, with a leap, is upon it? Watch one. I intend to act in the same way." The statement dates from April 21, 1940, and is quoted in Brian R. Sullivan, "The Impatient Cat: Assessments of Military Power in Fascist Italy, 1936–1940," in *Calculations: Net Assessment and the Coming of World War II*, ed. Williamson Murray and Allan R. Millet (New York: The Free Press, 1992), 97.

70. Mark Jones, *Children as Treasures: Childhood and the Middle Class in Early Twentieth-Century Japan* (Cambridge, MA: Harvard University Press, 2010), 117–18.

71. Ueda Sakuichi, *Mussorini shushō: Kinsei dai ijin* (Tokyo: Kōmin Kyōiku Kenkyūkai, 1927); Abe Sueo, *Mussorini: Shōnen sekai ijin dokuhon* (Osaka: Hōbunkan, 1930); Matsudaira Michio, *Mussorini* (Tokyo: Kin No Seisha, 1928); Ashima Kei, *Shōnen Mussorini den* (Tokyo: Bunkadō, 1932).

72. Abe, *Mussorini*. Introduction by the (unnamed) editor.

73. Koyama Shizuko examines the ideal of "good wife, wise mother" from Meiji to the 1930s, focusing on moral tracts; Koyama, *Ryōsai kenbo: The Educational Ideal of "Good wife, Wise mother" in Modern Japan* (Leiden: Brill, 2013).

74. Abe, *Mussorini*, 30–33. See also Ashima, *Shōnen Mussorini den*, 48.

75. Ashima, *Shōnen Mussorini den*, 48.

76. Abe, *Mussorini*, 16.

77. Matsudaira, *Mussorini*, 18–21. This recurrent episode is also narrated in Abe, *Mussorini*, 48–51. For Matsudaira, the young Benito's manly character also emerged in academic preferences. He had little time for subjects like Latin grammar or the history of religion: "Instead of spending his energies on insignificant subjects, he was completely engrossed in reading about Caesar and the heroes of ancient Rome" (Matsudaira, *Mussorini*, 32).

78. Duus, "Liberal Intellectuals and Social Conflict in Taishō Japan," 438.

79. Abe, *Mussorini*, 18–20.

80. Ashima, *Shōnen Mussorini den*, 333.

81. Ibid., 335.

82. As quoted in Yamazaki, "Itaria fashizumu, sono Nihon ni okeru jūyō to hyōgen keitai," 268.

83. Ashima, *Shōnen Mussorini den*, 4. This view was reiterated in the late 1930s by the philosopher Miki Kiyoshi in this theorization of "cooperativism" (*kyōdōshugi*). Mobilization from below—or self-mobilization—was needed to avoid "totalitarian control." "Cooperativism [does not] rest on abstract democracy; rather, it recognizes the important significance of leaders. The leaders required by cooperativism are not authoritarian dictators, nor are they separated from the people. Rather, they enter among the people, educate the people, and lead the people by taking up their demands"; Miki Kiyoshi in Duus, "Liberal Intellectuals and Social Conflict in Taishō Japan," 440.

3. THE CLASH OF FASCISMS, 1931–1937

1. Hugh Byas, *Government by Assassination* (New York: Knopf, 1942).

2. The argument that Manchuria represented the "jewel" in Japan's crown is made by Louise Young, *Japan's Total Empire: Manchuria and the Culture of Wartime Imperialism* (Berkeley: University of California Press, 1999), 21–52. Sandra Wilson relativizes the impact of the Manchurian Incident on Japanese society; Wilson, *The Manchurian Crisis and Japanese Society, 1931–33* (London: Routledge, 2002). For a contemporary account of how in the 1930s the world of the radical Right mixed with the criminal underworld, see Eiko Maruko Siniawer, *Ruffians, Yakuza, Nationalists: The Violent Politics of Modern Japan, 1860–1960* (Ithaca, NY: Cornell University Press, 2008), 108–38. For an examination of the February 26, 1936, attempted coup d'état, see Ben-Ami Shillony, *Revolt in Japan: The Young Officers and the February 26, 1936, Incident* (Princeton, NJ: Princeton University Press, 1973). The rise of the police state is described in Elise K. Tipton, *The Japanese Police State: The Tokkō in Interwar Japan* (Honolulu: University of Hawai'i Press, 1990). Janis Mimura analyzes the technocratic visions of Japan's "new bureaucrats" and the ideological connections to European fascist administrators; Mimura, *Planning for Empire: Reform Bureaucrats and the Japanese Wartime State* (Ithaca, NY: Cornell University Press, 2011). On the issue of "reformism" and reformist bureaucrats, see Itō Takashi, *Taishōki kakushinha no seiritsu* (Tokyo: Hanawa Sensho, 1978). A recent study of the February 26, 1936, Incident in the context of fascism is Hori Makiyo, *Nishida Mitsugi to Nihon Fashizumu Undō* (Tokyo: Iwanami, 2007).

3. An overview of fascist movements around the world can be found in Stanley G. Payne, *A History of Fascism, 1914–1945* (Madison: University of Wisconsin Press, 1995), 329–53. Recent works on fascism in China are Margaret Clinton, "Fascism, Cultural Revolution, and National Sovereignty in 1930s China" (New York University, 2009); Brian Kai Hin Tsui, "China's Forgotten Revolution: Radical Conservatism in Action, 1927–1949" (Columbia University, 2013).

4. One of the few exceptions is Richard Torrance, "The People's Library: The Spirit of Prose Literature versus Fascism," in *The Culture of Japanese Fascism*, ed. Alan Tansman (Durham, NC: Duke University Press, 2009), 74. Torrance precisely notes how widespread the term "fascism" was among left-wing writers, who used it to criticize repression of the Left and censorship. Another example is Miles Fletcher, *The Search for a New Order: Intellectuals and Fascism in Prewar Japan* (Chapel Hill: University of North Carolina Press, 1982). In Japanese, the recent work of Fuke Takahiro examines the debate on fascism among intellectuals: Fuke, *Nihon fashizumu ronsō: Taisen zenya no shisōka tachi* (Tokyo: Kawade Bukkusu, 2012), and *Senkanki Nihon no shakai shisō: "chōkokka" e no furontia* (Tokyo: Jinbun Shoin, 2010).

5. Carol Gluck discusses the *kokutai* in the context of late-nineteenth-century nation building; Gluck, *Japan's Modern Myths: Ideology in the Late Meiji Period* (Princeton, NJ: Princeton University Press, 1985). Konno Nobuyuki focuses on the function of the *kokutai* in the 1930s for the right-wing Pan-Asianist intellectual and Indologist Ōkawa Shūmei and

the historian Hiraizumi Kiyoshi; Konno, *Kindai Nihon no kokutairon: "Kōkoku shikan" saikō* (Tokyo: Perikan, 2008).

6. The economist Fukuda Tokuzō, an advocate of welfare economics, had studied with Lujo Brentano in Leipzig in 1899–1900; Tamotsu Nishizawa, "Lujo Brentano, Alfred Marshall, and Tokuzo Fukuda: The Reception and Transformation of the German Historical School in Japan," in *The German Historical School: The Historical and Ethical Approach to Economics*, ed. Yuichi Shionoya (London); Erich Pauer, *The Transfer of Technology between Germany and Japan from 1890 to 1945*, vol. 3 of *Japan and Germany: Two Latecomers to the World Stage, 1890–1945*, ed. Kudō Akira, Tajima Nobuo, and Erich Pauer, (Kent: Global Oriental, 2009), 466–510. Economic relations between Japan and Germany in the pre- and postwar periods have been examined by Kudō Akira; Kudō, *Nichi-Doku keizai kankeishi josetsu* (Tokyo: Sakurai Shoten, 2011).

7. Katō Tetsurō, "Personal Contacts in Japanese-German Cultural Relations during the 1920s and Early 1930s," in *Japanese-German Relations, 1895–1945: War, Diplomacy, and Public Opinion*, ed. Christian W. Spang and Rolf-Harald Wippich (London: Routledge, 2006). In 1929, 151 government-sponsored scholars studied in Germany as opposed to 34 in Great Britain and the United States and 29 in France.

8. Mimura, *Planning for Empire.*

9. Hijikata Seibi, *Fashizumu: shisō, undō, seisaku* (Tokyo: Iwanami, 1932), 253–54.

10. Particularly influential was Sombart's *Die Zukunft des Kapitalismus* (1932); Osamu Yanagisawa, "The Impact of German Economic Thought on Japanese Economists before World War II," in *The German Historical School: The Historical and Ethical Approach to Economics*, ed. Yuichi Shionoya (London: Routledge, 2001).

11. Mimura, *Planning for Empire*, 18–20, 36–39.

12. On Konoe's New Order Movement (*shintaisei undō*), see Yabe Teiji, "Konoe Fumimaro to shintaisei," in *Kindai Nihon o tsukutta hyakunin*, ed. Ōkōchi Kazuo and Ōya Sōichi (1965).

13. Fletcher, *Search for a New Order*, 53–57, 80–82, 120.

14. See, for example, a *Yomiuri shinbun* editorial entitled "The National Essence Party and the National Essence Association" (*kokusuitō to kokusuikai*), or the reference to Mussolini's 1922 cabinet as the "national essence cabinet" (*kokusui naikaku*): "Kokusuitō naikaku soshiki," *Yomiuri Shinbun*, November 1, 1922; "Kokusuitō to Kokusuikai," *Yomiuri shinbun*, October 31, 1922; ibid.

15. Fuke, *Nihon fashizumu ronsō*, 69–70, 72–75.

16. I use the term "national socialism" even though the literal translation of *kokkashugi* is "state socialism." This rendering reflects its proponents' emphasis on the state as an institution to solve economic and social problems. But the adherents of this ideology often translated *kokkashugi* as "national socialism," and contemporaries often remarked about the parallels with German National Socialism. For example, the title of the journal of this school of thought was *kokkashakaishugi*, which they translated as "national socialism."

17. Other examples of bibliographies on fascism are Gotō Toranosuke, *Fashizumu to wa nanika, fashizumu naigai bunken* (Tokyo: Rōnō Shobō, 1932); Toda Takeo, ed., *Fashizumu sankō bunken* (Tokyo: Tōkyō Shakai Kagaku Kenkyūjo, 1933). The political scientist Sassa Hiroo, who translated the philosopher H. W. Schneider's study on Fascism (1928), appended a lengthy and detailed bibliography of Japanese and foreign works relating to fascism; Sassa Hiroo and H. W. Schneider, *Fashizumu kokkagaku* (Tokyo: Chūō Kōronsha, 1934). For the Home Ministry's survey of fascism, see Naimushō keihōkyoku, ed., *Fashizumu no riron*, vol. 5, *Shuppan keisatsu kankei shiryō shūsei* (Tokyo: Fuji Shuppan, 1986 [1932]), 269–509.

18. Mussolini's inconclusive attempt to internationalize Fascism is the subject of Michael Ledeen, *Universal Fascism: The Theory and Practice of the Fascist International,*

1928–1936 (New York: H. Fertig, 1972). See also Luca De Caprariis, "'Fascism for Export'? The Rise and Eclipse of the Fasci Italiani all'Estero," *Journal of Modern History* 35, no. 2 (2000).

19. Ishikawa Sanshirō in "Fashizumu hihan," *Keizai no ōrai*, no. 11 (1927): 86.

20. The pamphlet published by the club stressed that "fascism, the hero of our times, is linked to the idea of a controlled economy; Nihon Kōgyō Kurabu Keizai Kenkyūkai, "Fassho Itari saikin no ugoki," *Keizai kenkyū sōsho* 19 (special edition; 1934): 1–2. As early as 1928, the Concordia Association (Kyōchōkai), a half-government half-industry–sponsored association tasked with harmonizing the relations between capital and labor, also conducted a study of Italy's agricultural labor contracts; Negishi Benji, *Itari no nōgyō ni okeru shūgōteki rōdō keiyaku* (Tokyo: Kyōchōkai Nōsonka, 1928).

21. Yoshino Sakuzō, "Fascism in Japan," *Contemporary Japan* 1, no. 1 (1932): 185.

22. Ibid.

23. Ibid.

24. Ibid., 185.

25. Ibid., 190–93.

26. Ibid., 193.

27. Ibid., 195.

28. Ibid., 185–86. Yoshino maintained some faith in Japan's political elites: "Fascism aims in theory at bringing democracy down to the ground, but it may well serve in practice, there and indeed elsewhere, to keep democratic politicians up to scratch"; ibid., 197.

29. Hasegawa Nyozekan, *Fashizumu hihan* (Tokyo: Ohata Shoten, 1932).

30. Ibid., 6–9, 26–29.

31. Ibid., 31. "Domestically the middle class did not feel the class anxieties of the development of the bourgeoisie and the rise of proletariat to such an intense degree"; ibid., 131.

32. Ibid., 46–47.

33. Ibid., 28.

34. Ibid., 14–15.

35. Ibid., 18.

36. Ibid., 20.

37. Maruyama Masao, "Theory and Psychology of Ultra-Nationalism, "in *Thought and Behaviour in Modern Japanese Politics*, ed. Ivan Morris (Oxford: Oxford University Press, 1969). For a more detailed discussion of liberal debates on fascism, see Hori, *Nishida Mitsugi to Nihon Fashizumu undō*, 64–72.

38. Tosaka appreciated his liberal colleague for being a "mature English-style bourgeois materialist" but found that his refusal to "recognize the use of dialectics" limited his understanding of the class dynamics of fascism; Tosaka Jun, *Nihon ideorogiiron* (Tokyo: Iwanami, 1977), 358–59.

39. Two studies that have taken seriously Tosaka's analysis of fascism are Naoki Sakai, "Imperial Nationalism and the Comparative Perspective," *Positions* 17, no. 1 (2008); Harry Harootunian, "The Black Cat in the Dark Room," *Positions* 13, no. 1 (2005). For an analytic overview of Tosaka's philosophy, see Harry Harootunian, "Time, Everydayness and the Specter of Fascism," in *Re-politicising the Kyoto School as Philosophy*, ed. Christopher Goto-Jones (London: Routledge, 2008).

40. Tosaka, *Nihon ideorogiiron*, 26–27, 134–35, 146–47.

41. Ibid., 18–20, 25–26, 29–30.

42. Ibid., 413.

43. Ibid., 420.

44. Ibid., 27. See also Harootunian, "The Black Cat in the Dark Room," 146–47.

45. Hiranuma Kiichirō, "Nihon no kakushin undō," *Kaizō* 14, no. 6 (1932): 94–95.

46. H. D. Harootunian and Tetsuo Najita, "Japan's Revolt against the West," in *Modern Japanese Thought*, ed. Bob Tadashi Wakabayashi (Cambridge: Cambridge University Press, 1999).

47. *Yomiuri shinbun*, May 25, 1933.

48. He had probably begun these works while still in Rome. See Shimoi Harukichi, *Fashizumu no shintai to Itari no sangyō tōsei*, ed. Katō Etsuzan (Osaka: Osaka Tosho Kabushikigaisha, 1933); *Ikoku no sangyō seisaku to rōdō kensho* (Tokyo: Kantō Sangyō Dantai Rengōkai, 1933); *Fassho undō to Itari no nōson shinkō seisaku ni tsuite* (Tokyo: Nagano kenjin Tokyo Rengōkai, 1933); and *Itari no kumiaisei kokka to nōgyō seisaku* (Tokyo: Dayamondosha, 1933). Three of these books were transcripts of talks Shimoi had given in various parts of the archipelago (one speech, exceeding one hundred pages, was delivered only a week after his arrival). But the fast pace of publication can also be explained by his parroting of Italian works. Shimoi, however, meticulously avoided literal translations of terms that might upset the censors. "Revolution," commonly used in Italian to refer to the "Fascist revolution," was rendered as "restoration," in line with the politically correct parlance of the day. Under corporatism, Shimoi argued, labor and capital had come to an agreement to set their differences aside for the sake of the state. In Italy the so-called Labor Charter (Carta del lavoro) sealed a historic arrangement that was "the greatest achievement of the Fascist restoration"; *Ikoku no sangyō seisaku to rōdō kensho*, 17.

49. Shimoi Harukichi, *Nekketsu netsuryū no daienzetsu* (Tokyo: Dai Nihon Yūbenkai Kōdansha, 1933), 130–32. *Kessoku* is also the literal translation of the Italian *fascio*.

50. SHPP. Shimoi probably met Banzai in 1932 or 1933 while the latter was visiting Italy as military attaché in Germany. Another business card found among Shimoi's papers is that of Nakano Fumi (1883–1966), the founder of a girls' school in Shiga.

51. Richard Smethurst examines the relationship between the military and the countryside in the 1930s; Smethurst, *A Social Basis for Prewar Japanese Militarism: The Army and the Rural Community* (Berkeley: University of California Press, 1974). Thomas R. H. Havens focuses on agrarianist thought (*nōhonshugi*); Havens, *Farm and Nation in Modern Japan: Agrarian Nationalism, 1870–1940* (Princeton, NJ: Princeton University Press, 1974).

52. The standard account of Ōmoto is Yoshio Yasumaru, *Deguchi Nao* (Tokyo: Asahi Shinbunsha, 1987). In English, see Emily Groszos Ooms, *Women and Millenarian Protest in Meiji Japan: Deguchi Nao and Ōmotokyō* (Ithaca, NY: Cornell University Press, 1993).

53. Nancy K. Stalker, *Prophet Motive: Deguchi Onisaburo, Oomoto, and the Rise of New Religions in Imperial Japan* (Honolulu: University of Hawai'i Press, 2008), 3, 12.

54. Ibid., 175–79.

55. On March 10, 1935, the Taiwan Nichi-nichi shinpō announced that Deguchi Onisaburō and his aide-de-camp, Shimoi Harukichi, had disembarked with its membership clad in khaki uniforms.

56. Ikeda Akira, ed., *Ōmoto shiryō shūsei*, vol. 3 (Tokyo: Sanichi Shobō, 1982–85), 470, 859.

57. Ibid., vol. 2, 759.

58. Ibid., vol. 2, 557. Another Shinseikai member declared that Fascism and Nazism had not reached the "great leadership principle of the imperial way [*kōdō*]" (ibid., 811). For other criticisms of fascism, see ibid., 583, 714.

59. Stalker, *Prophet Motive*, 184.

60. *Yomiuri shinbun*, January 18, 1932. See also Naoki Sanjūgo, *Fashizumu sengen sono ta*, vol. 14, *Naoki Sanjūgo zenshū* (Tokyo: Shijinsha, 1992), 121.

61. For a discussion of these authors, see Torrance, "People's Library."

62. The league's publications are lost.

63. An anonymous reviewer stated contemptuously that Naoki had many "joking sides" (*fuzaketa bunshi*) to him and that it was clearly difficult to tell how serious he was about fascism; "Bungei nōto," *Shinchō* 29, no. 3 (1932): 20.

64. *Yomiuri shinbun*, February 11 and 28, 1932.

65. See, for example, Nakamura Burafu et al., "Fassho to fashizumu bungaku ni tsuite," *Shinchō* 29, no. 4 (1932). This roundtable comprised twelve writers and journalists, including Tokuda Shūsei, Nii Itaru, Yoshikawa Eiji, Mikami Otokichi, and Murobuse Kōshin. Elsewhere, the philosopher and journalist Tsuchida Kyōson, an ex-liberal who had turned to the right in the 1930s, argued that there were no self-styled fascists in Japan, nor was there a reason for fascistization, but that there *was* a need for a debate on fascism; Tsuchida, "Fassho to bungaku," ibid., no. 3.

66. Nii Itaru, "Bungei jihyō," *Shinchō* 29, no. 3 (1932): 110–14.

67. Maedako Hiroichirō, "Fassho ryūkō," *Yomiuri shinbun*, March 8, 1932. See also Ōya Sōichi, "Gurando ruru no nai bundan (jō)," *Yomiuri shinbun*, March 27, 1932; "Gurando ruru no nai bundan (chū)," *Yomiuri shinbun*, March 29, 1932; and "Gurando ruru no nai bundan (ge)," *Yomiuri shinbun*, March 30, 1932.

68. "1934-nen no bungei dōkō zadankai," *Yomiuri shinbun*, January 9, 1934. The participants included Kikuchi Kan, Yamamoto Yūzō, Naoki Sanjūgo, Ishihama Tomoyuki, Nakamura Murao, Yokomitsu Riichi, Asahara Rokurō, Hayashi Fusao, Sugiyama Heisuke, and Fukada Kyūya.

69. Alan Tansman, *The Aesthetics of Japanese Fascism* (Berkeley: University of California Press, 2009).

70. Sakai, "Imperial Nationalism and the Comparative Perspective," 168.

71. Sugimori Kōjirō, *The Principles of the Moral Empire* (London: University of London Press, 1918), 6, 238–39.

72. Sugimori Kōjirō, "Fashizumu no bunseki oyobi hihan (1)," *Shakai seisaku jihō* 154 (1933): 118–20. Sugimori was pleased that this counterrevolutionary nationalism had emerged also in Japan: in this sense, he argued, "one has to recognize [fascism's] existence and development also in Japan"; Sugimori, "Fashizumu no bunseki oyobi hihan (2)," *Shakai seisaku jihō* 155 (1933): 110. He made the same claim in "Fuwasushizumu," *Kokuhon* 12, no. 3 (1932).

73. Sugimori, "Fashizumu no bunseki oyobi hihan (2)," 76–78.

74. Ibid., 80–81.

75. Richard Storry, *The Double Patriots, a Study of Japanese Nationalism* (Cambridge, MA: Riverside Press, 1957), 26.

76. Military-led groups are sometimes divided into the "imperial way" (*kōdō*) and "control" (*tōsei*) factions. The former tended to be comprised of young army and navy officers who favored direct, violent action against leading political and economic figures. The "control faction" included more senior officers, who were more inclined toward an organized, state-led reform of the institutions. The distinction, however, was often blurred, also because there was some significant crossover of individuals. For a discussion of these factions, see Maruyama Masao, "The Ideology and Dynamics of Japanese Fascism," in *Thought and Behaviour in Modern Japanese Politics*, ed. Ivan Morris (Oxford: Oxford University Press, 1969), 69–71. For a narrative of the factionalism, as well as the military and political intrigues of the early 1930s, see also James B. Crowley, *Japan's Quest for Autonomy: National Security and Foreign Policy, 1930–1938* (Princeton, NJ: Princeton University Press, 1966), 244–300.

77. For a critical overview of the right wing in the 1930s, see Tetsuo and Harootunian, "Japan's Revolt against the West."

78. The confrontation between Japanists and national socialists has also been analyzed in Fuke, *Senkanki Nihon no shakai shisō*, 251–321.

79. Kita was educated at the elite Waseda University and Harvard University. He had also spent time in France and Germany, where he had embraced Bergson's notions of élan vital. A hardened opponent of social science—this discipline could not possibly understand "the totality of life" (*seikatsu no zentai*)—he turned to philosophy as the only way to find an "immutability [*fuhensei*] that runs through the past, present, and future." For Kita, the spirit embodied in the people represented the fundamental "metahistorical" (*chōrekishiteki*) element in the life of the nation, and he therefore founded a society, the Sokokukai (Ancestral Land Association), to move from thought to action. He advocated restorationist politics: if the Meiji Restoration was a process from above, its Shōwa rehearsal would be "from below for above, from the many for the few, from the periphery to the center"; Kita Reikichi, "Sekai wa dō ugoku de arō ka," *Kaizō* 6, no. 1 (1924): 42–55.

Takabatake famously attempted a synthesis of Marxism and nationalism. After World War I he had authored the first Japanese translation of *Das Kapital*, before relinquishing socialist politics for *kokkashakaishugi*. For a discussion of Takabatake, see Germaine Hoston, "Marxism and National Socialism in Taishō Japan: The Thought of Takabatake Motoyuki," *Journal of Asian Studies* 44, no. 1 (1984).

80. Takabatake Motoyuki, *Mussorini to sono shisō* (Tokyo: Jitsugyō No Sekaisha, 1928), 107–9.

81. Takabatake Motoyuki, "Gokai sareta Mussorini," *Bungei shunjū*, no. 6 (1928): 16.

82. Takabatake Motoyuki, *Kokka shakaishugi daigi* (Tokyo: Nihon Shakaishugi Kenkyūjo, 1932), 1.

83. Kita Reikichi, *Fassho to kokka shakaishugi* (Tokyo: Nihon Shosō, 1937), 1.

84. Kita, *Fassho to kokka shakaishugi*, 152–53.

85. Kita Reikichi, *Shōwa ishin* (Tokyo: Sekai Bunkō Kankōkai, 1927), 39–40.

86. Takabatake, *Mussorini to sono shisō*, 91–92, 102–3.

87. The history of the term "totalitarianism" is the subject of Abbott Gleason, *Totalitarianism: The Inner History of the Cold War* (New York: Oxford University Press, 1995).

88. Fuke, *Nihon fashizumu ronsō*, 170–73; ibid.

89. On Kanokogi, see Christopher W. A. Szpilman, "Kanokogi Kazunobu: 'Imperial Asia,' 1937," in *Pan-Asianism: A Documentary History, Volume 2: 1920–Present*, ed. Sven Saaler and Christopher W. A. Szpilman (Lanham, MD: Rowman & Littlefield, 2011).

90. Nakatani Takeyo, "Fasushisuchi kokka no kokumin kyōiku (1)," *Kokuhon* 11, no. 4 (1931): 44–45.

91. Nakatani Takeyo, "Fasushisuchi kokka no kokumin kyōiku (2)," *Kokuhon* 11, no. 5 (1931): 48.

92. Nakatani Takeyo, "Fashizumu no honshitsu to sono kokka kannen," *Kokuhon* 12, no. 4 (1932): 21–23.

93. Tsukui Tatsuo, *Nihonshugi undō no riron to jissen* (Tokyo: Kensetsusha, 1935), 20–25.

94. Nakatani Takeyo, "Fashizumu yori kōdōshugi," *Kokuhon* 12, no. 11 (1932): 37–38.

95. Tosaka Jun, *Nihon ideorogiron* (Tokyo: Iwanami, 1977), 206.

96. Tansman, *Aesthetics of Japanese Fascism*, 152–53.

97. Japan, Ministry of Education, *Kokutai no hongi* (Tokyo: Nihon Tosho Senta, 2003), 1–7, 143–56. The translation is taken from "Fundamentals of Our National Polity (*Kokutai no hongi*)," in *Sources of Japanese Tradition*, ed. Theodore Wm. De Bary, Carol Gluck, and Arthur E. Tiedemann (New York: Columbia University Press, 2005 [1937]), 968–75. For a study of the language and aesthetics of *Kokutai no hongi*, see Tansman, *Aesthetics of Japanese Fascism*.

98. Murobuse Kōshin, *Fassho ka Marukusu ka* (Tokyo: Ichigensha, 1932), 183–84.

4. IMPERIAL CONVERGENCE: THE ITALO-ETHIOPIAN WAR AND JAPANESE WORLD-ORDER THINKING, 1935–1936

1. This is a revised version of an article that appeared in the *Journal of Contemporary History* in 2015.

2. Alexander De Grand argues that in 1935 the regime was at an "ideological dead-end." The corporatist experiment had failed, and Mussolini was feeling the competition from Nazi Germany. The more radical members of the regime, such as Giuseppe Bottai, found in the empire a way to reawaken a stalled revolution and toughen Italians; De Grand, "Mussolini's Follies: Fascism in Its Imperial and Racist Phase, 1935–1940," *Contemporary European History* 13, no. 2 (2004): 136–37. For a history of Italian imperialism, see Nicola Labanca, *Oltremare: Storia dell'espansione coloniale italiana* (Bologna: Il Mulino, 2002). For a study of the military and political elites in the lead-up to the Ethiopian war, see Giorgio Rochat, *Militari e politici nella preparazione della campagna d'Etiopia. Studio e documenti, 1932–1936* (Milan: Angeli, 1971). Davide Rodogno examines Fascist Italy's imperial policies in Europe and the Mediterranean; Rodogno, *Fascism's European Empire: Italian Occupation during the Second World War* (Cambridge: Cambridge University Press, 2006).

3. Protectionism was on the rise in these years, and the Fascist regime envisioned its colonies in Libya and East Africa as contributing to the goal of economic self-sufficiency, or "autarky." See Philip Morgan, "Corporatism and the Economic Order," in *The Oxford Handbook of Fascism*, ed. R. J. B. Bosworth (Oxford: Oxford University Press, 2010); Giovanni Federico, "Autarchia," in *Dizionario del Fascismo*, ed. Victoria de Grazia and Sergio Luzzatto (Turin: Einaudi, 2002). The émigré anti-Fascist Gaetano Salvemini weighed the usefulness of Ethiopia as a market and provider of raw materials in Salvemini, "Can Italy Live at Home?" *Foreign Affairs* 14, no. 2 (1936).

4. Sakai Tetsuya examines the transition from the post–World War I consent on internationalist foreign policy to propositions of a new international order; Sakai, *Kindai Nihon no kokusai chitsujoron* (Tokyo: Iwanami, 2007), 97–99, 103–5. See also Thomas W. Burkman, "Nitobe Inazō: From World Order to Regional Order," in *Culture and Identity: Japanese Intellectuals during the Interwar Years*, ed. J. Thomas Rimer (Princeton, NJ: Princeton University Press, 1990).

5. Prasenjit Duara, *Sovereignty and Authenticity: Manchukuo and the East Asian Modern* (Lanham, MD: Rowman & Littlefield, 2003), 9–40. Duara examines the intersection between nationalism and imperialism in the establishment of Manchukuo.

6. Furukawa Tetsushi has provided a critical examination of the pro-Ethiopian rhetoric in Japan, showing how it intermingled with a Japanese imperial mindset; Furukawa, "Japan and Ethiopia in the 1920s–30s: The Rise and Fall of 'Sentimental' Relations," *Ningen kankyōgaku* 8 (1999). For the most part, however, existing studies have read the Japanese response to the Italo-Ethiopian War in an anticolonial key. See Okakura Takashi, "1930 nendai no Nihon-Echiopia kankei: Echiopia sensō o chūshin ni," *Afurika kenkyū* 37, no. 12 (1990). Okakura also examined the anti-Western reaction among Japanese and Indian Pan-Asianists; Okakura, "Futatsu no Echiopia sensō to Nihon: Dai-Ajiashugisha o chūshin ni," *Tōyō kenkyū*, no. 122 (1996). Joseph Calvitt Clarke III proposes a similar argument, focusing on racial politics; Clarke, *Alliance of the Colored Peoples: Ethiopia and Japan before World War II* (Woodbridge, Suffolk: James Currey, 2011).

7. Not since Wilson's call for national self-determination had the colonized and semicolonized people around the world found a joint voice against imperial aggression. In India the war had so struck Gandhi that he ended his self-imposed silence, calling on the "Indian people to contribute to the Red Cross fund for Ethiopia" ("Datō Mussorini no koe. Botsuzen Indo ni okiru chinmoku yabutta Ganji shi," *Yomiuri shinbun*, July 27, 1935). In China, the fascist blue-shirts professed sympathy for Ethiopia, a weak nation at the mercy

of white imperialism; Margaret Clinton, "Fascism, Cultural Revolution, and National Sovereignty in 1930s China" (PhD diss., New York University, 2009). In Harlem, some twenty thousand African Americans were stirred to demonstrate against Italian imperialism; Clare Corbould, *Becoming African Americans: Black Public Life in Harlem, 1919–1939* (Cambridge, MA: Harvard University Press, 2009). See also Erez Manela, *The Wilsonian Moment: Self-Determination and the International Origins of Anticolonial Nationalism* (Oxford and New York: Oxford University Press, 2007).

8. Konoe made this point in a controversial article he published in 1918, "Reject the Anglo-American-Centered Peace"; Yoshitake Oka, *Konoe Fumimaro: A Political Biography* (Tokyo: University of Tokyo Press, 1992), 15. For Konoe's impression of the Versailles Peace Conference, see his own account. The prince was particularly irritated by the unwillingness of the Powers to grant Japan a foothold in China and by the question of racial equality; Konoe Fumimaro, *Ōbei kenbunki* (Tokyo: Chūō Kōronsha, 2006), 35–36, 136–37. Corradini and Pascoli advocated Italian expansion in Libya (1911), the poet famously calling on Italy, the "Great Proletarian," to "make a move."

9. For a discussion of the media's reaction to and role in the Japanese invasion of Manchuria, see Louise Young, *Japan's Total Empire: Manchuria and the Culture of Wartime Imperialism* (Berkeley: University of California Press, 1999), 55–113.

10. "Taigai mondai no kansatsuten," *Yomiuri shinbun*, September 26, 1935.

11. *Nihon gaikō bunsho* [Documents on Japanese Foreign Policy], *Shōwaki II*, 4 (Tokyo 1996), Hirota to Sato, December 4, 1935, 228–29.

12. *Yomiuri shinbun*, July 27, 1935. For Sugimura's role in the League, see Thomas W. Burkman, *Japan and the League of Nations: Empire and World Order, 1914–1938* (Honolulu: University of Hawai'i Press, 2008), esp. 179.

13. Commentators reminded people that this incident was in line with Mussolini's policy in East Asia: Rome opposed Japanese rights in China and sold weapons to Chiang Kai-shek, a policy that caused great irritation among Japanese leaders; Ashida Hitoshi, "Echiopia mondai o meguru kakkoku no dōkō," *Kokusei isshin ronsō* 8 (1935): 3–4.

14. Mussolini made immense war preparations. Nearly one million troops were mobilized for the invasion, strengthened by mechanized divisions and, crucially, the air force. Aerial bombardment played a central role in the Italian strategy: the fascists not only made use of it against military targets but indiscriminately bombed villages that were suspected of harboring resistance fighters, most notoriously using poison gas. See Angelo Del Boca, *I gas di Mussolini: Il fascismo e la guerra d'Etiopa* (Rome: Editori Riuniti, 1996).

15. *Yomiuri shinbun*, August 20, 1935.

16. Social management is the focus of Sheldon M. Garon, *Molding Japanese Minds: The State in Everyday Life* (Princeton, NJ: Princeton University Press, 1997).

17. *Yomiuri shinbun*, October 9, 1935.

18. Edamatsu Hideyuki, "Sensō to bokutachi," *Yomiuri shinbun*, October 20, 1935.

19. *Yomiuri shinbun*, August 6, 1935.

20. Though dated, Herbert Norman's study of right-wing societies and their leaders, such as Tōyama Mitsuru and Uchida Ryōhei, is still informative; Norman, "The Genyosha: A Study on the Origins of Japanese Imperialism," *Pacific Affairs* 17, no. 3 (1944).

21. Kokuryūkai, *I-E mondai to Echiopia jijō*, Echiopia mondai kondankai (Tokyo: Kokuryūkai Shuppan, 1935), 2. In a telegram, the Ethiopian foreign minister, Baltingheta Heroui, declared himself "touched" by Tōyama's commitment.

22. ASMAE, AP, Giappone, 1931–45, b. 10, conflitto Italia-Etiopia, 344, Scalise to War Minister (Mussolini), Tokyo, October 17, 1935.

23. "Echiopia e jūgun shigan," *Yomiuri shinbun*, August 6, 1935. For a hagiographic biography of Sasakawa, see Satō Seizaburō, *Sasakawa Ryoichi: A Life* (Norwalk, CT: Eastbridge, 2006).

24. ASMAE, AP, Giappone, 1931–45, b. 10, rapporti italo-giapponesi, 918/406, Auriti to Foreign Minister (Mussolini), Tokyo, November 7, 1935.

25. Naoko Shimazu, *Japan, Race, and Equality: The Racial Equality Proposal of 1919* (New York: Routledge, 1998), 13–37, 117–36. See also Noriko Kawamura, "Wilsonian Idealism and Japanese Claims at the Paris Peace Conference," *Pacific Historical Review* 66, no. 4 (1997).

26. The controversy over the London Naval Treaty is covered in James B. Crowley, *Japan's Quest for Autonomy: National Security and Foreign Policy, 1930–1938* (Princeton, NJ: Princeton University Press, 1966), 35–81. See also Kobayashi Tatsuo, "The London Naval Treaty, 1930," in *Japan Erupts: The London Naval Conference and the Manchurian Incident, 1928–1932*, ed. James William Morley (New York: Columbia University Press, 1984).

27. David John Lu, *Agony of Choice: Matsuoka Yōsuke and the Rise and Fall of the Japanese Empire, 1880–1946* (Lanham, MD: Lexington Books, 2002), 85.

28. Young, *Japan's Total Empire*, 115–80. Young, following John Dower, uses the term "go-fast imperialism" to refer to the accelerated drive toward expansion in the early 1930s. Thomas W. Burkman takes Japan's commitment to Wilsonianism more seriously, arguing that an old guard of internationalists such as Makino Nobuaki, Itō Myoji, Nitobe Inazō, and Ishii Kikujirō were dedicated to the League to the end; Burkman, *Japan and the League of Nations*, xi–xi, 46–50, 142–64.

29. *Gaikō jihō* (also known as *Revue Diplomatique*) was founded in 1898, and by the 1920s it had a readership that included academics and members of the educated public, making the bimonthly journal influential in both policy circles and public opinion.

30. "I-E mondai to Nihon (Sugimura taishi wa Ikoku ni riyō sareta)," *Gaikō jihō* 75, no. 736 (August 1, 1935): 4.

31. G. Bruce Strang, "Imperial Dreams: The Mussolini-Laval Accords of January 1935," *Historical Journal* 44, no. 3 (2001).

32. Matsuda Shōichi, "Ōshū kinjō no shoanken to kokusai renmei," *Gaikō jihō* 75, no. 737 (August 15, 1935): 13.

33. Ibid., 4.

34. Hori Makoto, "I-E funsō to kokusai seikyoku no dōkō," *Gaikō jihō* 737, no. 75 (August 15): 66.

35. Aoyama Kimihiko, "I-E funsō o meguru Ei-I no tachiba," *Gaikō jihō* 76, no. 743 (November 15): 96.

36. Kano Kizō, "I-E funsō no shinso," *Gaikō jihō* 75, no. 738 (September 1): 186.

37. Tachi Sakutarō, "I-E funsō to kokusaihō," *Kokusai chishiki* 15, no. 11 (1935): 8–9.

38. Ashida Hitoshi, "I-E funsō no kakudaisei," *Gaikō jihō* 76, no. 742 (November 1, 1935): 3–4.

39. Aoyama Kimihiko, "I-E funsō o meguru rekkyo no rigai kankei," *Gaikō jihō* 75, no. 739 (September 15): 54.

40. Baba Tsunego, "Seiji to dōtokusei," *Yomiuri shinbun*, July 7, 1935.

41. The *kokutai*, literally "the national body," referred to the spiritual and political structure of the Japanese state. In the 1920s constitutionalists argued that the emperor, though occupying a central position in the *kokutai*, was but an organ of the state. Although this interpretation had gained widespread acceptance, in the 1930s nationalists fought for a revision (or, as they called it, "clarification") that cast the emperor as a figure that transcended the state. The debates about this vision peaked in late 1935 and gradually replaced the earlier assumptions that had regarded the emperor as a constitutional monarch.

42. "Honnen no Nihon gaikō (jishu, jiritsu, jishin no kakuritsu)," *Gaikō jihō* 76, no. 745 (1935): 1–4. Kajima Morinosuke put it more poetically. For him, Japanese had rediscovered the principles of bushido (*gi*, duty). The morality of bushido, though, "transcended class and time" because it was a "universal value" that Japanese had to bring to Asia. See Kajima, "Bushidō no taishūka," *Kokusai chishiki* 15, no. 10 (1935): 64–66.

43. The role of military in the move toward autarky is discussed in Michael A. Barnhart, *Japan Prepares for Total War: The Search for Economic Security* (Ithaca, NY: Cornell University Press, 1987), 22–49, 64–76. Louise Young examines the interplay between army and business in the framing of Manchuria's economic development; Young, *Japan's Total Empire*, 183–240.

44. An example of managerial attempts to bring unions under control can be found in Andrew Gordon, *The Evolution of Labor Relations in Japan: Heavy Industry, 1853–1955* (Cambridge, MA: Harvard University Press, 1985), esp. 211–35.

45. Takafusa Nakamura, *Lectures on Modern Japanese Economic History* (Tokyo: LTCB International Library Foundation, 1994), 67–77. For a discussion of the new industrial conglomerates (new *zaibatsu*) and reform bureaucrats, see Janis Mimura, *Planning for Empire: Reform Bureaucrats and the Japanese Wartime State* (Ithaca, NY: Cornell University Press, 2011), 21–29. On the reform bureaucrats, see also Hashikawa Bunzō, "Kakushin kanryō," in *Kenryoku no shisō*, ed. Kamishima Jirō (Tokyo: Chikuma Shobō, 1965). Louise Young has examined the relationship between army and civilian planners in Manchuria; Young, *Japan's Total Empire*, 183–240. Ramon Hawley Myers outlines the economic protectionism and development policies that Japanese introduced in Manchuria and North China in what he calls an "enclave economy"; Myers, "Creating a Modern Enclave Economy: The Economic Integration of Japan, Manchuria, and North China, 1932–1945," in *The Japanese Wartime Empire, 1931–1945*, ed. Peter Duus et al. (Princeton, NJ: Princeton University Press, 1996).

46. Mark Metzler, *Lever of Empire: The International Gold Standard and the Crisis of Liberalism in Prewar Japan* (Berkeley: University of California Press, 2006), 240–42, 252–56.

47. Unno Yoshirō, "Dai-niji Itaria-Echiopia sensō to Nihon," *Hōsei riron* 16, no. 2 (1983): 188. According to Unno, between 1922 and 1926 Japanese exports more than doubled. By the early 1930s, Japan had almost a monopoly in the export of silk and rayon. See also Furukawa Tetsushi, "Kindai Nihon ni totte no Echiopia: Shōwa shoki ni okeru keizai kanshin to Heruy shisetsudan rainichi o chūshin ni," *Ōtani gakuhō* 86, no. 2 (2007): 2.

48. *Chūgai shōgyō shinbun*, "Echiopia," November 8–10, 1931.

49. "Japanese in Abyssinia, No Sign of Territorial Ambitions," *Cape Times*, January 4, 1935.

50. *Chūgai shōgyō shinbun*, "Echiopia."

51. Katsuta Teiji, "I-E kōsō to zaikai. Ōshū masu kuraushite, Nihon iyoiyo akarushi," *Yomiuri shinbun*, October 7, 1935.

52. *I-E mondai kakudai to kabushiki sōba no eikyō* (Tokyo: Daiyamondo 1935), "Preface."

53. Ibid., 73–98.

54. "Mussorini to jinken," *Yomiuri shinbun*, September 5, 1935.

55. Kajiwara Nakaji, "Fukakudai demo resei jisshitsu kai tsudsukan," *Ekonomisuto* 13, no. 31 (1935): 18.

56. "Jūshi subeki I-E funsō. Waga zaikai ni wa kō zairyō," *Osaka Asahi shinbun*, September 2, 1935. Other interlocutors included Ogizaka Yasoba, business manager at the platemaking section of Kawasaki Shipping; Sogame Moritsugu, managing director of Sumitomo Bank; Kawasaki Hisaichi, head of the Kobe branch of Japan Raw Silk (Nihon Kiito); and Yagi Seitarō, board member of Japan Cotton (Nihon Menka).

57. Educated at Tokyo Imperial University, Matsui had pursued an unremarkable career as a bureaucrat in the Home Ministry, where he was the director of the Resources Bureau (Shigenkyoku), before becoming governor of Osaka Prefecture and holding other administrative posts in the central government and industry groups—he was director (*riji*) of the Japanese Chamber of Commerce and Industry (1937). See Mimura, *Planning for Empire*, 20, 68.

58. Katsuta, "I-E kōsō to zaikai."

59. Iida Seizō, "Senji keiki mitōshi. Handōrai wa hisshi: Ōshū taisenji to no hikaku," *Yomiuri shinbun*, September 9, 1935.

60. Matsui Haruo, "Sekai no dōran to keizai Nihon no shinro: atarashiki tsūshō jiyū," *Yomiuri shinbun*, January 7, 1936.

61. Katsuta Teiji, "Shihonshugi no tessoku. Shokuminchi bunkatsu sen: I-E funsō ni odoru kabushiki," *Yomiuri shinbun*, September 9, 1935.

62. Takahashi Korekiyo, as quoted in "Ōbei shihon ni taikō Hokushi kaihatsu ni sonoeyo," *Tōkyō Nichinichi shinbun*, September 4, 1935. Richard J. Smethurst absolves Takahashi of collusion with "militarism," suggesting that his budgets merely allowed "the military to fund the conquest of Manchuria and thus to take a preliminary step toward militarism and total war." The point, however, is precisely to show that the central idea that moved the erstwhile liberal was not "militarism" but a notion of political economy based on empire; Smethurst, *From Foot Soldier to Finance Minister. Takahashi Korekiyo: Japan's Keynes* (Cambridge, MA: Harvard University Press, 2007), 268–70.

63. Takeuchi Kenji, "I-E sensō no eikyō ikan. Kono kikai ni tekkō kokuze o kakuritsu seyo," *Ekonomisuto* 13, no. 30 (1935): 21.

64. Nogami Yaeko, "Shō ojisan," *Yomiuri shinbun*, December 11, 1935.

65. Baba Tsunego, "Seiji to dōtokusei," *Yomiuri shinbun*, July 7, 1935.

66. Tsurumi Yūsuke and Komai Jūji, *Fūun no rutsubo no Echiopia!* (Tokyo: Yashima Shobō, 1935), 19–20, 39–40, 47–49, 54.

67. Kanezaki Ken, "I-E funsō kara hoku-shi kōsaku," *Gaikō jihō* 743, no. 76 (November 1, 1935): 35–36, 37.

68. Ashida Hitoshi, "I-E funsō no kakudaisei," *Gaikō jihō* 76, no. 742 (November 1): 5–6.

69. For the response of a Pan-Asianist group to the Italo-Ethiopian War, see Okakura, "Futatsu no Echiopia sensō to Nihon," 14–21.

70. Kita Reikichi, "Echiopia mondai to Nihon," *Keizai ōrai* 10, no. 9 (1935): 91.

71. ASMAE, AP, Giappone, 1931–45, b.10, rapporti politici, Relazione sulla propaganda svolta in Giappone dal 1 ottobre al 24 dicembre 1935.

72. Stefan Tanaka, *Japan's Orient: Rendering Pasts into History* (Berkeley: University of California Press, 1993).

73. Masamune Hakuchō, "Korai no bunka," *Yomiuri shinbun*, June 6, 1936.

74. Uramoto Secchō, "Minzoku seibutsuryoku to minzoku jumyō,"*Yomiuri shinbun*, October 27, 1935.

75. Mutō Naoyoshi, *Sekai dōran no dōka-sen I-E no sono go?* (Tokyo: Tō-A Shobō, 1936), 17, 49.

76. Katakura Tōjirō, *Nihon wa Itaria o shiji shite Ei-Bei no appaku ni sonoeyo* (Tokyo: Konnichi No Mondaisha, 1935), 11–12. Another anti-Ethiopian cliché was the argument, dear to Italian Fascist propaganda, that Ethiopia was a backward country that still practiced slavery; *Kore ga Echiopia da: dorei monogatari* (Tokyo: Okuchōsha, 1935).

77. Furukawa, "Japan and Ethiopia in the 1920s–30s," 140.

78. SMEUS, H3, b.5, forniture militari, f. 2, Scalise-Ministero Guerra, telegram 389 Scalise-Ministero Guerra, December 3, 1935. The military dispatched Hattori Takushirō, a rising star in the army, to observe the war operations. Hattori's diary can be found in the National Institute for Defense Studies in Tokyo (*Nisshi kaisō* 658). Hattori spent almost six months in Ethiopia, observing operations from the Ethiopian side. He commented that aerial bombardment was the order of the day and that the greatest weakness of the Ethiopians was not having an air force (December 1).

79. SMEUS, H3, b. 5, forniture militari, f. 2, Scalise-Ministero Guerra, prot. 303, 4 settembre 1935.

80. Kajima Morinosuke, "Shinsei naru rikoshugi (*sacro egoismo*) (naniga Ōshū kokumin o sensō ni mukawashimen to suru ka)," *Gaikō jihō* 76, no. 740 (October 15, 1935): 100–101.

81. "I-E funsō no jitsubutsu kyōkun (hattenteki minzoku ni wa ryōdo ga hitsuyō da)," *Gaikō jihō* 76, no. 742 (November 1, 1935): 1–4.

82. Murobuse Kōshin, "Rokujūnen o okuru," *Yomiuri shinbun*, December 29, 1936; Murobuse Kōshin, "I-E sen to sekaisen," *Yomiuri shinbun*, October 8, 1935.

83. The Kyoto School was a philosophical movement based at Kyoto Imperial University that during the war years sought to lay the metaphysical foundations for Japan's empire and its new order. The members of this group—leading philosophers and literary critics—strove to go beyond the strictures of the Western modern and to define Japan's role in bringing about a world-historical change. They convened at two symposia in July 1942, one known as the "Overcoming modernity" symposium and the other as "The World-Historical Position and Japan" symposium. For a discussion, see Harry Harootunian, *Overcome by Modernity: History, Culture, and Community in Interwar Japan* (Princeton, NJ: Princeton University Press, 2000).

84. Mark Mazower, *Governing the World: The History of an Idea* (New York: Penguin, 2012), 166–67.

85. ASMAE, AP, Giappone, 1931–45, b. 10, rapporti italo-giapponesi, 918/406, Auriti to Minister of Foreign Affairs (Mussolini), November 7, 1935.

86. Karl Polanyi, *The Great Transformation: The Political and Economic Origins of Our Time* (Boston: Beacon Press, 2001), 30.

87. Tagawa Daikichirō, "Nichi-Doku-I to Ei-Futsu-Bei," *Kokusai chishiki* 15, no. 10 (1935): 41–42. See also Tagawa, "Nichi-Doku-I to Ei-Futsu-Bei," *Kokusai chishiki* 15, no. 11 (1935).

88. Konoe was inspired by some declarations made by Colonel Edward M. House, an American diplomat, whose stance he mistook as pro-Japanese; Konoe Fumimarō, "Kokusai heiwa no konpon mondai," in *Kenryoku no shisō*, ed. Kamishima Jirō, Gendai Nihon shisō taikei, vol. 10 (Tokyo: Chikuma Shobō, 1965), 312. See also Kazuo Yagami, *Konoe Fumimaro and the Failure of Peace in Japan, 1937–1941: A Critical Appraisal of the Three-Time Prime Minister* (Jefferson, NC: McFarland, 2006), 31.

89. Mark Mazower, *Hitler's Empire: How the Nazis Ruled Europe* (New York: Penguin, 2008), 580–81.

5. FASCISM IN WORLD HISTORY, 1937–1943

1. "The Tripartite Alliance of Germany, Italy, and Japan and Accompanying Notes, September 27, 1940," in *Deterrent Diplomacy: Japan, Germany, and the USSR, 1935–1940*, ed. James William Morley (New York: Columbia University Press, 1976).

2. The tortuous decision-making process, often pushed forth by midlevel bureaucrats and diplomatic personnel, is described in Hosoya Chihiro, "The Tripartite Pact, 1939–1940," in *Deterrent Diplomacy: Japan, Germany, and the USSR, 1935–1940*, ed. James William Morley (New York: Columbia University Press, 1976), 191–257. Germany's perspectives can be found in Ernst Leopold Presseisen, *Germany and Japan: A Study in Totalitarian Diplomacy, 1933–1941* (The Hague: M. Nijhoff, 1958); Theo Sommer, *Deutschland und Japan zwischen den Mächten, 1935–1940. Vom antikominternpakt zum Dreimächtepakt: Eine Studie zur diplomatischen Vorgeschichte des Zweiten Weltkriegs* (Tübingen: Mohr, 1962); Bernd Martin, *Deutschland und Japan im Zweiten Weltkrieg. Vom Angriff auf Pearl Harbor bis z. dt. Kapitulation* (Göttingen, Zürich: Musterschmidt, 1969), issued also as a thesis, Marburg, 1967. For a comparative study of the Japanese and German wartime empires, see L. H. Gann, "Reflections on the Japanese and German Empires of World War II," in *The Japanese*

Wartime Empire, 1931–1945, ed. Peter Duus et al. (Princeton, NJ: Princeton University Press, 1996). Italy's foreign policy toward Japan can be found in Valdo Ferretti, *Il Giappone e la politica estera italiana* (Rome: Giuffrè, 1983).

3. Mark Mazower, *Hitler's Empire: How the Nazis Ruled Europe* (New York: Penguin, 2008), 580–81.

4. Masaki Minagawa, *Konoe shintaisei no shisō to seiji: Jiyūshugi kokufuku no jidai* (Tokyo: Yūshisha, 2009).

5. The policies and thought behind the Greater East Asian Co-Prosperity Sphere can be found in Joyce C. Lebra, *Japan's Greater East Asia Co-Prosperity Sphere in World War II: Selected Readings and Documents* (Kuala Lumpur: Oxford University Press, 1975). Walter Skya examines the religious dimensions in Japanese politics and imperialism; Skya, *Japan's Holy War: Ideology of Radical Shintō Ultranationalism* (Durham, NC: Duke University Press, 2009).

6. Harry Harootunian, *Overcome by Modernity: History, Culture, and Community in Interwar Japan* (Princeton, NJ: Princeton University Press, 2000).

7. Konoe Fumimaro Papers (Yomei Bunkō), *Kokusaku ni tsuite no josōbun* [Imperial conference on national policy] Konoe Fumimaro, July 1940, 188–89.

8. For the rapid degeneration of ordinary life in wartime Japan, see Thomas R. H. Havens, *Valley of Darkness: The Japanese People and World War Two* (New York: Norton, 1978).

9. Kenneth J. Ruoff, *Imperial Japan at Its Zenith: The Wartime Celebration of the Empire's 2,600th Anniversary* (Ithaca, NY: Cornell University Press, 2010), 18. The wide-ranging and multifaceted propaganda efforts of the Japanese state are examined in Barak Kushner, *The Thought War: Japanese Imperial Propaganda* (Honolulu: University of Hawai'i Press, 2007).

10. During this period, the Japanese Foreign Ministry periodically conducted surveys of Fascist Italy's economy, legal system, agriculture, and foreign affairs. See Gaimushō, "Nichi-Doku-I no bōkyōtei: Itari dattai to renmei," *Shūhō* 63, no. 12.29 (1937); *Nichi-Doku-I sankoku bōkyōtei ni tsuite* (Tokyo: Gaimushō Jōhōbu, 1937); *Nichi-Doku-I kokubō kyōtei ni tsuite* (Tokyo: Gaimushō Jōhōbu, 1937); *Bōkyō Doku-I no Yudayajin mondai*, vol. 4, *Bōkyō kyōteikoku kokujō chōsa* (Tokyo: Gaimushō Chōsabu, 1938); *Itari no keizai kikō to gensei (zenpen)*, vol. 1, *Bōkyō kyōteikoku kokujō chōsa* (Tokyo: Gaimushō Chōsabu, 1938); *Nachisu oyobi Fashisuto no kokka kan* (Tokyo: Nihon Kokusai Kyōkai, 1939); *Fashisuto Itari no seiji soshiki to sono unyō narabini hantaiha seiryoku*, vol. 13, *Bōkyō kyōteikoku kokujō chōsa* (Tokyo: Gaimushō Chōsabu, 1939); *I sansen ori sankoku jōyaku seiritsu*, Taisen gaikō dokuhon (Tokyo: Gaimushō Jōhōkyoku Daisanbu, 1940); *Itari fassho kumiai giin seido* (Tokyo: Gaimushō Chōsabu, 1940); *Sengo no Ōshū keizai kyōchō ni kansuru Doku-I ryōgoku no keikakuan* (Tokyo: Gaimushō Chōsabu, 1941); *Itari no shokuryō mondai* (Tokyo: Gaimushō Chōsabu, 1942).

11. Kawai Tatsuo, *Nichi-Doku-I sangoku bōkyō kyōtei ni tsuite* (Tokyo: Gaimushō Jōhōbu, 1937), 10–11. For anticommunism as an element in Japanese foreign policy since the Manchurian Incident, see Sakai Tetsuya, "The Soviet Factor in Japanese Foreign Policy, 1928–1937," in *Imperial Japan and the World, 1931–1945*, ed. Antony Best (London: Routledge, 2010 [1988]).

12. ASMAE, AP, Giappone, 1931–45, b. 13, rapporti Italian-giapponesi, telegram 448 PR/107, May 9, 1936.

13. Ferretti, *Il Giappone e la politica estera italiana*, 121. Hirota Kōki, the foreign minister, welcomed the scenario of an understanding between Japan and Italy, two powers that had left the League of Nations. He received the emperor's approval, yet on condition that such an agreement must not damage Japan's relations with Great Britain. From that moment, according to Ferretti, Japanese diplomacy set out to formulate a policy that would balance good relations with Britain and a rapprochement with Italy.

14. Italy, like Germany, was involved in training the Chinese Nationalists under Chiang Kai-shek. Japan objected in particular to Italian weapon sales. The Italian foreign minister, Count Galeazzo Ciano, had served as consul in Shanghai (1930–1933) with his wife Edda, Mussolini's daughter. In China Ciano is said to have forged a friendship with Zhang Xueliang, the Manchurian warlord whose father had been assassinated by the Japanese. Zhang's antipathy toward Japan seems to have influenced Ciano. It was only with the Japanese invasion of China on July 7, 1937, that Ciano was won over to a pro-Japanese foreign policy.

15. Hashikawa Bunzō, "Nachisu shisō no shintō to sankoku dōmei," in *Kindai Nihon shisōshi no kiso chishiki*, ed. Hashikawa Bunzō, Kano Masanao, and Hiraoka Toshio (Tokyo: Yūhikaku, 1971), 395–97.

16. Louise Young, *Japan's Total Empire: Manchuria and the Culture of Wartime Imperialism* (Berkeley: University of California Press, 1999), 55–114.

17. ACS, SPD, CO, 195.044, Kimpaci Miyamoto.

18. ACS, SPD, CO, 191.772, Giappone, Cantiere di Amama, società anonima.

19. *Yomiuri shinbun*, January 29, 1938. On January 23, 1938, a girls' school in Shibuya had also readied a batch of dolls to be delivered to the two dictators (*Yomiuri shinbun*, January 23, 1938).

20. ACS, SPD, CO, 184.057, Giappone, Patto Tripartito Anticomunista.

21. The documentary (*Missione del Partito Nazionale Fascista nel Giappone*, 1938) is available online through the archive of the Istituto Luce. A copy is also hosted at NARA, Record Group 242: National Archives Collection of Foreign Records Seized, 1675–1958, ARC 43829 / 242-MID-2819. Ruth Ben-Ghiat has examined the role of cinematography in the making of Fascist culture; Ben-Ghiat, *Fascist Modernities: Italy, 1922–1945* (Berkeley: University of California Press, 2001), 131–34 (for the activities of the Istituto Luce).

22. *Japan Times*, April 13, 1938. The role of department stores in showcasing current affairs and cultural trends has been examined in Louise Young, "Marketing the Modern: Department Stores, Consumer Culture, and the New Middle Class in Interwar Japan," *International Labor and Working-Class History* 55 (1999); Kim Brandt, *Kingdom of Beauty: Mingei and the Politics of Folk Art in Imperial Japan* (Durham, NC: Duke University Press, 2007).

23. "Yomiuri shinbun chokugen," *Yomiuri shinbun*, March 18, 1938.

24. Ibid., March 21, 1938.

25. Ibid., April 3, 1938.

26. ASMAE, AP, Giappone, 1931–45, b. 18, rapporti Italian-giapponesi. Undated text (but probably November 1937) of an article by the Stefani news agency.

27. Interview with *Nichi-nichi shinbun*, November 17, 1937, as translated in Italian in ASMAE, AP, Giappone, 1931–45, b. 18, rapporti Italian-giapponesi, "L'amicizia oltre il 'patto.'"

28. Nakano was the charismatic leader of the Society of the East (Tōhōkai). His members mimicked European fascist practices and paraphernalia such as black shirts and rallies and won eleven seats in the Diet in 1937. Nakano sat on the board of directors of the Imperial Rule Assistance Association, but he failed to give it a more marked Fascist or Nazi imprint. See Ben-Ami Shillony, *Politics and Culture in Wartime Japan* (New York: Oxford University Press, 1981), 22–23.

29. ASMAE, AP, Giappone, 1931–45, b. 18, rapporti Italian-giapponesi, telegram n.469, Auriti to Ministry of Foreign Affairs, November 21, 1937.

30. Chichibu had contacts with Tōyama Mitsuru. Kita Ikki gave the prince a copy of the infamous "Plan for the Fundamental Reorganization of Japan"; Herbert P. Bix, *Hirohito and the Making of Modern Japan* (New York: Harper Collins, 2000), 100–101. Chichibu was

also close to rebels in the army. See David Bergamini, *Japan's Imperial Conspiracy* (New York: William Morrow, 1972), 680.

31. ASMAE, AP, Giappone, 1931–45, b.18, rapporti Italian-giapponesi, telegrams 198 and 220, Auriti to Ministry of Foreign Affairs, March 19 and 25, 1938.

32. ASMAE, AP, Giappone, 1931–45, b.18, rapporti Italian-giapponesi, letter Sakai to Mussolini, Berlin, January 1938.

33. *Itaria no tomonokai kaisoku* (Tokyo: Itaria No Tomonokai, 1941), 19–20, 27–31.

34. MCP, Gab., b.1, Case Salesiane del Giappone, presidente Istituto Nazionale Luce to Dino Alfieri, October 31, 1938. In 1935 a request for funds to pay local Japanese for propaganda activities met the resistance of the Italian government organ in charge of these matters, the Ministry of Popular Culture—the costs were excessive; ACS, MCP, reports, b. 12, f. 119, Auriti-Stampa, October 5, 1935. Later Dino Alfieri, the deputy secretary for press and propaganda, authorized the modest sum of five thousand lire "for an experimental organization of a press service in Japan for the period of two months"; ibid., Lettera Riservata, Alfieri-Italian Embassy, Tokyo (October 16, 1935).

35. Ardemagni was from Cremona, the fiefdom of Roberto Farinacci, a die-hard fascist whose squads were infamous for their brutality. Ardemagni claimed to have participated in the 1919 "punitive expeditions" against "subversives." Later, when working for the regime's official mouthpiece, the *Popolo d'Italia*, he seemingly became close with the newspaper's director, Mussolini's brother Arnaldo. Ardemagni was also a keen traveler, publishing books about his trips to Latin America and Italian-held Africa. One reason behind his dispatch to Tokyo was that he earned himself a reputation as a troublemaker. The file on Ardemagni can be found in ACS, MCP, Gabinetto, Secondo versamento, b.1, Ardemagni Mirko. An account of early Fascism and *squadrismo* can be found in Paul Corner, *Fascism in Ferrara, 1915–1925* (London: Oxford University Press, 1975).

36. *Itaria no tomonokai kaisoku.*

37. For a discussion of the Tripartite alliance at the highest levels, see Japan Imperial Japanese Army General Staff Office, *Sugiyama memo*, vol. 1 (Tokyo: Hara Shobō, 1989), 27–55.

38. *Itaria no tomonokai kaisoku*, 20.

39. Tokutomi Sohō, "Wareware wa Itaria o aisu," *Itaria*, no. 10 (1941): 22.

40. Shiratori Toshio, "Sangoku dōmei to shinsekai," *Itaria*, no. 4: 50–52.

41. Wada Kojirō, "Fashizumu no kokka kan," *Itaria*, no. 12: 27.

42. Ueda Tatsunosuke, "Sekai shinchitsujo to kumiai kokkasei," *Itaria*, no. 6 (1942): 14, 19.

43. Kamei Katsuichirō, "Itari e no yume," *Itaria*, no. 10: 119.

44. Kiyosawa's critical stance over the wartime state can be found in his diary; Kiyosawa Kiyoshi, *A Diary of Darkness: The Wartime Diary of Kiyosawa Kiyoshi*, trans. Eugene Soviak (Princeton, NJ: Princeton University Press, 1999).

45. "Kaisō no Itaria: sono geijutsu to seiji," *Itaria*, no. 4 (1941): 91. Kiyosawa had already vacationed in Italy in 1930.

46. Saitō Mōkichi, "Fumetsu," *Itaria*, no. 3 (1942): 54–55.

47. Harootunian, *Overcome by Modernity*.

48. For the discourse on culture in Fascist Italy and Nazi Germany, see Benjamin G. Martin, "A New Order for European Culture: The German-Italian Axis and the Reordering of International Cultural Exchange, 1936–1943" (PhD diss., Columbia University, 2006). For an examination of how writers envisaged reforming European culture, see Martin's "European Literature in the Nazi New Order: The Cultural Politics of the European Writers' Union, 1941–3," *Journal of Contemporary History* 48, no. 3 (2013). Naoki Sakai has discussed the philosopher Watsuji Tetsurō's quest for authenticity, showing how the positionality between East and West was central to his thought; Sakai, "Return to the West/

Return to the East: Watsuji Tetsuro's Anthropology and Discussions of Authenticity," *Boundary 2* 18, no. 3 (1991).

49. For a history of the *Nichi-I kyōkai*, see Reto Hofmann, "The Fascist Reflection: Japan and Italy, 1919–1950" (PhD diss., Columbia University, 2010), 269–77.

50. ACS, MCP, reports, b.12, f.119 prop 39–43, "Relazione sulla situazione giapponese," 7350.A.10 G.G, Rome, October 21, 1939.

51. Morita Tetsurō, in Nichi-I Kyōkai, *Nichi-I kyōkaishi* (Tokyo: Nichi-I Kyōkai, 1993), 21–22.

52. Simonetta Falasca-Zamponi, *Fascist Spectacle: The Aesthetics of Power in Mussolini's Italy* (Berkeley: University of California Press, 1997); Emilio Gentile, *The Sacralization of Politics in Fascist Italy* (Cambridge, MA: Harvard University Press, 1996). See also Romke Visser, "Fascist Doctrine and the Cult of Romanità," *Journal of Contemporary History* 27, no. 1 (1992).

53. Dan Inō, "'Nichi-I bunka kenkyū' zōkan no ji," in Nichi-I Kyōkai, *Nichi-I kyōkaishi*, 252–53.

54. Ōrui Noboru, "Runessansuteki ningen," *Nichi-I bunka kenkyū* 6 (1942): 84.

55. Kamo Giichi, "Runessansu no kagaku ni tsuite," *Nichi-I bunka kenkyū* 3 (1941): 85, 89–90.

56. Niizeki Ryōzō, "Kinsei engekishi ni okeru Itaria engeki," *Nichi-I bunka kenkyū* 5 (1942): 35–36.

57. Nishiwaki Junzaburō, "Itari bunka," *Nichi-I bunka kenkyū* 5, 14–16.

58. Hani Gorō, "Gioconda no hohoemi," *Nichi-I bunka kenkyū* 8 (1942): 61. Hani argued against the hagiographical reading of the Renaissance as a high point in Italian national history. Rather, he stated that the Renaissance developed qualities that were universal. The Italian states of this period achieved their greatness not through force (*buryoku*) but through culture (*bunka*)—a subtle criticism of Japanese imperialism. For a closer examination of Hani's article, see Hofmann, "The Fascist Reflection," 287–89.

59. Martin, "New Order for European Culture."

60. The literature on the Kyoto School of Philosophy and the "Overcoming the Modern" symposium is vast. See, for example, Harootunian, *Overcome by Modernity*; Naoki Sakai and Isomae Jun'ichi, eds., *"Kindai no chōkoku" to Kyōto gakuha: kindaisei, teikoku, fuhensei* (Tokyo: Ibunsha, 2010). See also the essays in Christopher Goto-Jones, ed., *Re-politicising the Kyoto School as Philosophy* (London: Routledge, 2008). For the relationship between Zen and the Kyoto School, see the essays in James W. Heisig and John C. Maraldo, eds., *Rude Awakenings: Zen, the Kyoto School, and the Question of Nationalism* (Honolulu: University of Hawai'i Press, 1995). On the Romantic School, see Kevin Michael Doak, *Dreams of Difference: The Japan Romantic School and the Crisis of Modernity* (Berkeley: University of California Press, 1994).

61. The career and writings of Kobayashi Hideo are the subject of James Dorsey, *Critical Aesthetics: Kobayashi Hideo, Modernity, and Wartime Japan* (Cambridge, MA: Harvard University Press, 2009). Paul Anderer provides an introductory essay on Kobayashi, followed by translations of seminal texts; Anderer, *Literature of the Lost Home: Kobayashi Hideo—Literary Criticism, 1927–1939* (Stanford, CA: Stanford University Press, 1995).

62. Kobayashi Hideo, "Kodai Roma no bunka izan," *Nichi-I bunka kenkyū*, no. 5 (1942): 62–63.

63. Ibid., 61.

64. Yoshimitsu Yoshihiko, "Sei Tomasu to Dante: Shinkyoku no shingaku ni tsuite," *Nichi-I bunka kenkyū*, no. 5 (1942): 76–77.

65. Yoshimitsu Yoshihiko, as quoted in Richard F. Calichman, ed., *Overcoming Modernity: Cultural Identity in Wartime Japan* (New York: Columbia University Press, 2008), 154, 156–58.

66. For a discussion on this symposium, see Harootunian, *Overcome by Modernity*, 42–43. He argues that this group focused to "explain the war within the broader context of the movement of world history, and to analyze what this meant for the Japanese state in a future world order once the Anglo-American alliance was destroyed."

67. Kosaka Masaaki et al., *Sekaishiteki tachiba to Nihon* (Tokyo: Chūō Kōronsha, 1942), 185–92.

68. Ibid., 194–97.

69. Ibid., 200–201.

70. Tōjō pronounced these words in the Diet in 1942. As quoted in Peter Duus, "Imperialism without Colonies: The Vision of a Greater East Asian Co-Prosperity Sphere," *Diplomacy and Statecraft* 7, no. 1 (1996): 64.

71. A basic account of Japanese conceptions of "Greater Asia" can be found in Tsurumi Shunsuke, *An Intellectual History of Wartime Japan, 1931–1945* (New York: KPI, 1986), 33–41.

72. Miwa Kimitada, "'Tōa shinchitsujo' sengen to 'daitōa kyōeiken' kōzō no dansō," in *Saikō taiheiyō sensō zenya: Nihon no 1930 nendairon to shite*, ed. Miwa Kimitada (Tokyo: Sōseki Sensho, 1981), 207–8. On Ishiwara, see Mark R. Peattie, *Ishiwara Kanji and Japan's Confrontation with the West* (Princeton, NJ: Princeton University Press, 1975). In the late 1930s Ishiwara notoriously theorized a "final war" between Japan and the Western powers; see Ishiwara Kanji, *Saishūsenron* (Tokyo: Keizai Ōraisha, 1978). For a study of the relationship between Pan-Asianism and fascism, including the thought of Ishiwara Kanji, see Matsuzawa Tetsunari, *Ajiashugi to fashizumu: Tennō teikokuron hihan* (Tokyo: Renga Shobō, 1979).

73. Duus, "Imperialism without Colonies," 297–98.

74. On Rōyama, see Miwa Kimitada, "'Tōa shinchitsujo' sengen to 'daitōa kyōeiken' kōzō no dansō," 236–39; Mitani Taichirō, *Taishō demokurashii ron: Yoshino Sakuzō no jidai to sono ato* (Tokyo: Tokyo Daigaku Shuppankai, 1995). On Haushofer, see Christian W. Spang, "Karl Haushofer Re-examined: Geopolitics as a Factor within Japanese-German Rapprochement in the Inter-War Years?" in *Japanese–German Relations, 1895–1945: War, Diplomacy and Public Opinion*, ed. Christian W. Spang and R. Wippich (London: Routledge, 2006).

75. Martin, "New Order for European Culture," 309–10.

76. Rōyama in Mitani, *Taishō demokurashii ron*, 254–56.

77. Martin, "New Order for European Culture," 2–4.

78. Kajima Morinosuke, "Dai-Tōa to Ōshū no shinchitsujo," in *Kajima Morinosuke gaikō ron senshū* (Tokyo: Kajima Kenkyūjo Shuppan, 1973 [1941]), 121.

79. Tosaka Jun, "Chūkanteki gaikō kaisetsu—Kajima, Radekku shi nado no ronbun," *Yomiuri shinbun*, February 27, 1936.

80. Mitani, *Taishō demokurashii ron*, 240–43.

81. Kajima Morinosuke, "Renmei no kaiso to pan-Europpa mondai," in *Kajima Morinosuke gaikōron senshū* (Tokyo: Kajima Kenkyūjo Shuppan, 1973 [1936]), 54, 60.

82. "Nichi-Doku-I bōkyō kyōtei no igi," *Chūō kōron* 52, no. 13 (1937): 172.

83. Takayanagi Kenzō, "Japan's View of the Struggle in the Far East," in *Imperial Japan and the World, 1931–1945*, ed. Anthony Best (London: Routledge, 2010 [1939]), 134.

84. Kajima, "Dai-Tōa to Ōshū no shinchitsujo," 122–27.

85. Kajima Morinosuke, "Doku-So sengo no kokusai jōsei," in *Sekai shinchitsujo o meguru gaikō: Dai-Tōa sensō to Dai-Tōa kyōeiken* (Tokyo: Kajima Kenkyūjo Shuppan, 1973 [1941]), 293–94. For Kajima's views on the Tripartite Pact, see Kajima, "Sekai no shinchitsujo to warera no shinro," in *Kajima Morinosuke gaikōron senshū* (Tokyo: Kajima Kenkyūjo Shuppan, 1973 [1940]).

86. "Mare naru gogaku no tensai. Fujisawa Chikao kun: Kokusaiteki shin shisōka," *Yomiuri shinbun*, May 16, 1920. In later years Fujisawa also published in Esperanto: Fujisawa Chikao, *Pri historia evoluado de moderna Japanujo: Kondukinta al la Renovigo de Imperiestra Regimo en 1868* (Fukuoka: Kyushu Imperial University, 1926).

87. Fujisawa Chikao, "Capitalism, Marxism, and the Japanese National Thoughts," *Annals of the Faculty of Law and Letters of the Kyushu Imperial University* 1, no. 3 (1928): 6.

88. Fujisawa Chikao, "Fashizumu no seiji tetsugaku ni tsuite," *Gaikō jihō*, no. 592 (1929): 16, 20, 24.

89. Fujisawa Chikao, "Sekaiteki nihonshugi e no yakushin," *Gaikō jihō*, no. 671 (November 15, 1932): 79.

90. Fujisawa Chikao, "Nihon seishin no gendaiteki igi," *Risō*, no. 415 (January 1934): 33–34.

91. Fujisawa Chikao, "Sekaiteki nihonshugi e no yakushin," 86.

92. Fujisawa Chikao, "Hittora to Ōdōshugi," *Gaikō jihō*, no. 681 (April 15, 1933).

93. Fujisawa Chikao, "Nichi-Doku bōkyō kyōtei to shisō kokusaku," *Gaikō jihō*, no. 787 (September 15, 1937): 61–63. He had expressed the same line in a three-part series in the daily *Yomiuru shinbun* ("Nichi-Doku bōkyō kyōtei shisōteki haikei," *Yomiuri shinbun*, December 10, 12, and 13, 1936).

94. Fujisawa cited one Fascist intellectual, Bruno Damiani, to show how Italians were shifting from the notion of "imperialism" to that of "empire"—two rather different things as far as Fujisawa was concerned, for the former was exploitative, the latter harmonizing. See Fujisawa Chikao, "Itaria no atarashiki kokusai rinen," *Nihon hyōron* 15, no. 5 (1940): 135–37.

95. For the background of Schmitt's article, see Mazower, *Hitler's Empire*, 577.

96. Mitani, *Taishō demokurashii ron*, 260–63.

97. Fujisawa Chikao, "Doku-I sūjiku no dōgisei," *Gaikō jihō*, no. 865 (December 15, 1940): 36–39.

98. Nishida Kitarō, "Sekai shinchitsujo no genri," http://www.aozora.gr.jp/cards/000182/files/3668_16431.html (accessed May 13, 2014).

99. Benoît Jacquet has examined the production of monuments such as that drafted by Tange in the context of the Overcoming Modernity debate; Jacquet, "Compromising Modernity: Japanese Monumentality during World War II," in *Front to Rear: Architecture and Planning during WWII* (New York University, Institute of Fine Arts, 2009). See also Jonathan M. Reynolds, *Maekawa Kunio and the Emergence of Japanese Modernist Architecture* (Berkeley: University of California Press, 2001), 126. Arata Isozaki has examined Tange's plan of the memorial for its meaning in the longer Japanese quest for Japan-ness in architecture; Arata, *Japan-ness in Architecture* (Cambridge, MA: MIT Press, 2006), 15–21.

EPILOGUE: FASCISM AFTER THE NEW WORLD ORDER, 1943–1952

1. Shimoi Harukichi, "Badorio gensui," *Jikyoku zasshi* 2, no. 7 (1943).

2. Tōjō Hideki, in Ito Takashi, Hirohashi Tadamitsu, and Katashima Norio, eds., *Tōjō Naikaku Sōri Daijin kimitsu kiroku: Tōjō Hideki Taishō genkōroku* (Tokyo: Tokyo Daigaku Shuppankai, 1990), 246.

3. *Yomiuri shinbun hōchi*, September 11, 1943.

4. ASMAE, AP, Giappone, 1931–45, b. 34, unnamed folder, report "Italiani in Estremo Oriente," Tokyo, November 1945. In 1948 an ex-internee claimed that by late 1945 they were on the verge of starvation, each having lost between fifteen and twenty kilos of weight (ibid., illegible name to Brusasca, undersecretary to the Ministry of Foreign Affairs, Pretoria, July 8, 1948). The postwar Italian government took the issue of the internment of its

citizens very seriously, requesting a Japanese apology and compensation before normalizing relations in 1952.

5. Luca Valente, *Il mistero della missione giapponese* (Rome: Cierre Edizioni, 2004).

6. Italian diplomats also considered the possibility of taking part in the Allied Treaty of Peace with Japan; ASMAE, AP, Giappone, 1931–45, b. 34, telespresso 24911/6, "Trattato di pace col Giappone," June 6, 1947.

7. William Henry Chamberlin, *Japan over Asia* (Boston: Little, Brown, 1937), 282, 286.

8. Hugh Byas, *The Japanese Enemy, His Power and His Vulnerability* (New York: Knopf, 1942), 97.

9. William C. Johnstone, "The Future of Japan," in *Ninth Conference of the Institute of Pacific Relations* (Hot Springs, VA: American Council Institute of Pacific Relations, 1945), 10.

10. Bruce Cumings, "Japan's Position in the World System," in *Postwar Japan as History*, ed. Andrew Gordon (Berkeley: University of California Press, 1993). Naoki Sakai makes a similar argument with regard to the relegitimation of the Kyoto School after the war; Sakai, "Resistance to Conclusion: The Kyoto School Philosophy under the Pax Americana," in *Re-Politicising the Kyoto School as Philosophy*, ed. Christopher Goto-Jones (London: Routledge, 2008).

11. In 1963, the German historian Ernst Nolte, for example, published a (controversial) book in which he espoused a theory about generic fascism, but by the mid-1970s he dropped the concept of fascism in favor of "totalitarianism." In Italy, Renzo De Felice argued that Fascism was a sui generis modernizing ideology that had nothing in common with Nazi Germany. See Ernst Nolte, *Three Faces of Fascism: Action Française, Italian Fascism, National Socialism* (New York: Holt, 1966); Renzo De Felice and Michael Arthur Ledeen, *Intervista sul fascismo* (Bari: Laterza, 1975). In the English-speaking world, representatives of this scholarship include Gilbert Allardyce and, for Japan, Peter Duus: Gilbert Allardyce, "What Fascism Is Not: Thoughts on the Deflation of a Concept," *American Historical Review* 84, no. 2 (1979); Peter Duus and Daniel Okimoto, "Fascism and the History of Pre-War Japan: The Failure of a Concept," *Journal of Asian Studies* 39 (1979): 65–76.

12. To be sure, postwar Marxists still used the term "fascism," but in a narrative of national pathology constituted by the emperor system. Hirai Kazuomi has noted how postwar Japanese Marxists and liberals, as well as the American understandings that underpinned the Tokyo War Crimes Tribunal, shared the assumption that the pathologically peculiar emperor system that was established in Meiji was responsible for what happened in the 1930s; Hirai, "Nihon fashizumu ron saikō," *Nihonshi kenkyū*, no. 576 (2010): 61–63. In this sense, Katō Yōko's observation that the transwar continuity in the Japanese interpretations of fascism is due to the "merits of social science" needs to be qualified. For although there were significant prewar contributions to the study of fascism, social science was also instrumental in reconverting the fascist critique of fascism into the postwar narratives of "ultranationalism" and "militarism." For Katō's survey of the debates on fascism, see Katō Yōko, "Fashizumu ron," *Nihon rekishi*, no. 9 (2006). The central role of social science and modernization theory in the "banishment" of fascism after World War II is discussed in Harry Harootunian, "The Black Cat in the Dark Room," *Positions* 13, no. 1 (2005): 137–38; and Harootunian, "The Imperial Present and the Second Coming of Fascism," *Boundary 2* 34, no. 1 (2007): 9–10.

13. Takashi Fujitani has written on the American wartime and postwar discussions to absolve the emperor from wartime responsibility, with a focus on the scholar and diplomat Edwin O. Reischauer; Fujitani, "The Reischauer Memo: Mr. Moto, Hirohito, and Japanese American Soldiers," *Critical Asian Studies* 33, no. 3 (2001).

14. After the war, Hatoyama went to great lengths to style himself as a long-standing believer in American-style liberal democracy. Accordingly, he took on board the Cold War nostrum of totalitarianism that cast fascism and communism as enemies of liberty.

See, for example, Hatoyama Ichirō, *Watakushi no shinjō* (Tokyo: Tōkyō bunkō, 1951), 105–13.

15. George B. Sansom, *Postwar Relations with Japan*, Tenth Conference of the Institute of Pacific Relations, Stratford-upon-Avon, England (London: The Royal Institute of International Affairs, 1947), 8. Sansom's contribution to this conference was a reissue of an earlier, wartime paper. Robert Craigie, the British ambassador to Japan from 1937 to 1942, also singled out the "primitive lust for power and dominion among a powerful section of Japan's warrior caste" as the driving force of Japanese politics. See Craigie, *Behind the Japanese Mask* (London and New York: Hutchinson, 1945), 162.

16. "Mizukara handō o kakunin. Jinmin no jikaku assatsu no tate," *Yomiuri shinbun*, February 23, 1946. The Marxist Okada Takeo, for example, published a book in the early postwar period in which he linked the history of prewar fascism to that of the "new fascism" of postwar Japan; Okada, *Fashizumu* (Tokyo: Gyōmeisha, 1949).

17. "Han fassho jinmin taikai," *Asahi shinbun*, August 12, 1948.

18. SHPP, scrap paper.

19. Indro Montanelli, *L'impero bonsai, cronaca di un viaggio in Giappone, 1951–2* (Milan: Rizzoli, 2007), 170.

20. Ibid.

21. Ibid., 168.

Bibliography

PRIVATE ARCHIVES

SHPP	Shimoi Harukichi Private Papers (Private collection, Tokyo)

PUBLIC ARCHIVES AND MANUSCRIPTS

Japan

BKJ	Bōei Kenkyūjo (National Institute for Defense Studies, Tokyo)
GGSK	Gaimushō Gaikō Shiryōkan (Diplomatic Record Office of the Ministry of Foreign Affairs of Japan, Tokyo)
KKK	Kokuritsu Kōbunshokan (National Archives of Japan, Tokyo)
Konoe Fumimarō	*Yōmei bunkō*. Microfilm. Tokyo: Waseda University Library
NHK	Shadan Hojin Nihon Hōsō Kyōkai (NHK Archives, Tokyo)
Ōkura Kishichirō	"Ōkura Kishichirō hasshin hikae." Tokyo: Waseda University Library, 1924–25
OSK	Ōkura Shūkokan (Archives of the Okura Museum of Art, Tokyo)

Italy

ACS	Archivio Centrale dello Stato (Government Archives, Rome)	
	CO	Carteggio Ordinario
	CS	Carteggio Riservato
	DGP	Divisione Generale Propaganda, n.u.p.i.e
	DGPS	Divisione Generale Pubblica Sicurezza
	G	Gabinetto
	MCP	Ministero della Cultura Popolare
	MI	Ministero dell'Interno
	PP	Polizia Politica
	R	Reports A16
AION	Archivio Istituto Orientale Napoli (The University of Naples, Oriental Institute, Naples)	
ASMAE	Archivio Storico Ministero degli Affari Esteri (Foreign Ministry Archives, Rome)	
	AP	Affari Politici, 1919–30, Giappone
	AP	Affari Politici, 1930–43, Giappone
AV	Archivio Vittoriale (Gabriele D'Annunzio Archives, Gardone)	
	AF	Archivio Fiumano
	AG	Archivio Generale
	AP	Archivio Personale

SMEUS	Stato Maggiore dell'Esercito, Ufficio Storico (Army General Staff, Historical Archives, Rome)
SPD	Segreteria Particolare del Duce

United States

NARA	National Archives and Records Administration (College Park)
	Record Group 331: Records of Allied Operational and Occupation Headquarters, World War II, 1907–1966 (Select files)

COLLECTIONS

NGB	Gaimushō. *Nihon gaikō bunsho* [Documents on Japanese foreign policy], *Shōwaki II*, vol. 4. Tokyo: Gaimushō Hensan, 1996
Ugaki Kazushige	*Ugaki Kazushige nikki.* 3 vols., vol. 1. Tokyo: Misuzu Shobō, 1968–71

NEWSPAPERS

Japan

Asahi shinbun, 1919–1950
Kōbe shinbun, 1935
Taiwan nichi-nichi shinpō, 1935
Tōkyō nichi-nichi shinbun, 1935
Yomiuri shinbun, 1919–1950
Yūshin nippō, 1935

Italy

Il Popolo d'Italia, 1919–1943

PUBLISHED SOURCES

Abel, Jessamyn R. "Warring Internationalisms: Multilateral Thinking in Japan, 1933–1964." PhD diss., Columbia University, 2004.

Abe Sueo. *Mussorini. Shōnen sekai ijin dokuhon*. Tokyo: Osaka Dōbunkan, 1930.

Adamson, Walter L. *Avant-Garde Florence: From Modernism to Fascism*. Cambridge, MA: Harvard University Press, 1993.

——. "Modernism and Fascism: The Politics of Culture in Italy, 1903–1922." *American Historical Review* 95 (1990): 359–90.

Allardyce, Gilbert. "What Fascism Is Not: Thoughts on the Deflation of a Concept." *American Historical Review* 84, no. 2 (1979): 367–88.

Ambaras, David. *Bad Youth: Juvenile Delinquency and the Politics of Everyday Life in Modern Japan*. Berkeley: University of California Press, 2006.

Amemiya Shōichi. "Self-Renovation of Existing Social Forces and Gleichschaltung: The Total-War System and the Middle Classes." In *Total War and "Modernization,"* edited by Yasushi Yamanouchi, J. Victor Koschmann, and Ryūichi Narita, 209–38. Ithaca, NY: Cornell University Press, 1998.

Anderer, Paul. *Literature of the Lost Home: Kobayashi Hideo—Literary Criticism, 1927–1939.* Stanford, CA: Stanford University Press, 1995.

Aoyama Kimihiko. "I-E funsō o meguru Ei-I no tachiba." *Gaikō jihō* 76, no. 743 (November 15, 1935): 87–97.

——. "I-E funsō o meguru rekkyo no rigai kankei." *Gaikō jihō* 75, no. 739 (September 15, 1935): 37–55.

Arata Isozaki. *Japan-ness in Architecture*. Cambridge, MA: MIT Press, 2006.

Arzeni, Flavia. *L'immagine e il segno*. Bologna: Il Mulino, 1987.

Ashida Hitoshi. "Echiopia mondai o meguru kakkoku no dōkō." *Kokusei isshin ronsō* 8 (1935): 1–23.

——. "I-E funsō no kakudaisei." *Gaikō jihō* 76, no. 742 (November 1, 1935): 1–8.

Ashima Kei. *Shōnen Mussorini den*. Tokyo: Bunkadō, 1932.

Baba Tsunego. "Seiji to dōtokusei." *Yomiuri shinbun*, July 7, 1935.

Barnhart, Michael A. *Japan Prepares for Total War: The Search for Economic Security*. Ithaca, NY: Cornell University Press, 1987.

Beasley, W. G. *Japan Encounters the Barbarian: Japanese Travellers in America and Europe, 1860–1873*. New Haven, CT: Yale University Press, 1995.

Ben-Ghiat, Ruth. *Fascist Modernities: Italy, 1922–1945*. Berkeley: University of California Press, 2001.

Bergamini, David. *Japan's Imperial Conspiracy*. New York: William Morrow, 1972.

Bix, Herbert P. *Hirohito and the Making of Modern Japan*. New York: Harper Collins, 2000.

Bonomi, Ivanoe. *From Socialism to Fascism, a Study of Contemporary Italy*. London: M. Hopkinson, 1924.

Bosworth, R. J. B. *The Italian Dictatorship: Problems and Perspectives in the Interpretation of Mussolini and Fascism*. London: Arnold, 1998.

——. *Mussolini*. London and New York: Arnold, 2002.

——. *Mussolini's Italy: Life under the Dictatorship, 1915–1945*. New York: Allen Lane, 2005.

Brandon, James R. *Kabuki's Forgotten War, 1931–1945*. Honolulu: University of Hawai'i Press, 2009.

——. "*Mussolini* in Kabuki: Notes and Translation." In *Japanese Theatre Transcultural: German and Italian Intertwinings*, edited by Stanca Scholz-Cionca and Andreas Regelsberger, 71–94. Munich: Iudicium, 2011.

Brandt, Kim. *Kingdom of Beauty: Mingei and the Politics of Folk Art in Imperial Japan*. Durham, NC: Duke University Press, 2007.

"Bungei nōto." *Shinchō* 29, no. 3 (1932): 20–23.

Burkman, Thomas W. *Japan and the League of Nations: Empire and World Order, 1914–1938*. Honolulu: University of Hawai'i Press, 2008.

——. "Nitobe Inazō: From World Order to Regional Order." In *Culture and Identity: Japanese Intellectuals during the Interwar Years*, edited by J. Thomas Rimer, 191–216. Princeton, NJ: Princeton University Press, 1990.

Byas, Hugh. *Government by Assassination*. New York: Knopf, 1942.

——. *The Japanese Enemy: His Power and His Vulnerability*. New York: Knopf, 1942.

Calichman, Richard F., ed. *Overcoming Modernity: Cultural Identity in Wartime Japan*. New York: Columbia University Press, 2008.

Chamberlin, William Henry. *Japan over Asia*. Boston: Little, Brown, 1937.

Clarke, Joseph Calvitt. *Alliance of the Colored Peoples: Ethiopia and Japan before World War II*. Woodbridge, Suffolk: James Currey, 2011.

Clinton, Margaret. "Fascism, Cultural Revolution, and National Sovereignty in 1930s China." PhD diss., New York University, 2009.

Corbould, Clare. *Becoming African Americans: Black Public Life in Harlem, 1919–1939*. Cambridge, MA: Harvard University Press, 2009.

Corner, Paul. *Fascism in Ferrara, 1915–1925*. London and New York: Oxford University Press, 1975.

Craigie, Robert. *Behind the Japanese Mask*. London, New York: Hutchinson, 1945.

Crowley, James B. *Japan's Quest for Autonomy: National Security and Foreign Policy, 1930–1938*. Princeton, NJ: Princeton University Press, 1966.
Cumings, Bruce. "Japan's Position in the World System." In *Postwar Japan as History*, edited by Andrew Gordon, 34–63. Berkeley: University of California Press, 1993.
D'Annunzio, Gabriele. "Le pagine di D'Annunzio." In *La guerra Italiana* (no page numbers). Naples: Libreria della Diana, 1919.
D'Antuono, Nicola. *Avventura intellettuale e tradizione culturale in Gherardo Marone*. Naples: Laveglia, 1984.
Dan Inō. *Itaria bijutsu kikō*. Tokyo: Shunyōdō, 1922.
De Caprariis, Luca. "'Fascism for Export'? The Rise and Eclipse of the Fasci Italiani all'Estero." *Journal of Modern History* 35, no. 2 (2000): 151–83.
De Felice, Renzo, and Luigi Goglia. *Mussolini, il mito. Grandi opere*. Rome: Laterza, 1983.
De Felice, Renzo, and Michael Arthur Ledeen. *Intervista sul fascismo*. Bari: Laterza, 1975.
De Grand, Alexander. "Mussolini's Follies: Fascism in Its Imperial and Racist Phase, 1935–1940." *Contemporary European History* 13, no. 2 (2004): 127–47.
de Grazia, Victoria. *How Fascism Ruled Women: Italy, 1922–1945*. Berkeley: University of California Press, 1992.
Dei, Adele. *"La Diana" (1915–1917), saggio e antologia*. Rome: Bulzoni, 1981.
Del Boca, Angelo. *I gas di Mussolini: Il fascismo e la guerra d'Etiopa*. Rome: Editori Riuniti, 1996.
Diggins, John P. *Mussolini and Fascism: The View from America*. Princeton, NJ: Princeton University Press, 1972.
Doak, Kevin Michael. *Dreams of Difference: The Japan Romantic School and the Crisis of Modernity*. Berkeley: University of California Press, 1994.
Dogliani, Patrizia. "Propaganda and Youth." In *The Oxford Handbook of Fascism*, edited by R. J. B. Bosworth, 185–202. Oxford: Oxford University Press, 2009.
Doi Bansui. *Su le orme dell'ippogrifo*. Translated by Shimoi Harukichi and Elpidio Jenco. Naples: Sakura, 1920.
——. "Tenba no michi ni: Gaburiere Danunuchio o mukauru chōshi." *Chūō kōron* 35 (1920): 177.
Dorsey, James. *Critical Aesthetics: Kobayashi Hideo, Modernity, and Wartime Japan*. Cambridge, MA: Harvard University Press, 2009.
Duara, Prasenjit. *Sovereignty and Authenticity: Manchukuo and the East Asian Modern*. Lanham, MD: Rowman & Littlefield, 2003.
Duus, Peter. "Imperialism without Colonies: The Vision of a Greater East Asian Co-Prosperity Sphere." *Diplomacy and Statecraft* 7, no. 1 (1996): 54–72.
——. "Liberal Intellectuals and Social Conflict in Taishō Japan." In *Conflict in Modern Japanese History*, edited by Tetsuo Najita and J. Victor Koschmann, 412–40. Princeton, NJ: Princeton University Press, 1982.
——. "Nagai Ryūtarō and the 'White Peril,' 1905–1944." *Journal of Asian Studies* 31, no. 1 (1971): 41–48.
——. *Party Rivalry and Political Change in Taishō Japan*. Cambridge, MA: Harvard University Press, 1968.
Duus, Peter, and Daniel Okimoto. "Fascism and the History of Pre-War Japan: The Failure of a Concept." *Journal of Asian Studies* 39 (1979): 65–76.
Duus, Peter, and Irwin Scheiner. "Socialism, Liberalism, and Marxism, 1901–1931." In *Modern Japanese Thought*, edited by Bob Tadashi Wakabayashi, 147–206. Cambridge: Cambridge University Press, 1998.
Falasca-Zamponi, Simonetta. *Fascist Spectacle: The Aesthetics of Power in Mussolini's Italy*. Berkeley: University of California Press, 1997.
"Fashizum hihan." *Keizai no ōrai*, no. 11 (1927): 80–89.

Federico, Giovanni. "Autarchia." In *Dizionario del Fascismo*, edited by Victoria de Grazia and Sergio Luzzatto, 116–20. Turin: Einaudi, 2002.
Ferrero, Guglielmo. *Four Years of Fascism*. London: P. S. King, 1924.
Ferretti, Valdo. *Il Giappone e la politica estera italiana*. Rome: Giuffrè, 1983.
Finchelstein, Federico. *Transatlantic Fascism: Ideology, Violence, and the Sacred in Argentina and Italy, 1919–1945*. Durham, NC, and London: Duke University Press, 2010.
"Fior di ciliegio." *Sakura*, nos. 1–2 (1920): 1–2.
Fiumi, Lionello. "Appello neoliberista." In *Opere poetiche*, edited by Beatrice Fiumi Magnani and Gianpaolo Marchi, 3–7. Verona: Fiorini, 1994.
Fletcher, Miles. *The Search for a New Order: Intellectuals and Fascism in Prewar Japan*. Chapel Hill: University of North Carolina Press, 1982.
Franzinelli, Mimmo. "Squadrism." In *The Oxford Handbook of Fascism*, edited by R. J. B. Bosworth, 91–108. Oxford: Oxford University Press, 2009.
Fujii Tei. "Sekaiteki fuwasshizumu to Nihon no kensei." *Chūō kōron* 8 (1927): 4–43.
Fujioka Hiromi. "Shimoi Harukichi to Itaria, Fashizumu: Danunchio, Mussorini, Nihon." *Fukuoka Kokusai Daigaku kiyō* 25 (2011): 53–66.
Fujisawa Chikao. "Capitalism, Marxism, and the Japanese National Thoughts." *Annals of the Faculty of Law and Letters of the Kyushu Imperial University* 1, no. 3 (1928): 1–80.
———. "Doku-I sūjiku no dōgisei." *Gaikō jihō*, no. 865 (December 15, 1940): 29–39.
———. "Fashizumu no seiji tetsugaku ni tsuite." *Gaikō jihō*, no. 592 (1929): 10–26.
———. "Hittora to Ōdōshugi." *Gaikō jihō*, no. 681 (April 15, 1933): 17–32.
———. "Itaria no atarashiki kokusai rinen." *Nihon hyōron* 15, no. 5 (1940).
———. "Nichi-Doku bōkyō kyōtei to shisō kokusaku." *Gaikō jihō*, no. 787 (September 15, 1937): 60–68.
———. "Nihon seishin no gendaiteki igi." *Risō*, no. 415 (January 1934).
———. *Pri historia evoluado de moderna Japanujo: Kondukinta al la Renovigo de Imperiestra Regimo en 1868*. Fukuoka: Kyushu Imperial University, 1926.
———. "Sekaiteki nihonshugi e no yakushin." *Gaikō jihō*, no. 671 (November 15, 1932): 69–86.
Fujitani, Takashi. "The Reischauer Memo: Mr. Moto, Hirohito, and Japanese American Soldiers." *Critical Asian Studies* 33, no. 3 (2001): 379–402.
Fuke Takahiro. *Nihon fashizumu ronsō: Taisen zenya no shisōka tachi*. Tokyo: Kawade Bukkusu, 2012.
———. *Senkanki Nihon no shakai shisō: "Chōkokka" e no furontia*. Tokyo: Jinbun Shoin, 2010.
Furukawa Tetsushi. "Japan and Ethiopia in the 1920s–30s: The Rise and Fall of 'Sentimental' Relations." *Ningen kankyōgaku* 8 (1999): 133–45.
———. "Kindai Nihon ni totte no Echiopia: Shōwa shoki ni okeru keizai kanshin to Heruy shisetsudan rainichi o chūshin ni." *Ōtani gakuhō* 86, no. 2 (2007): 1–17.
Gaimushō. *Bōkyō Doku-I no Yudayajin mondai*. Bōkyō kyōteikoku kokujō chōsa, vol. 4. Tokyo: Gaimushō Chōsabu, 1938.
———. *Fashisuto Itari no seiji soshiki to sono unyō narabini hantaiha seiryoku*. Bōkyō kyōteikoku kokujō chōsa, vol. 13. Tokyo: Gaimushō Chōsabu, 1939.
———. *I sansen ori sankoku jōyaku seiritsu*. Taisen gaikō dokuhon, vol. 3. Tokyo: Gaimushō Jōhōkyoku Daisanbu, 1940.
———. *Itari fassho kumiai giin seido*. Tokyo: Gaimushō Chōsabu, 1940.
———. *Itari no keizai kikō to gensei (zenpen)*. Bōkyō kyōteikoku kokujō chōsa, vol. 1. Tokyo: Gaimushō Chōsabu, 1938.
———. *Itari no shokuryō mondai*. Tokyo: Gaimushō Chōsabu, 1942.
———. *Nachisu oyobi Fashisuto no kokka kan*. Tokyo: Nihon Kokusai Kyōkai, 1939.
———. *Nichi-Doku-I kokubō kyōtei ni tsuite*. Tokyo: Gaimushō Jōhōbu, 1937.
———. "Nichi-Doku-I no bōkyōtei: Itari dattai to renmei." *Shūhō* 63, no. 12.29 (1937): 39–45.

——. *Nichi-Doku-I sankoku bōkyōtei ni tsuite*. Tokyo: Gaimushō Jōhōbu, 1937.
——. *Sengo no Ōshū keizai kyōchō ni kansuru Doku-I ryōgoku no keikakuan*. Tokyo: Gaimushō Chōsabu, 1941.
Gallifuoco, Silvana, ed. *Lettere di Lionello Fiumi*. Naples: Macchiaroli, 2003.
Gann, L. H. "Reflections on the Japanese and German Empires of World War II." In *The Japanese Wartime Empire, 1931–1945*, edited by Peter Duus, Ramon Hawley Myers, Mark R. Peattie, and Wanyao Zhou, 335–62. Princeton, NJ: Princeton University Press, 1996.
Garon, Sheldon M. *Molding Japanese Minds: The State in Everyday Life*. Princeton, NJ: Princeton University Press, 1997.
Gentile, Emilio. *The Sacralization of Politics in Fascist Italy*. Cambridge, MA: Harvard University Press, 1996.
Gibelli, Antonio. *L'officina della guerra e le trasformazioni del mondo mentale*. Turin: Bollati Boringhieri, 2007.
Gleason, Abbott. *Totalitarianism: The Inner History of the Cold War*. New York: Oxford University Press, 1995.
Gluck, Carol. *Japan's Modern Myths: Ideology in the Late Meiji Period*. Princeton, NJ: Princeton University Press, 1985.
Gordon, Andrew. *The Evolution of Labor Relations in Japan: Heavy Industry, 1853–1955*. Cambridge, MA: Harvard University Press, 1985.
——. *Labor and Imperial Democracy in Prewar Japan*. Berkeley: University of California Press, 1991.
Gorgolini, Pietro. *The Fascist Movement in Italian Life*. London: Unwin, 1923.
Gotō Toranosuke. *Fashizumu to wa nanika, fashizumu naigai bunken*. Tokyo: Rōnō Shobō, 1932.
Goto-Jones, Christopher, ed. *Re-politicising the Kyoto School as Philosophy*. London: Routledge, 2008.
Gramsci, Antonio. *Quaderni del carcere*. 4 vols., vol. 3. Turin: Einaudi, 2007.
——. *Selections From the Prison Notebooks of Antonio Gramsci*. New York: International Publishers, 1971.
"Han fassho jinmin taikai." *Asahi shinbun*, August 12, 1948.
Han, Jung-Sun N. "Envisioning a Liberal Empire in East Asia: Yoshino Sakuzō in Taishō Japan." *Journal of Japanese Studies* 33, no. 2 (2007): 357–82.
——. *An Imperial Path to Modernity: Sakuzō and a New Liberal Order in East Asia, 1905–1937*. Cambridge, MA: Harvard University Press, 2012.
Harootunian, Harry. "Between Politics and Culture: Authority and the Ambiguities of Intellectual Choice in Imperial Japan." In *Japan in Crisis: Essays on Taishō Democracy*, edited by Bernard S. Silberman and Harry Harootunian, 110–55. Princeton, NJ: Princeton University Press, 1974.
——. "The Black Cat in the Dark Room." *Positions* 13, no. 1 (2005): 137–55.
——. "Figuring the Folk: History, Poetics, and Representation." In *Mirror of Modernity*, edited by Stephen Vlastos, 144–59. Berkeley: University of California Press, 1998.
——. "The Imperial Present and the Second Coming of Fascism." *Boundary 2* 34, no. 1 (2007): 1–15.
——. "Introduction: A Sense of an Ending and the Problem of Taishō," In *Japan in Crisis: Essays on Taishō Democracy*, ed. Bernard Silberman and Harry Harootunian, 3–28. Princeton, NJ: Princeton University Press, 1974.
——. *Overcome by Modernity: History, Culture, and Community in Interwar Japan*. Princeton, NJ: Princeton University Press, 2000.
——. "Time, Everydayness and the Specter of Fascism." In *Re-politicising the Kyoto School as Philosophy*, edited by Christopher Goto-Jones, 96–112. London: Routledge, 2008.

Harootunian, H. D., and Tetsuo Najita. "Japan's Revolt against the West." In *Modern Japanese Thought*, edited by Bob Tadashi Wakabayashi, 207–72. Cambridge: Cambridge University Press, 1999.

Hasegawa Nyozekan. *Fashizumu hihan*. Tokyo: Ohata Shoten, 1932.

Hashikawa Bunzō. "Kakushin kanryō." In *Kenryoku no shisō*, edited by Kamishima Jirō, 251–73. Tokyo: Chikuma Shobō, 1965.

——. "Nachisu shisō no shintō to sankoku dōmei." In *Kindai Nihon shisōshi no kiso chishiki*, edited by Hashikawa Bunzō, Kano Masanao, and Hiraoka Toshio, 395–97. Tokyo: Yūhikaku, 1971.

Hatoyama Ichirō. *Watakushi no shinjō*. Tokyo: Tōkyō Bunkō, 1951.

Hattori Shisō. *Tennōsei zettaishugi no kakuritsu*. Tokyo: Chūō Kōron, 1948.

Havens, Thomas R. H. *Farm and Nation in Modern Japan: Agrarian Nationalism, 1870–1940*. Princeton, NJ: Princeton University Press, 1974.

——. *Valley of Darkness: The Japanese People and World War Two*. New York: Norton, 1978.

Heisig, James W., and John C. Maraldo, eds. *Rude Awakenings: Zen, the Kyoto School, and the Question of Nationalism*. Honolulu: University of Hawai'i Press, 1995.

Hijikata Seibi. *Fashizumu: shisō, undō, seisaku*. Tokyo: Iwanami, 1932.

Hirai Kazuomi. "Nihon fashizumu ron saikō." *Nihonshi kenkyū*, no. 576 (2010): 50–67.

Hirakawa Sukehiro. "Japan's Turn to the West." In *Modern Japanese Thought*, edited by Bob Tadashi Wakabayashi, 30–97. Cambridge: Cambridge University Press, 1998.

Hiranuma Kiichirō. "Nihon no kakushin undō." *Kaizō* 14, no. 6 (1932): 94–95.

Hofmann, Reto. "The Fascist Reflection: Japan and Italy, 1919–1950." PhD diss., Columbia University, 2010.

Hori Makiyo. *Nishida Mitsugi to Nihon Fashizumu Undō*. Tokyo: Iwanami Shoten, 2007.

Hori Makoto. "I-E funsō to kokusai seikyoku no dōkō." *Gaikō jihō* 737, no. 75 (August 15) (1935): 59–66.

Hosoya Chihiro. "The Tripartite Pact, 1939–1940." In *Deterrent Diplomacy: Japan, Germany, and the USSR, 1935–1940*, edited by James William Morley. New York: Columbia University Press, 1976, 191–257.

Hoston, Germaine. "Marxism and National Socialism in Taishō Japan: The Thought of Takabatake Motoyuki." *Journal of Asian Studies* 44, no. 1 (1984): 43–64.

"I-E funsō no jitsubutsu kyōkun (hattenteki minzoku ni wa ryōdo ga hitsuyō da)." *Gaikō jihō* 76, no. 742 (November 1, 1935): 1–4.

I-E mondai kakudai to kabushiki sōba no eikyō. Tokyo: Daiyamondo 1935.

"I-E mondai to Nihon (Sugimura taishi wa Ikoku ni riyō sareta)." *Gaikō jihō* 75, no. 736 (August 1, 1935): 1–4.

Ikeda Akira, ed. *Ōmoto shiryō shūsei*. Vol. 2. Tokyo: Sanichi Shobō, 1982–85.

Ikeda Akira, ed. *Ōmoto shiryō shūsei*. Vol. 3. Tokyo: Sanichi Shobō, 1982–85.

Iida Seizō. "Senji keiki mitōshi. Handōrai wa hisshi: Ōshū taisenji to no hikaku." *Yomiuri shinbun*, September 9, 1935.

Inahara Katsuji. "Mussorini kōtei ni naruka." *Gaikō jihō* 577, no. 12 (1928): 13–28.

Inomata Keitarō. *Nakano Seigō*. Tokyo: Yoshikawa Kōbunkan, 1960.

Inoue Kiyoshi. *Tennōsei zettaishugi no hatten*. Tokyo: Chūō Kōron, 1951.

Ishiwara Kanji. *Saishūsenron*. Tokyo: Keizai Ōraisha, 1978.

Itaria no tomonokai kaisoku. Tokyo: Itaria No Tomonokai, 1941.

Itō Takashi. "Shōwa seijishi kenkyū e no isshikaku." *Shisō*, no. 624 (1976): 949–62.

——. *Taishōki kakushinha no seiritsu*. Tokyo: Hanawa Sensho, 1978.

Itō Takashi, Hirohashi Tadamitsu, and Katashima Norio. *Tōjō Naikaku Sōri Daijin kimitsu kiroku: Tōjō Hideki Taishō genkōroku*. Tokyo: Tokyo Daigaku Shuppankai, 1990.

Jacquet, Benoît. "Compromising Modernity: Japanese Monumentality during World War II." In *Front to Rear: Architecture and Planning during WWII*. New York University, Institute of Fine Arts, 2009.

Japan Imperial Japanese Army General Staff Office. *Sugiyama memo*. Vol. 1. Tokyo: Hara Shobō, 1989

Japan. Ministry of Education. "Fundamentals of Our National Polity (*Kokutai no hongi*)." In *Sources of Japanese Tradition*, edited by Theodore Wm. De Bary, Carol Gluck, and Arthur E. Tiedemann, 968–75. New York: Columbia University Press, 2005 (1937).

——. *Kokutai no hongi*. Tokyo: Nihon Tosho Senta, 2003.

Johnstone, William C. "The Future of Japan." In *Ninth Conference of the Institute of Pacific Relations*. Hot Springs, VA: American Council Institute of Pacific Relations, 1945.

Jones, Mark. *Children as Treasures: Childhood and the Middle Class in Early Twentieth-Century Japan*. Cambridge, MA: Harvard University Press, 2010.

Jünger, Ernst. *Storm of Steel*. London: Allen Lane, 2003.

Kajima Morinosuke. "Bushidō no taishūka." *Kokusai chishiki* 15, no. 10 (1935): 64–66.

——. "Dai-Tōa to Ōshū no shinchitsujo." In *Kajima Morinosuke gaikō ron senshū*, 112–34. Tokyo: Kajima Kenkyūjo Shuppan, 1973 (1941).

——. "Doku-So sengo no kokusai jōsei." In *Sekai shinchitsujo o meguru gaikō—Dai-Tōa sensō to Dai-Tōa kyōeiken*, 283–94. Tokyo: Kajima Kenkyūjo Shuppan, 1973 (1941).

——. "Nichi-Doku-I bōkyō kyōtei no igi." *Chūō kōron* 52, no. 13 (1937): 167–72.

——. "Renmei no kaiso to pan-Europpa mondai." In *Kajima Morinosuke gaikōron senshū*, 44–65. Tokyo: Kajima Kenkyūjo Shuppan, 1973 (1936).

——. "Sekai no shinchitsujo to warera no shinro." In *Kajima Morinosuke gaikōron senshū*, 313–23. Tokyo: Kajima Kenkyūjo Shuppan, 1973 (1940).

——. "Shinsei naru rikoshugi (sacro egoismo) (naniga Ōshū kokumin o sensō ni mukawashimentosuru ka)." *Gaikō jihō* 76 (October 15), no. 740 (1935): 89–103.

Kajiwara Nakaji. "Fukakudai demo resei jisshitsu kai tsudsukan." *Ekonomisuto* 13, no. 31 (1935): 18–19.

Kamei Katsuichirō. "Itari e no yume." *Itaria*, no. 10 (1942): 119–26.

Kamo Giichi. "Runessansu no kagaku ni tsuite." *Nichi-I bunka kenkyū* 3 (1941): 84–90.

Kanezaki Ken. "I-E funsō kara hoku-shi kōsaku." *Gaikō jihō* 743, no. 76 (November 1) (1935): 33–51.

Kano Kizō. "I-E funsō no shinso." *Gaikō jihō* 75, no. 738 (September 1, 1935): 167–86.

Karlin, Jason. "The Gender of Nationalism: Competing Masculinities in Meiji Japan." *Journal of Japanese Studies* 28, no. 1 (2002): 41–77.

Kasza, Gregory. "Fascism from Below? A Comparative Perspective on the Japanese Right, 1931–1936." *Journal of Contemporary History* 19 (1984): 607–29.

——. *The State and the Mass Media in Japan*. Berkeley: University of California Press, 1988.

Katakura Tōjirō. *Nihon wa Itaria o shiji shite Ei-Bei no appaku ni sonoeyo*. Tokyo: Konnichi No Mondaisha, 1935.

Katayama Sen. "Fuwashizumu to Ōshū no genjō." *Kaizō* 5, no. 9 (1923): 72–84.

Katō Tetsurō. "Personal Contacts in Japanese–German Cultural Relations during the 1920s and Early 1930s." In *Japanese–German Relations, 1895–1945: War, Diplomacy, and Public Opinion*, edited by Christian W. Spang and Rolf-Harald Wippich. London: Routledge, 2006.

Katō Yōko. "Fashizumu ron." *Nihon rekishi*, no. 9 (2006): 143–53.

Katsuta Teiji. "I-E kōsō to zaikai. Ōshū masu kuraushite, Nihon iyoiyo akarushi." *Yomiuri shinbun*, October 7, 1935.

——. "Shihonshugi no tessoku. Shokuminchi bunkatsu sen: I-E funsō ni odoru kabushiki." *Yomiuri shinbun*, September 9, 1935.

Kawai Tatsuo. *Nichi-Doku-I sangoku bōkyō kyōtei ni tsuite*. Tokyo: Gaimushō Jōhōbu, 1937.
Kawamura, Noriko. "Wilsonian Idealism and Japanese Claims at the Paris Peace Conference." *Pacific Historical Review* 66, no. 4 (1997): 503–26.
Kershaw, Ian. *Making Friends with Hitler: Lord Londonderry, the Nazis, and the Road to War*. New York: Penguin, 2004.
Kersten, Rikki. "Japan." In *The Oxford Handbook of Fascism*, edited by R. J. B. Bosworth, 526–44. Oxford: Oxford University Press, 2009.
Kinmonth, Earl H. *The Self-Made Man in Meiji Japanese Thought: From Samurai to Salary Man*. Berkeley: University of California Press, 1981.
Kitamura Mitsuko. *Seinen to kindai: Seinen to seinen o meguru gensetsu no keifugaku*. Yokohama: Seori Shobō, 1998.
Kita Reikichi. "Echiopia mondai to Nihon." *Keizai ōrai* 10, no. 9 (1935): 86–91.
——. *Fassho to kokkashakaishugi*. Tokyo: Nihon Shosō, 1937.
——. "Sekai wa dō ugoku de arō ka." *Kaizō* 6, no. 1 (1924): 42–54.
——. *Shōwa ishin*. Tokyo: Sekai Bunkō Kankōkai, 1927.
Kiyosawa Kiyoshi. *A Diary of Darkness: The Wartime Diary of Kiyosawa Kiyoshi*. Translated by Eugene Soviak. Princeton, NJ: Princeton University Press, 1999.
——. "Kaisō no Itaria: Sono geijutsu to seiji." *Itaria*, no. 4 (1941): 86–91.
Kobayashi Hideo. "Kodai Roma no bunka izan." *Nichi-I bunka kenkyū*, no. 5 (1942): 58–63.
Kobayashi Tatsuo. "The London Naval Treaty, 1930." In *Japan Erupts: The London Naval Conference and the Manchurian Incident, 1928–1932*, edited by James William Morley, 11–117. New York: Columbia University Press, 1984.
Kokuryūkai. *I-E mondai to Echiopia jijō*. Echiopia mondai kondankai. Tokyo: Kokuryūkai Shuppan, 1935.
"Kokusuitō naikaku soshiki." *Yomiuri shinbun*, November 1, 1922.
"Kokusuitō to Kokusuikai." *Yomiuri shinbun*, October 31, 1922.
Konno Nobuyuki. *Kindai Nihon no kokutairon: "Kōkoku shikan."* Tokyo: Perikan, 2008.
Konoe Fumimarō. "Kokusai heiwa no konpon mondai." In *Kenryoku no shisō*, edited by Kamishima Jirō. Gendai Nihon shisō taikei, vol. 10, 312–18. Tokyo: Chikuma Shobō, 1965.
——. *Ōbei kenbunki*. Tokyo: Chūō Kōronsha, 2006.
Kore ga Echiopia da: dorei monogatari (Tokyo: Okuchōsha, 1935).
Kosaka Masaaki, Nishitani Keiji, Kōyama Iwao, and Suzuki Shigetaka. *Sekaishiteki tachiba to Nihon*. Tokyo: Chūō Kōronsha, 1942.
Koyama Shizuko. *Ryōsai kenbo: The Educational Ideal of "Good wife, Wise mother" in Modern Japan*. Leiden: Brill, 2013.
Kubizek, August. *The Young Hitler I Knew*. London: Greenhill Books, 2006.
Kudō Akira. *Nichi-Doku keizai kankeishi josetsu*. Tokyo: Sakurai Shoten, 2011.
Kushner, Barak. *The Thought War: Japanese Imperial Propaganda* Honolulu: University of Hawai'i Press, 2007.
Labanca, Nicola. *Oltremare: Storia dell'espansione coloniale italiana*. Bologna: Il Mulino, 2002.
Larsen, Stein Ugelvik. *Fascism Outside Europe: The European Impulse against Domestic Conditions in the Diffusion of Global Fascism*. Boulder, CO: Social Science Monographs, 2001.
Lebra, Joyce C. *Japan's Greater East Asia Co-Prosperity Sphere in World War II: Selected Readings and Documents*. Kuala Lumpur: Oxford University Press, 1975.
Ledeen, Michael. *The First Duce: D'Annunzio at Fiume*. Baltimore, MD: Johns Hopkins University Press, 1977.
——. *Universal Fascism: The Theory and Practice of the Fascist International, 1928–1936*. New York: H. Fertig, 1972.

Lu, David John. *Agony of Choice: Matsuoka Yōsuke and the Rise and Fall of the Japanese Empire, 1880–1946*. Lanham, MD: Lexington Books, 2002.

Lukács, György. *History and Class Consciousness: Studies in Marxist Dialectics*. Cambridge, MA: MIT Press, 1971.

Lyttelton, Adrian. *The Seizure of Power: Fascism in Italy, 1919–1939*. London and New York: Routledge, 2004.

Maedako Hiroichirō. "Fassho ryūkō." *Yomiuri shinbun*, March 8, 1932.

Maida Minoru. "Itari no seikyoku (jō)." *Gaikō jihō* 493 (1925): 59–70.

——. "Itari no seikyoku (ge)." *Gaikō jihō* 495 (1925): 23–34.

Manela, Erez. *The Wilsonian Moment: Self-Determination and the International Origins of Anticolonial Nationalism*. Oxford and New York: Oxford University Press, 2007.

"Mare naru gogaku no tensai. Fujisawa Chikao kun: Kokusaiteki shin shisōka." *Yomiuri shinbun*, May 16, 1920.

Martin, Benjamin G. "European Literature in the Nazi New Order: The Cultural Politics of the European Writers' Union, 1941–3." *Journal of Contemporary History* 48, no. 3 (2013): 486–508.

——. "A New Order for European Culture: The German–Italian Axis and the Reordering of International Cultural Exchange, 1936–1943." PhD diss., Columbia University, 2006.

Martin, Bernd. *Deutschland und Japan im Zweiten Weltkrieg. Vom Angriff auf Pearl Harbor bis z. dt. Kapitulation*. Göttingen and Zurich: Musterschmidt, 1969. Issued also as a thesis, Marburg, 1967.

Maruyama Masao. "The Ideology and Dynamics of Japanese Fascism." In *Thought and Behaviour in Modern Japanese Politics*, edited by Ivan Morris, 25–83. Oxford: Oxford University Press, 1969.

——. "Theory and Psychology of Ultra-Nationalism." In *Thought and Behaviour in Modern Japanese Politics*, edited by Ivan Morris, 1–24. Oxford: Oxford University Press, 1969.

Masamune Hakuchō. "Korai no bunka." *Yomiuri shinbun*, June 6, 1936.

Matsudaira Michio. *Mussorini*. Tokyo: Kin No Seisha, 1928.

Matsuda Shōichi. "Ōshū kinjō no shoanken to kokusai renmei." *Gaikō jihō* 75, no. 737 (August 15, 1935): 1–13.

Matsui Haruo. "Sekai no dōran to keizai Nihon no shinro—atarashiki tsūshō jiyū." *Yomiuri shinbun*, January 7, 1936.

Matsuzawa Tetsunari. *Ajiashugi to fashizumu: Tennō teokokuron hihan*. Tokyo: Renga Shobō, 1979.

Mattioli, Guido. *Mussolini aviatore e la sua opera per l'aviazione*. Rome: Casa Editrice Pinciana, 1936.

Mazower, Mark. *Governing the World: The History of an Idea*. New York: Penguin, 2012.

——. *Hitler's Empire: How the Nazis Ruled Europe*. New York: Penguin, 2008.

Metzler, Mark. *Lever of Empire: The International Gold Standard and the Crisis of Liberalism in Prewar Japan*. Berkeley: University of California Press, 2006.

Mimura, Janis. *Planning for Empire: Reform Bureaucrats and the Japanese Wartime State*. Ithaca, NY: Cornell University Press, 2011.

Minagawa Masaki. *Konoe shintaisei no shisō to seiji: Jiyūshugi kokufuku no jidai*. Tokyo: Yūshisha, 2009.

Minami Hiroshi. *Shōwa bunka*. Tokyo: Keisō Shobō, 1987.

——. *Taishō bunka*. Tokyo: Shinsōban, 1988.

Minichiello, Sharon. *Retreat from Reform: Patterns of Political Behavior in Interwar Japan*. Honolulu: University of Hawai'i Press, 1984.

Mitani Taichirō. *Taishō demokurashii ron: Yoshino Sakuzō no jidai to sono ato*. Tokyo: Tokyo Daigaku Shuppankai, 1995.
Mitchell, Richard H. *Thought Control in Prewar Japan*. Ithaca, NY: Cornell University Press, 1976.
Miwa Kimitada. "'Tōa shinchitsujo' sengen to 'daitōa kyōeiken' kōzō no dansō." In *Saikō taiheiyō sensō zenya: Nihon no 1930 nendairon to shite*, edited by Miwa Kimitada, 195–231. Tokyo: Sōseki Sensho, 1981.
"Mizukara handō o kakunin. Jinmin no jikaku assatsu no tate." *Yomiuri shinbun*, February 23, 1946.
Mizuno Hironori. "Fasshizumu to Nihon." *Keizai ōrai*, no. 11 (1927): 81–83.
Montanelli, Indro. *L'impero bonsai, cronaca di un viaggio in Giappone, 1951–2*. Milan: Rizzoli, 2007.
Morgan, Philip. "Corporatism and the Economic Order." In *The Oxford Handbook of Fascism*, edited by R. J. B. Bosworth, 150–65. Oxford: Oxford University Press, 2010.
Mosse, George. *Fallen Soldiers: Reshaping the Memory of the World Wars*. New York: Oxford University Press, 1990.
Mosse, George L. "The Poet and the Exercise of Political Power: Gabriele D'Annunzio." In *Masses and Man: Nationalist and Fascist Perceptions of Reality*, 87–103. Detroit, MI: Wayne State University Press, 1987.
Murobuse Kōshin. *Fassho ka Marukusu ka*. Tokyo: Ichigensha, 1932.
——. "I-E sen to sekaisen." *Yomiuri shinbun*, October 8, 1935.
Mussolini, Benito. "Fascism's Myth: The Nation." In *Fascism*, edited by Roger Griffin, 43–44. Oxford: Oxford University Press, 1995 (1922).
Mussolini, Benito, Shimoi Harukichi, and Adriano Alberti. *Nihon gunbu ni tsugu*. Tokyo: Kokutai Meichō kai, 1936.
Mutō Naoyoshi. *Sekai dōran no dōka-sen I-E no sono go?* Tokyo: Tōa Shobō, 1936.
Myers, Ramon Hawley. "Creating a Modern Enclave Economy: The Economic Integration of Japan, Manchuria, and North China, 1932–1945." In *The Japanese Wartime Empire, 1931–1945*, edited by Peter Duus, Ramon Hawley Myers, Mark R. Peattie, and Wanyao Zhou, 136–70. Princeton, NJ: Princeton University Press, 1996.
Nagai Ryūtarō. "Mussorini shushō no shojo enzetsu." *Yūben* 18, no. 1 (1927): 22–27.
——. "Uiruson kara Mussorini made." In *Yūkō kurabu kōenshū*, 1–24. Tokyo, 1927.
Naimushō keihōkyoku, ed. *Fashizumu no riron*. Shuppan keisatsu kankei shiryō shūsei, vol. 5. Tokyo: Fuji Shuppan, 1986 (1932).
Najita, Tetsuo. *Japan: The Intellectual Foundations of Modern Japanese Politics*. Chicago: University of Chicago Press, 1974.
Najita, Tetsuo, and Harry Harootunian. "Japan's Revolt against the West." In *Modern Japanese Thought*, edited by Bob Tadashi Wakabayashi, 207–72. Cambridge: Cambridge University Press, 1998.
Nakagawa Shigeru. *Mussorini*. Ijin denki bunkō, vol. 52. Tokyo: Nihonsha, 1935.
Nakahira Akira. "Mussorini no gaikō." *Gaikō jihō* 518, no. 7.1 (1926): 65–82.
Nakamura Burafu et al. "Fassho to fashizumu bungaku ni tsuite." *Shinchō* 29, no. 4 (1932): 125–46.
Nakamura, Takafusa. *Lectures on Modern Japanese Economic History*. Tokyo: LTCB International Library Foundation, 1994.
Nakano Seigo. "Entakukei no Mussorini to yōchina rōnōtō." *Chūō kōron* 43, no. 5 (1928): 81–84.
Nakatani Takeyo. "Fashizumu no honshitsu to sono kokka kannen." *Kokuhon* 12, no. 4 (1932): 19–23.
——. "Fashizumu yori kōdōshugi." *Kokuhon* 12, no. 11 (1932): 33–38.
——. "Fasushisuchi kokka no kokumin kyōiku (1)." *Kokuhon* 11, no. 4 (1931): 44–48.

——. "Fasushisuchi kokka no kokumin kyōiku (2)." *Kokuhon* 11, no. 5 (1931): 45–48.
Naoki Sanjūgo. *Fashizumu sengen sono ta.* Naoki Sanjūgo zenshū, vol. 14. Tokyo: Shijinsha, 1992.
Narita Ryūichi. *Taishō demokurashii.* Shiriizu Nihon kingendaishi, vol. 4. Tokyo: Iwanami, 2007.
——. "Women in the Motherland: Oku Mumeo through Wartime and Postwar." In *Total War and "Modernization,"* edited by Yasushi Yamanouchi, J. Victor Koschmann, and Ryūichi Narita, 137–58. Ithaca, NY: Cornell University Press, 1998.
Negishi Benji. *Itari no nōgyō ni okeru shūgōteki rōdō keiyaku.* Tokyo: Kyōchōkai Nōsonka, 1928.
Neocleous, Mark. *Fascism.* Minneapolis: University of Minnesota Press, 1997.
Nichi-I Kyōkai. *Nichi-I kyōkaishi.* Tokyo: Nichi-I Kyōkai, 1993.
Nihon kōgyō kurabu keizai kenkyūkai. "Fassho Itari saikin no ugoki." *Keizai kenkyū sōsho* 19 (special edition) (1934).
Nii Itaru. "Bungei jihyō." *Shinchō* 29, no. 3 (1932): 110–19.
Niizeki Ryōzō. "Kinsei engekishi ni okeru Itaria engeki." *Nichi-I bunka kenkyū* 5 (1942): 29–38.
Ninagawa Arata. "Fuasichizumu no kōryū to rōdō sōgi no gentai." *Tōtaku geppō* 5, no. 1 (1924): 1–3.
——. "Ikoku no saikin kakumei to sono kōka." *Gaikō jihō* 4, no. 1 (1923): 154–64.
"1934-nen no bungei dōkō zadankai." *Yomiuri shinbun*, January 9, 1934.
Nishida Kitarō. "Sekai shinchitsujo no genri." http://www.aozora.gr.jp/cards/000182/files/3668_16431.html. Accessed June 12, 2014.
Nishiwaki Junzaburō. "Itari bunka." *Nichi-I bunka kenkyū*, no. 5 (1942): 14–16.
Nishizawa, Tamotsu. "Lujo Brentano, Alfred Marshall, and Tokuzo Fukuda: The Reception and Transformation of the German Historical School in Japan." In *The German Historical School: The Historical and Ethical Approach to Economics*, edited by Yuichi Shionoya, 155–72. London and New York: Routledge, 2001.
Nitobe Inazō. *Ijin gunzō.* Tokyo: Jitsugyō no Nihonsha, 1931.
Nogami Yaeko. "Shō ojisan." *Yomiuri shinbun*, December 11, 1935.
Nolte, Ernst. *Three Faces of Fascism: Action Française, Italian Fascism, National Socialism.* New York: Holt, 1966.
Nolte, Sharon H. *Liberalism in Modern Japan: Ishibashi Tanzan and His Teachers, 1905–1960.* Berkeley: University of California Press, 1987.
Norman, Herbert. "The Genyosha: A Study on the Origins of Japanese Imperialism." *Pacific Affairs* 17, no. 3 (1944): 261–84.
Oates, Leslie Russell. *Populist Nationalism in Prewar Japan: A Biography of Nakano Seigo.* Sydney: Allen & Unwin, 1985.
Oka, Yoshitake. *Konoe Fumimaro: A Political Biography.* Tokyo: University of Tokyo Press, 1992.
Okada Tadahiko. *Senpūri no Ōshū.* Tokyo: Teikoku shoin, 1936.
Okada Takeo. *Fashizumu.* Tokyo: Gyōmeisha, 1949.
Okakura Takashi. "Futatsu no Echiopia sensō to Nihon: Dai-Ajiashugisha o chūshin ni." *Tōyō Kenkyū*, no. 122 (1996): 1–24.
Okumura Takeshi. *Jidōsha ō Henri Fōdo.* Osaka: Enomoto Shoten, 1928.
——. *Kaiketsu Mussorini.* Osaka: Enomoto Shoten, 1928.
Ooms, Emily Groszos. *Women and Millenarian Protest in Meiji Japan: Deguchi Nao and Ōmotokyō.* Ithaca, NY: Cornell University Press, 1993.
Ōrui Noboru. "Runessansuteki ningen." *Nichi-I bunka kenkyū* 6 (1942): 10–14.
Ōya Sōichi. "Gurando ruru no nai bundan (jō)." *Yomiuri shinbun*, March 27, 1932.
——. "Gurando ruru no nai bundan (chū)." *Yomiuri shinbun*, March 29, 1932.

———. "Gurando ruru no nai bundan (ge)." *Yomiuri shinbun*, March 30, 1932.
Papini, Giovanni. "Lettres italiennes." *Mercure de France*, nos. 11–12 (1917): 149–52.
Passerini, Luisa. *Mussolini immaginario*. Rome: Laterza, 1991.
Pauer, Erich. *The Transfer of Technology between Germany and Japan from 1890 to 1945*. Vol. 3 of *Japan and Germany: Two Latecomers to the World Stage, 1890–1945*, edited by Kudō Akira, Tajima Nobuo, and Erich Pauer. Kent, UK: Global Oriental, 2009.
Paxton, Robert O. *The Anatomy of Fascism*. London: Penguin, 2004.
Payne, Stanley G. *A History of Fascism, 1914–1945*. Madison: University of Wisconsin Press, 1995.
Peattie, Mark R. *Ishiwara Kanji and Japan's Confrontation with the West*. Princeton, NJ: Princeton University Press, 1975.
Polanyi, Karl. *The Great Transformation: The Political and Economic Origins of Our Time*. Boston: Beacon Press, 2001.
Presseisen, Ernst Leopold. *Germany and Japan: A Study in Totalitarian Diplomacy, 1933–1941*. The Hague: M. Nijhoff, 1958.
Prezzolini, Giuseppe. *Fascism*. New York: E. P. Dutton, 1927.
Pyle, Kenneth. "Meiji Conservatism." In *Modern Japanese Thought*, edited by Bob Tadashi Wakabayashi, 99–146. Cambridge: Cambridge University Press, 1999.
Reynolds, Jonathan M. *Maekawa Kunio and the Emergence of Japanese Modernist Architecture*. Berkeley: University of California Press, 2001.
Robertson, Jennifer Ellen. *Takarazuka : Sexual Politics and Popular Culture in Modern Japan*. Berkeley: University of California Press, 1998.
Rochat, Giorgio. *Militari e politici nella preparazione della campagna d'Etiopia. Studio e documenti, 1932–1936*. Milan: Angeli, 1971.
Roden, Donald. *Schooldays in Imperial Japan: A Study in the Culture of a Student Elite*. Berkeley: University of California Press, 1980.
Rodogno, Davide. *Fascism's European Empire: Italian Occupation during the Second World War*. Translated by Adrian Belton. Cambridge: Cambridge University Press, 2006.
Ruoff, Kenneth J. *Imperial Japan at Its Zenith: The Wartime Celebration of the Empire's 2,600th Anniversary*. Ithaca, NY: Cornell University Press, 2010.
Saguchi Kazurō. "The Historical Significance of the Industrial Patriotic Association: Labor Relations in the Total-War State." In *Total War and "Mobilization,"*, edited by Yasushi Yamanouchi, J. Victor Koschmann, and Ryūichi Narita, 261–87. Ithaca, NY: Cornell University Press, 1998.
Saitō Mōkichi. "Fumetsu." *Itaria*, no. 3 (1942): 54–55.
Sakai, Naoki. "Imperial Nationalism and the Comparative Perspective." *Positions* 17, no. 1 (2008): 159–205.
———. "Resistance to Conclusion: The Kyoto School of Philosophy under the Pax Americana." In *Re-Politicising the Kyoto School as Philosophy*, edited by Christopher Goto-Jones, 183–98. London: Routledge, 2008.
———. "Return to the West/Return to the East: Watsuji Tetsuro's Anthropology and Discussions of Authenticity." *Boundary 2* 18, no. 3 (1991): 157–90.
Sakai, Naoki, and Isomae Jun'ichi, eds. *"Kindai no chōkoku" to Kyōto gakuha: Kindaisei, teikoku, fuhensei*. Tokyo: Ibunsha, 2010.
Sakai Tetsuya. *Kindai Nihon no kokusai chitsujoron*. Tokyo: Iwanami, 2007.
———. "The Soviet Factor in Japanese Foreign Policy, 1928–1937." In *Imperial Japan and the World, 1931–1945*, edited by Antony Best, 167–83. London: Routledge, 2010 (1988).
Salaris, Claudia. *Alla festa della rivoluzione*. Bologna: Il Mulino, 2002.
Salierno, Vito. "Il mancato volo di D'Annunzio in Giappone." In *Un capitolo di storia: Fiume e D'Annunzio, Atti del Convegno, Gardone Riviera, San Pelagio, 27–8 ottobre 1989*, edited by Elena Ledda and Guglielmo Salotti. Rome: Lucarini, 1991.

Salvemini, Gaetano. "Can Italy Live at Home?" *Foreign Affairs* 14, no. 2 (1936): 243–58.
Samuels, Richard. *Machiavelli's Children: Leaders and Their Legacies in Italy and Japan.* Ithaca: Cornell University Press, 2003.
Sano Manabu. "Fashizumu ni tsuite no danpen." *Keizai ōrai* (1927): 88–89.
Sansom, George B. *Postwar Relations with Japan.* Tenth Conference of the Institute of Pacific Relations, Stratford-upon-Avon, England. London: The Royal Institute of International Affairs, 1947.
Sassa Hiroo and H. W. Schneider. *Fashizumu kokkagaku.* Tokyo: Chūō Kōronsha, 1934.
Satō Seizaburō. *Sasakawa Ryoichi: A Life.* Translated by Hara Fujiko. Norwalk, CT: Eastbridge, 2006.
Sawada Ken. *Mussorini den.* Tokyo: Dai Nihon Yūbenkai Kōdansha, 1928.
Schieder, Wolfgang. *Mythos Mussolini. Deutsche in Audienz beim Duce.* Munich: Oldenbourg Wissenschaftsverlag, 2013.
Shillony, Ben-Ami. *Politics and Culture in Wartime Japan.* New York: Oxford University Press, 1981.
——. *Revolt in Japan: The Young Officers and the February 26, 1936, Incident.* Princeton, NJ: Princeton University Press, 1973.
Shimazu, Naoko. *Japan, Race, and Equality: The Racial Equality Proposal of 1919.* New York: Routledge, 1998.
Shimoi Harukichi. "Badorio gensui." *Jikyoku zasshi* 2, no. 7 (1943): 4–8.
——"Duello di poesia." *Sakura* 1, no. 1 (1920): 26–27.
——. *Fashizumu no shintai to Itari no sangyō tōsei*, edited by Katō Etsuzan. Osaka: Osaka Tosho Kabushikigaisha, 1933.
——. *Fassho undō.* Tokyo: Minyūsha, 1925.
——. *Fassho undō to Itari no nōson shinkō seisaku ni tsuite.* Tokyo: Nagano Kenjin Tokyo Rengōkai, 1933.
——. *Fassho undō to Mussorini.* Tokyo: Bunmei Kyōkai, 1927.
——. *Gyorai no se ni matagarite.* Tokyo: Shingidō, 1926.
——. *Ikoku no sangyō seisaku to rōdō kensho.* Tokyo: Kantō Sangyō Dantai Rengōkai, 1933.
——. *Itari no kumiaisei kokka to nōgyō seisaku.* Tokyo: Dayamondosha, 1933.
——. *La guerra italiana.* Naples: Libreria della Diana, 1919.
——. *Mussorini no shishiku.* Tokyo: Dai Nihon Yūbenkai Kōdansha, 1929.
——. *Nekketsu netsuryū no daienzetsu.* Tokyo: Dai Nihon Yūbenkai Kōdansha, 1933.
——. *Ohanashi no shikata.* Tokyo: Dōbunkan, 1926 (1917).
——. *Taisenchū no Itaria.* Tokyo: Shingidō, 1926.
——. *Taisen ga unda Ikoku no niyūshi.* Tokyo: Teikoku Bunka Kyōkai, 1926.
Shimoi Harukichi and Gherardo Marone, eds. *Lirici giapponesi.* Lanciano: G. Carabba, 1926.
——. *Poesie giapponesi.* Naples: Riccardo Ricciardi Editore, 1917.
Shiotsu Seisaku. "Mussorini no kōka." *Kokusai chishiki* 8, no. 8 (1928): 52–60.
Shiratori Toshio. "Sangoku dōmei to shinsekai." *Itaria*, no. 4 (1941): 50–55.
Silberman, Bernard, and Harry Harootunian, eds. *Japan in Crisis: Essays on Taishō Democracy.* Princeton, NJ: Princeton University Press, 1974.
Silverberg, Miriam. "Constructing a New Cultural History of Prewar Japan." In *Japan in the World*, edited by Masao Miyoshi and H. D. Harootunian, 115–43. Durham, NC: Duke University Press, 1993.
——. "Constructing a New Cultural History of Prewar Japan." In *Japan in the World*, edited by Masao Miyoshi and Harry Harootunian, 115–43. Durham, NC: Duke University Press, 1993.
——. *Erotic Grotesque Nonsense: The Mass Culture of Japanese Modern Times.* Berkeley: University of California Press, 2009.

Siniawer, Eiko Maruko. *Ruffians, Yakuza, Nationalists: The Violent Politics of Modern Japan, 1860–1960*. Ithaca, NY: Cornell University Press, 2008.
Skya, Walter A. *Japan's Holy War: Ideology of Radical Shintō Ultranationalism*. Durham, NC, and London: Duke University Press, 2009.
Smethurst, Richard. *From Foot Soldier to Finance Minister. Takahashi Korekiyo: Japan's Keynes*. Cambridge, MA: Harvard University Press, 2007.
——. *A Social Basis for Prewar Japanese Militarism: The Army and the Rural Community* Berkeley: University of California Press, 1974.
Sommer, Theo. *Deutschland und Japan zwischen den Mächten, 1935–1940. Vom antikominternpakt zum Dreimächtepakt: Eine Studie zur diplomatischen Vorgeschichte des Zweiten Weltkriegs*. Tübingen: Mohr, 1962.
Spang, Christian W. "Karl Haushofer Re-examined: Geopolitics as a Factor within Japanese–German Rapprochement in the Inter-War Years?" In *Japanese-German Relations, 1895–1945: War, Diplomacy and Public Opinion*, edited by Christian W. Spang and R. Wippich. London: Routledge, 2006.
Stalker, Nancy K. *Prophet Motive: Deguchi Onisaburo, Oomoto, and the Rise of New Religions in Imperial Japan*. Honolulu: University of Hawai'i Press, 2008.
Storry, Richard. *The Double Patriots, a Study of Japanese Nationalism*. Cambridge, MA: Riverside Press, 1957.
Strang, G. Bruce. "Imperial Dreams: The Mussolini–Laval Accords of January 1935." *Historical Journal* 44, no. 3 (2001): 799–809.
Sturzo, Luigi. *Italy and Fascismo*. New York: Harcourt, 1926.
Suga Atsuko. "Ungaretti e la poesia giapponese." In *Atti del Convegno Internazionale su Giuseppe Ungaretti*. Urbino, 1979.
Sugimori Kojirō. "Fashizumu no bunseki oyobi hihan (1)." *Shakai seisaku jihō* 154 (1933): 107–26.
——. "Fashizumu no bunseki oyobi hihan (2)." *Shakai seisaku jihō* 155 (1933): 64–81.
——. "Fuwasushizumu." *Kokuhon* 12, no. 3 (1932): 33–42.
——. *The Principles of the Moral Empire*. London: University of London Press, 1918.
Sullivan, Brian R. "The Impatient Cat: Assessments of Military Power in Fascist Italy, 1936–1940." In *Calculations: Net Assessment and the Coming of World War II*, edited by Williamson Murray and Allan R. Millet, 97–135. New York: The Free Press, 1992.
Suzaki Shinichi. *Nihon fashizumu to sono jidai: Tennōsei, gunbu, sensō, minshū*. Tokyo: Ōtsuki Shoten, 1998.
Szpilman, Christopher W. A. "Fascist and Quasi-Fascist Ideas in Interwar Japan, 1918–1941." In *Japan in the Fascist Era*, edited by Bruce E. Reynolds, 73–106. New York: Palgrave Macmillan, 2004.
——. "Kanokogi Kazunobu: 'Imperial Asia,' 1937." In *Pan-Asianism: A Documentary History, Volume 2: 1920–Present*, edited by Sven Saaler and Christopher W. A. Szpilman, 149–54. Lanham, MD: Rowman & Littlefield, 2011.
Tachi Sakutatō. "I-E funsō to kokusaihō." *Kokusai chishiki* 15, no. 11 (1935): 1–13.
Tagawa Daikichirō. "Nichi-Doku-I to Ei-Futsu-Bei." *Kokusai chishiki* 15, no. 10 (1935): 41–53.
——. "Nichi-Doku-I to Ei-Futsu-Bei." *Kokusai chishiki* 15, no. 11 (1935): 30–40.
Takabatake Motoyuki. "Gokai sareta Mussorini." *Bungei shunju*, no. 6 (1928): 13–16.
——. *Kokka shakaishugi daigi*. Tokyo: Nihon Shakaishugi Kenkyūjo, 1932.
——. *Mussorini to sono shisō*. Tokyo: Jitsugyō No Sekaisha, 1928.
Takaishi Shinjirō. "Ningen Mussorini to kataru." In *Itaria no inshō*, 153–58. Tokyo: Itaria Tomo No Kai, 1943.
Takayanagi Kenzō. "Japan's View of the Struggle in the Far East." In *Imperial Japan and the World, 1931–1945*, edited by Anthony Best. London: Routledge, 2010 (1939).

Takeuchi Kenji. "I-E sensō no eikyō ikan. Kono kikai ni tekkō kokuze o kakuritsu seyo." *Ekonomisuto* 13, no. 30 (1935): 19–21.
Tamburello, Adolfo, ed. *Italia-Giappone, 450 anni*. 2 vols. Naples: Istituto italiano per l'Africa e l'Oriente, Università degli studi di Napoli "l'Orientale," 2003.
Tanaka, Stefan. *Japan's Orient: Rendering Pasts into History*. Berkeley: University of California Press, 1993.
Tansman, Alan. *The Aesthetics of Japanese Fascism*. Berkeley: University of California Press, 2009.
——. *The Culture of Japanese Fascism*. Durham, NC: Duke University Press, 2009.
Tipton, Elise K. *The Japanese Police State: The Tokkō in Interwar Japan*. Honolulu: University of Hawai'i Press, 1990.
Toda Takeo, ed. *Fashizumu sankō bunken*. Tokyo: Tōkyō Shakai Kagaku Kenkyūjo 1933.
Tokutomi Rōka. *Nihon kara Nihon e*. Rōka zenshū, vol. 13. Tokyo: Shinchōsha, 1929.
Tokutomi Sohō. "Wareware wa Itaria o aisu." *Itaria*, no. 10 (1941): 22–25.
Torrance, Richard. "*The People's Library*: The Spirit of Prose Literature versus Fascism." In *The Culture of Japanese Fascism*, edited by Alan Tansman, 56–79. Durham, NC: Duke University Press, 2009.
Tosaka Jun. "Chūkanteki gaikō kaisetsu: Kajima, Radekku shi nado no ronbun." *Yomiuri shinbun*, February 27, 1936.
——. *Nihon ideorogiiron*. Tokyo: Iwanami, 1977.
"The Tripartite Alliance of Germany, Italy, and Japan and Accompanying Notes, September 27, 1940." In *Deterrent Diplomacy: Japan, Germany, and the USSR, 1935–1940*, edited by James William Morley. New York: Columbia University Press, 1976.
Tsubouchi Shikō. "Mussorini." In *Nihon gikyoku zenshū. Gendai hen*. Tokyo: Shunyōdō, 1928–30.
Tsuchida Kyōson. "Fassho to bungaku." *Shinchō* 29, no. 3 (1932): 24–33.
Tsuda Shun. "Casupole giapponesi di campagna." *Sakura* 1, no. 4 (1920): 101–2.
Tsui, Brian Kai Hin. "China's Forgotten Revolution: Radical Conservatism in Action, 1927–1949." PhD diss., Columbia University, 2013.
Tsukui Tatsuo. *Nihonshugi undō no riron to jissen*. Tokyo: Kensetsusha, 1935.
——. *Nihonteki shakaishugi no teishō*. Tokyo: Senshinsha, 1932.
Tsurumi Shunsuke. *An Intellectual History of Wartime Japan, 1931–1945*. New York: KPI, 1986.
Tsurumi Yūsuke. *Eiyū taibō ron*. Tokyo: Dai Nihon Yūbenkai Kōdansha, 1928.
——. *Ōbei tairiku yūki*. Tokyo: Dai Nihon Yūbenkai Kōdansha, 1933.
Tsurumi Yūsuke and Komai Jūji. *Fūun no rutsubo no Echiopia!* Tokyo: Yashima Shobō, 1935.
Ueda Sakuichi. *Mussorini shushō: Kinsei dai ijin*. Tokyo: Kōmin Kyōiku Kenkyūkai, 1927.
Ueda Tatsunosuke. "Sekai shinchitsujo to kumiai kokkasei." *Itaria*, no. 6 (1942): 4–19.
Uesugi Shinkichi. "Dōri to seigi no teki Mussorini ron." *Chūō Kōron* 43, no. 2 (1928): 29–40.
Ugaki Kazushige. *Ugaki Kazushige nikki*. 3 vols., vol. 1. Tokyo: Misuzu Shobō, 1968–71.
Ungaretti, Giuseppe. *Lettere dal fronte a Gherardo Marone (1916–1918)*. Milan: Mondadori, 1978.
Unno Yoshirō. "Dai-niji Itaria-Echiopia sensō to Nihon." *Hōsei riron* 16, no. 2 (1983): 188–240.
Uramoto Secchō. "Minzoku seibutsuryoku to minzoku jumyō." *Yomiuri shinbun*, October 27, 1935.
Usuda Zan'un. *Wagahai wa Mussorini de aru*. Tokyo: Chūseidō, 1928.
Valente, Luca. *Il mistero della missione giapponese*. Rome: Cierre Edizioni, 2004.
Villari, Luigi. *The Awakening of Italy*. London and New York: Methuen, 1924.

Visser, Romke. "Fascist Doctrine and the Cult of Romanità." *Journal of Contemporary History* 27, no. 1 (1992): 5–22.
Wada Kojirō. "Fashizumu no kokka kan." *Itaria*, no. 12 (1941).
Wanrooij, Bruno. "The Rise and Fall of Italian Fascism as a Generational Revolt." *Journal of Contemporary History* 22 (1987): 401–18.
Weber, Max. *Wirtschaft und Gesellschaft. Grundrisse der verstehenden Soziologie*. Grundrisse der Sozialökonomik, vol. 3. Tübingen, 1922.
Wilson, G. M. "A New Look at the Problem of 'Japanese Fascism.'" In *Reappraisals of Fascism*, edited by Henry Ashby Turner, 199–214. New York: New Viewpoints, 1975.
Wilson, Sandra. *The Manchurian Crisis and Japanese Society, 1931–33*. London: Routledge, 2002.
Winter, Jay. *Sites of Memory, Sites of Mourning: The Great War in European Cultural History*. Cambridge: Cambridge University Press, 1995.
Wohl, Robert. *The Spectacle of Flight: Aviation and the Western Imagination, 1920–1950*. New Haven, CT: Yale University Press, 2005.
Yabe Teiji. "Konoe Fumimaro to shintaisei." In *Kindai Nihon o tsukutta hyakunin*, edited by Ōkōchi Kazuo and Ōya Sōichi. Tokyo: Mainichi Shinbunsha, 1965.
Yagami, Kazuo. *Konoe Fumimaro and the Failure of Peace in Japan, 1937–1941: A Critical Appraisal of the Three-Time Prime Minister*. Jefferson, NC: McFarland, 2006.
Yamane seishi kaihō, August 15 and 19, 1926, 2.
Yamazaki Mitsuhiko. "'Fashisuto' Mussorini wa Nihon de ika egakareta ka: hyōgen bunka ni okeru seijiteki eiyūzō." *Ryūkoku daigaku kokusai sentā kenkyū nenpō*, no. 15 (2006): 201–26.
——. "Itaria fashizumu, sono Nihon ni okeru jūyō to hyōgen keitai." Chap. 10 in "*Taishō*" *saikō*, edited by Seki Shizuo, 243–87. Tokyo: Mineruba, 2007.
Yanagisawa, Osamu. "The Impact of German Economic Thought on Japanese Economists before World War II." In *The German Historical School: The Historical and Ethical Approach to Economics*, edited by Yuichi Shionoya, 173–87. London: Routledge, 2001.
Yasumaru Yoshio. *Deguchi Nao*. Tokyo: Asahi Shinbunsha, 1987.
Yosano, Akiko. *Onde del mare azzurro*. Translated by Shimoi Harukichi and Elpidio Jenco. Naples: Sakura, 1920.
Yoshida Yakuni. "Mussorini enzetsu no inshō." *Kaizō* 11, no. 3 (1929): 119–20.
Yoshimitsu Yoshihiko. "Sei Tomasu to Dante: Shinkyoku no shingaku ni tsuite." *Nichi-I bunka kenkyū* 5 (1942): 76–85.
Yoshimura Michio. "Shōwa shoki no shakai jōkyōka ni okeru Nihonjin no Mussorini zō." *Nihon rekishi*, no. 497 (1989): 66–85.
Yoshino Sakuzō. "Fascism in Japan." *Contemporary Japan* 1, no. 1 (June 1932): 185–97.
Young, Louise. *Japan's Total Empire: Manchuria and the Culture of Wartime Imperialism*. Berkeley: University of California Press, 1999.
——. "Marketing the Modern: Department Stores, Consumer Culture, and the New Middle Class in Interwar Japan." *International Labor and Working-Class History* 55 (1999): 52–70.

Index

Page numbers in *italics* refer to illustrations.

Studies of the Weatherhead East Asian Institute

Columbia University

Selected Titles

(Complete list at http://www.columbia.edu/cu/weai/weatherhead-studies.html)

The Proletarian Wave: Literature and Leftist Culture in Colonial Korea, 1910–1945, by Sunyoung Park. Harvard University Asia Center, 2014.

Neither Donkey nor Horse: Medicine in the Struggle over China's Modernity, by Sean Hsiang-lin Lei. University of Chicago Press, 2014.

When the Future Disappears: The Modernist Imagination in Late Colonial Korea, by Janet Poole. Columbia University Press, 2014.

Bad Water: Nature, Pollution, and Politics in Japan, 1870–1950, by Robert Stolz. Duke University Press, 2014.

Rise of a Japanese Chinatown: Yokohama, 1894–1972, by Eric C. Han. Harvard University Asia Center, 2014.

Beyond the Metropolis: Second Cities and Modern Life in Interwar Japan, by Louise Young. University of California Press, 2013.

From Cultures of War to Cultures of Peace: War and Peace Museums in Japan, China, and South Korea, by Takashi Yoshida. MerwinAsia, 2013.

Imperial Eclipse: Japan's Strategic Thinking about Continental Asia before August 1945, by Yukiko Koshiro. Cornell University Press, 2013.

The Nature of the Beasts: Empire and Exhibition at the Tokyo Imperial Zoo, by Ian J. Miller. University of California Press, 2013.

Public Properties: Museums in Imperial Japan, by Noriko Aso. Duke University Press, 2013.

Reconstructing Bodies: Biomedicine, Health, and Nation-Building in South Korea since 1945, by John P. DiMoia. Stanford University Press, 2013.

Taming Tibet: Landscape Transformation and the Gift of Chinese Development, by Emily T. Yeh. Cornell University Press, 2013.

Tyranny of the Weak: North Korea and the World, 1950–1992, by Charles K. Armstrong. Cornell University Press, 2013.

The Art of Censorship in Postwar Japan, by Kirsten Cather. University of Hawai'i Press, 2012.

Asia for the Asians: China in the Lives of Five Meiji Japanese, by Paula Harrell. MerwinAsia, 2012.

Lin Shu, Inc.: Translation and the Making of Modern Chinese Culture, by Michael Gibbs Hill. Oxford University Press, 2012.

Occupying Power: Sex Workers and Servicemen in Postwar Japan, by Sarah Kovner. Stanford University Press, 2012.

Redacted: The Archives of Censorship in Postwar Japan, by Jonathan E. Abel. University of California Press, 2012.

Empire of Dogs: Canines, Japan, and the Making of the Modern Imperial World, by Aaron Herald Skabelund. Cornell University Press, 2011.

Planning for Empire: Reform Bureaucrats and the Japanese Wartime State, by Janis Mimura. Cornell University Press, 2011.

Realms of Literacy: Early Japan and the History of Writing, by David Lurie. Harvard University Asia Center, 2011.

Russo-Japanese Relations, 1905–17: From Enemies to Allies, by Peter Berton. Routledge, 2011.

Behind the Gate: Inventing Students in Beijing, by Fabio Lanza. Columbia University Press, 2010.

Imperial Japan at Its Zenith: The Wartime Celebration of the Empire's 2,600th Anniversary, by Kenneth J. Ruoff. Cornell University Press, 2010.

Passage to Manhood: Youth Migration, Heroin, and AIDS in Southwest China, by Shao-hua Liu. Stanford University Press, 2010.

Postwar History Education in Japan and the Germanys: Guilty Lessons, by Julian Dierkes. Routledge, 2010.

The Aesthetics of Japanese Fascism, by Alan Tansman. University of California Press, 2009.

The Growth Idea: Purpose and Prosperity in Postwar Japan, by Scott O'Bryan. University of Hawai'i Press, 2009.

Leprosy in China: A History, by Angela Ki Che Leung. Columbia University Press, 2008.

National History and the World of Nations: Capital, State, and the Rhetoric of History in Japan, France, and the United States, by Christopher Hill. Duke University Press, 2008.